Lecture Notes in Computer Science 12021

More information about this series at http://www.springer.com/series/7409

Christian Grimme · Mike Preuss ·
Frank W. Takes · Annie Waldherr (Eds.)

Disinformation in Open Online Media

First Multidisciplinary International Symposium, MISDOOM 2019
Hamburg, Germany, February 27 – March 1, 2019
Revised Selected Papers

 Springer

Editors
Christian Grimme (ID)
Institut für Wirtschaftsinformatik
WWU Münster
Münster, Nordrhein-Westfalen, Germany

Mike Preuss (ID)
LIACS
Leiden University
Leiden, Zuid-Holland, The Netherlands

Frank W. Takes (ID)
LIACS
Leiden University
Leiden, Zuid-Holland, The Netherlands

Annie Waldherr (ID)
Department of Communication
University of Münster
Münster, Germany

ISSN 0302-9743   ISSN 1611-3349 (electronic)
Lecture Notes in Computer Science
ISBN 978-3-030-39626-8   ISBN 978-3-030-39627-5 (eBook)
https://doi.org/10.1007/978-3-030-39627-5

LNCS Sublibrary: SL3 – Information Systems and Applications, incl. Internet/Web, and HCI

This Springer imprint is published by the registered company Springer Nature Switzerland AG
The registered company address is: Gewerbestrasse 11, 6330 Cham, Switzerland

Preface

Online media has become a politically, economically, and organizationally critical infrastructure. Internet users all over the world can directly use it to interact and share private and open arguments. They can participate in political discussion or find and share information. Through online media, journalists have access to enormous amounts of information and public sentiment that increasingly become part of reporting. Politicians refine their positions and actions based on the (seemingly) public opinion, which they distill from online media. Others use these channels to distribute their views. Companies and retailers allow product reviews by users to provide crowd-based quality assurance.

In an ideal world, participation and openness will foster free and democratic processes as well as beneficial societal interactions. However, beyond the desired space for free expression of public opinions, such openness also provides opportunities for large-scaled and orchestrated manipulations, i.e., "disinformation". Groups of humans (so-called "trolls" or semi- to fully-automated systems (so-called "social bots") are able to bias or manipulate societal streams, perceptions, and multiplicators in society.

One advantage of online media is that its contents are digitally stored and as such relatively easily available for automated analysis. Although often hindered by privacy and security restrictions, data from online platforms may serve as a powerful starting point for a solution to the complex problem of disinformation. In particular, recent methodological advances in machine learning, information retrieval, and data-driven social network analysis have the potential to create a better understanding of the credibility and shareability of online content. However, we are still far from automated methods that can actively detect and predict the behavior of, for example, the aforementioned trolls and social bots.

Under the acronym of MISDOOM, the Multidisciplinary International Symposium on Disinformation in Open Online Media is a newly established platform for the international and interdisciplinary exchange of scientific results on the above topic. The founding organizers of this first MISDOOM event are active and established researchers from computer science, communication science, and journalism, who are convinced that this topic cannot be handled by one scientific discipline and from one (be it the technical or societal) perspective alone. Their goal is to establish a platform that provides a multifaceted view on an important topic, to establish a new scientific forum and provide an innovative outlet for research contributions aimed at identifying, tracing, and curtailing disinformation.

The need for this platform and the overwhelming multidisciplinarity of the field becomes obvious from the list of MISDOOM 2019 participants. Besides scientists from the mentioned disciplines, colleagues from psychology, political science, statistics, information systems, and humanities were present. Additionally, many media professionals, governmental and public organizations, as well as representatives of non-governmental organizations participated.

In our view, such a multidisciplinary approach comes with some difficulties induced by different schools of thought, scientific terms, and even publication traditions in separate disciplines. However, we are convinced that for this research area as well as for many other challenges brought to us by rapid scientific and societal changes, multidisciplinarity is of key importance. We thus did our best to accommodate many different perspectives and expectations in this proceedings volume, even if it happens to be published in computer science.

At MISDOOM 2019, 15 research groups presented their work in scientific sessions. The topics ranged from populism and conspiracy over propaganda as well as fake and hate detection towards technical aspects such as social bots and infrastructures. The scientific program was framed by five invited keynotes provided by André Calero Valdez (University of Aachen), Greg Barber (Washington Post), Juliane von Reppert-Bismarck (Project Lie Detectors), Stefano Cresci (IIT-CNR, University of Pisa), and Christian Stöcker (HAW Hamburg).

The current post-proceedings volume is the result of scientific articles that could be submitted in the aftermath of the symposium by presenters and invited speakers based on their presentation abstracts. The articles were evaluated in a single-blind peer-review process by 20 international reviewers from multiple disciplines, with a minimum of 3 referees per paper. The 14 accepted papers present a very broad view on the topic of disinformation in online media and certainly contribute to the current scientific discussion from multiple angles.

Needless to say that the success of such a conference depends on authors, reviewers, and local organizers. We are very grateful to all participants of MISDOOM for intensive interaction on the topic, to all authors for submitting their best and latest work, to all the referees for their generously spent time and valuable expertise in preparing the reviews, to the program chairs for their hard work in a broad scientific field, to the keynote speakers for their inspiring talks and insights, to the proceedings and publicity chairs for managing the MISDOOM post-proceedings and website, and to the local organizers who actually made MISDOOM 2019 happen.

We would also like to thank the Deutsche Forschungsgemeinschaft (DFG), the European Research Center for Information Systems (ERCIS), and the University of Applied Science HAW Hamburg for their generous financial support.

December 2019

Christian Grimme
Mike Preuss
Frank Takes
Annie Waldherr

Opening Remarks

By Dr. Carsten Brosda

Minister of Culture and Media, Free and Hanseatic City of Hamburg

Even those who have power must be able to convince. Those who do not have the best arguments on their side may be easily tempted to give their cases a helping hand. The history books are full of examples of rulers and business leaders who have tried to deceive the public. The crude propaganda that often results is an expression of the argumentative weakness that we have learnt to deal with in our modern media democracies.

But new challenges lie ahead: today around 3.5 billion people use social media services. What at first looked to be the fulfilment of the promise of non-hierarchical and free communication is increasingly turning out to be a serious democratic challenge. Technological development has led, in particular by means of algorithmically driven channels, to an exponential increase in the quantity of available news and thus to disinformation on a scale that existing mechanisms of our public communication are evidently unable to deal with. While it has become very easy to express and disseminate personal opinions, we still seem to find it very hard to distil the many individual voices into a public opinion that would make social and political action possible.

At the moment, therefore, we are discussing the politicization of the Internet primarily from a negative perspective, whereas at the outset (as in the case of the Arab Spring) the focus was on the enormous democratic potential of the oppositional alternative public sphere and self-empowerment strategies – we are now seeing ever more clearly how communication on the web can be loaded or used as an instrument for manipulative deception. We need a lot more research to better understand and respond to these changes at the heart of our democratic process. Papers by the Hans Bredow Institute in Hamburg show that the statements that determine the climate of opinion on algorithmically organized intermediaries, and thus are certain to distort it in comparison with overall public opinion, originate above all on the political extremes. The London Institute for Strategic Dialogue was able to show in research that hate campaigns on the web are often orchestrated by a relatively small minority. And a paper by the Massachusetts Institute of Technology (MIT) shows strikingly, using Twitter as an example, that "fake news" spreads six times as fast on average as accurate reporting. Radicalism and populism are very much at home in a communication landscape where listening is distinctly subordinate to speaking and where any position, however outlandish, can elicit an amplifying echo.

The blatant strategy of drowning the distinction between fact and fiction in the sheer complexity of information (flood them with shit was the command of Steve Bannon, Donald Trump's former Chief Strategist) is now putting something fundamental at risk, namely trust in the credibility and authenticity of content. The increasingly far-reaching production of fake news and of content created or manipulated by AI threatens to completely erode trust in text, images, audio, and film. Producers of content, website operators, and users have a common interest in averting this danger. In an open democracy we depend on intact and trustworthy processes of information dissemination and opinion-forming that we can only standardize to a limited extent by legislation; they also rely on support from culture and society. Therefore, research concepts in this field such as "MISDOOM" are so extremely important if we are to tackle these challenges jointly from a range of disciplinary perspectives.

As a leading media location with strong research and teaching facilities in the media and IT sector, Hamburg is exactly the right place for researching this topic. I am confident that it will be possible to make up ground in the race against attempted manipulation and mass dissemination of lies and hate speech and to establish trustworthy structures for the digital public sphere. Perhaps we will see in the not too distant future the fulfilment of the great promise of comprehensive, equal communication after all.

Organization

MISDOOM 2019 was organized by the Department of Information, Hamburg University of Applied Sciences, Germany, and the Department of Information Systems and Statistics, University of Münster, Germany.

General Chairs

Christian Grimme	University of Münster, Germany
Christian Stöcker	Hamburg University of Applied Sciences, Germany
Thorsten Quandt	University of Münster, Germany

Program Chairs

Frank Takes	LIACS, University of Leiden, The Netherlands
Annie Waldherr	University of Münster, Germany

Proceeding and Publicity Chairs

Mike Preuss	LIACS, University of Leiden, The Netherlands
Dennis Assenmacher	University of Münster, Germany

Local Organizers

Petra Petruccio	Hamburg University of Applied Sciences, Germany
Philipp Kessling	Hamburg University of Applied Sciences, Germany

Program Committee

Dennis Assenmacher	University of Münster, Germany
Ebrahim Bagheri	Ryerson University, Canada
Antonio Barata	LIACS, Leiden University, The Netherlands
Alessio Maria Braccini	Tuscia University, Italy
Gerrit Jan de Bruin	Leiden University, The Netherlands
Lena Frischlich	University of Münster, Germany
Christian Grimme	University of Münster, Germany
Dietmar Janetzko	Cologne Business School, Germany
Neta Kligler-Vilenchik	Hebrew University of Jerusalem, Israel
Judith Moeller	University of Amsterdam, The Netherlands
Mehwish Nasim	The University of Adelaide, Australia
Christina Peter	Ludwig Maximilian University of Munich, Germany
Mike Preuss	LIACS, Leiden University, The Netherlands

Hyunjin Song   University of Vienna, Austria
Stefan Stieglitz   University of Duisburg-Essen, Germany
Frank Takes   Leiden University and University of Amsterdam,
                              The Netherlands
Diliara Valeeva   University of Amsterdam, The Netherlands
Suzan Verberne   LIACS, Leiden University, The Netherlands
Annie Waldherr   University of Münster, Germany
Martin Wettstein   University of Zurich, Switzerland

Contents

Media and Disinformation

Human Computer Interaction and Disinformation

Human and Algorithmic Contributions to Misinformation Online - Identifying the Culprit

André Calero Valdez[✉] (iD)

Human-Computer Interaction Center, RWTH Aaachen University,
Campus Boulevard 57, 52074 Aachen, Germany
calero-valdez@comm.rwth-aachen.de

Abstract. In times of massive fake news campaigns in social media, one may ask who is to blame for the spread of misinformation online. Are humans, in their limited capacity for rational self-reflection or responsible information use, guilty because they are the ones falling for the misinformation? Or are algorithms that provide the basis for filter bubble phenomena the cause of the rise of misinformation in particular in the political public discourse? In this paper, we look at both perspectives and see how both sides contribute to the problem of misinformation and how underlying metrics shape the problem.

Keywords: Misinformation · Recommender systems · Cognitive biases · Opinion formation

1 Introduction

The spread of misinformation in the public sphere is not new to humankind. It has not arisen with the digital age, but has always been present. Emperor Augustus has been found to manipulate his life's work [33] for the archives. And so have other tyrants and dictators throughout history. Still, the effect digitization has had on misinformation seems to change the game drastically.

As early as 1996, Floridi [19] was the first to mention the challenges addressing misinformation in conjunction with the technologies that were to appear in the near future. He warned that with an increase in personalization misinformation online would take novel paths.

For him misinformation would suffer from one of the following: lack of *objectivity*, as in the case of propaganda, lack of *completeness*, as in a case of damnatio memoriae, or lack of *pluralism*, as in the case of censorship.

He writes: "Things may easily become more problematic in the future, for reasons connected to two variables—the number of provusers and the physical integration of the various mass media into a unique digital instrument [...]" [19].

This research was supported by the Digital Society research program funded by the Ministry of Culture and Science of the German State of North Rhine-Westphalia.

C. Grimme et al. (Eds.): MISDOOM 2019, LNCS 12021, pp. 3–15, 2020.
https://doi.org/10.1007/978-3-030-39627-5_1

Not only did Floridi correctly foresee the problems personalization on a large scale would bring, but he also recognized the need to arrange the increasing amount of information for end users.

One class of algorithms, so called recommender systems [60] try to achieve this by selecting items that are relevant for the individual user. Relevance is derived from the users' previous decisions. What did they like? What did they buy? Where did they spend time?

In 2011, Pariser published his book the filter bubble [54] explaining how such algorithms take part in designing the web differently for each user. Every user is only exposed to content that matches their preferences, their interests, and their political opinion. The Internet, which used to be praised for allowing free access to information for all, has become an accomplice in mass deception, or more specifically in mass-self deception. However, the existence of filter bubbles or echo chambers has been doubted or moved to the societal fringes of hyper-partisanship [53].

The success of social media in recent years has brought about another drastic change. Initially, intended to improve social interaction and to connect friends across the world, Facebook has become the entry point to the Internet for large parts of the population. It has also become the source of political information for many users. Further, since everyone is now a publisher with a potential 1 Bn people reach in social media, algorithms are required to sort through the large amount of published items to allow users to cope with information overload.

This is also the case for "fake news", i.e., political propaganda in the disguise of news items [59]. Fake news are subject to the same recommendation algorithms as regular content and are thus often recommended on the basis of other users' interaction with them. The filter bubble dramatically increases the reach of fake news [65], as a positive interaction with such news posts triggers the exposure of this item to other users who are also likely to interact with it positively.

Social media—thus the misinformation on social media—has shown to have an influence on election outcomes in the 2017 elections in Great Britain and the USA [1]. However, it is unclear how large the impact of algorithms were, or whether the sole possibility to spread information (or misinformation) may have contributed to election outcomes opposing what election polls had predicted.

A challenge in predicting real-world outcomes in a digitally connected world lies in the complexity of the underlying interactions. Users' opinions are assumed to be influenced by media exposure and users' choices then influence the algorithms underlying social media. Small effects on either sides (the micro level) can yield drastically different outcome on the whole setting (the macro level) [34]. So, how can we disentangle this mishmash and determine ways to reduce the spread of misinformation?

2   Opinions, Information, and Misinformation

To reduce the spread of misinformation, we must understand what misinformation is, how it is related to information, and how it relates to opinion. For all terms, different definitions exist in different disciplines. Here, we will focus on the following definitions.

What are opinions? **Opinions** are beliefs or convictions of people that contain a sentiment towards an opinion object [26]. Opinions are subjective, thus they are neither correct nor incorrect. When such judgments are held privately they are often referred to as attitudes [51]; only when known to the public are they referred to as opinion. One must ensure to disentangle the concept of public opinion and opinions: the first refers to opinions held by groups of people, while the latter are held by individuals. It is important to note that opinions are not necessary factual or positivistic, but that may solely be normative. Opinions may be based on factual knowledge (i.e. beliefs), but do not have to be.

Information are descriptions of positivistic nature. They describe things as they are. Information is different from facts or data, as it is contextualized and provides references for understanding its meaning. Information often has an author providing these additions to data and facts. Abstract "[i]nformation is seen as an objective commodity defined by the dependency relations between distinct events" [16]. In the realm of online information, information is often considered to be the factual part of an article, a news post, a blog post, or any other form of media.

Misinformation is information that is considered to be counter-factual. This means it contradicts other information that is available. Typically misinformation is referred to as information that is counter-factual, but it is so by mere misinterpretation of data, lack of facts, or knowledge. Authors of misinformation have no ill intent.

Disinformation on other hand is objectively counter-factual information designed in spite of differing data or facts [59]. Disinformation is fabricated and designed to convey counter-factual information. Authors of disinformation have the intent to affect opinions by exposing readers to counter-factual information. Often information is embedded in context that is highly arousal to trigger sharing reactions in recipients. From the reception point of view misinformation is hard—if not impossible—to distinguish from disinformation when facts and data are missing. Thus, disinformation is considered to be a subset of misinformation.

It is important to note that the spread of information and opinion formation processes are closely related. On the one hand opinions are often justified by and based on (mis-)information. On the other hand opinion is then used to filter what information to process [35] and to look for [36].

3 Humans as a Culprit in Spreading Misinformation

We first look at how, social media and media in general affects human opinion formation. To understand the specificities of social media we look at the interaction of how human behavior and human decision making affect the spread of misinformation in social media. We then look at how users use social media, before we address the underlying cognitive biases that partially put the blame in the spread of misinformation on humans.

3.1 Opinion Formation and Media Effects

Understanding how people arrive at their opinions has been studied scientifically since the early to mid 20th century. Early research focused in particular on how individuals shape the opinions of others. So called *opinion leaders* are people that have a high interest in a topic and are consulted by their peers [61]. Efforts were invested to understand how to identify opinion leaders and to understand what personality traits play a role in how someone becomes an opinion leader [11]. Interestingly, opinion leadership is not solely personality dependent, but may change with different domains and topics of interest [49].

When looking at how media affects opinion formation several media effects theories have been proposed. *Agenda setting theory* [47] assumes that the media affects the content of the public discourse by providing a gateway function to curated information. According to the theory, media does not directly influence opinion formation in voting for example. But, by setting the agenda to a topic that is relevant for the election, media can indirectly affect opinion formation with regard to elections.

Cultivation theory [24] goes a little further assuming that the consumption of mass media products has a significant influence on the socialization of human beings, providing reference frames for norms, habits, and fears in a socially constructed reality. It particularly addresses television as a mass media outlet, but mapping it to social media, and in particular filter bubbles in social media, raises critical concerns about the spread of misinformation in social media. People exposed to fake news encultivate perceptions in accordance with said fake news and may become a victim of their own pseudo-realities.

In light of the spiral of silence theory [50], such pseudo-realities become even more worrying. According to the theory, minorities refrain from speaking their opinion to prevent possible backlash and repression. This again decreases the exposure of this particular opinion, increasing fear in others to voice their opinion as well. As a consequence, only majority opinions are heard in the public sphere.

Such effects have been witnessed in social media as well [22], indicating that users might refrain from voicing their opinion online, if they feel to be part of the minority regarding their opinion. Together with filter-bubble pseudo-realities, it becomes hard to determine, whose opinions actually are majorities, whose majorities were created by algorithms, and for whom?

3.2 Use of Social Media

Not every human being is an active social media user. In fact, most people are mostly passive readers online. However, when studying users of Facebook, it shows that people who score highly on the openness scale of the big five personality model are more avid users in particular [2]. This means that people who are more likely to believe new information are more frequently active on social media. Further, they also tend to interact more in social media, increasing the amount of data used by the underlying recommender system.

On one hand, it was shown that active social media use has positive effects on political participation [15]. Users are more interested in politics and interact more frequently with political content online. However, interest is not awareness and interest does not necessarily increase knowledge about politics [72]. For this, factual knowledge must be tested directly.

On the other hand, Lee et al. [41] showed that more active social media usage leads to higher network heterogeneity. This means that more active users have more diverse online friends. This supposedly combats political polarization, although it is unclear how this is achieved.

More active usage also provides more data to the social media provider. This type of information can in theory be used to manipulate the user in elections. Kosinski et al. [40] were able to predict very delicate private information from the seemingly inconspicuous usage data—facebook likes. The researchers were able to accurately predict political orientation, sexual orientation, and substance abuse from a set of likes all publicly shared on facebook. This brings the threat of hacking elections by personal profiling [28]. By providing personalized election commercials or even matching fake news, voting behavior can be manipulated shortly before elections.

Others studies investigated, whether a malevolent agent was even required to shift opinions towards a polarized state. They found that social network structure alone can cause emergent polarization [43] and that differences between users can be generated from first principles in simulation with no prior direction [45].

A particular problem with the spread of misinformation in social media are the negative effects of polarization [17]. By separating users with extreme opinions into subgroups (into their own echo chambers), norm violations in echo chambers are more likely to occur due the perception of anonymity online [32]. These types of incivility can trigger cascades of norm violation [46], as only few individuals deescalate in such cases.

3.3   Cognitive Biases

Some of these problems occur, because human beings have "irrational" thought processes—cognitive biases. Strictly speaking, these thought processes are, from an evolutionary standpoint, well adapted to the tribal life of a great ape. They are only irrational from a modern world perspective with science to show their irrationality. There is nothing inherently bad with cognitive biases. We all have them. The problem is that disinformation often leverages these bias to ensure users share the disinformation.

A strong bias that humans have is the outgroup homogeneity [55] bias. This makes us believe that "the others", be them political enemies, foreigners, or opposing team members, are all alike. People perceive variability in groups smaller for "them" and perceive variability larger in "us". This bias is an open invitation for the spread of disinformation that addresses or discredits single individuals in outgroups to discredit the whole group. Targeted recipients find confirmatory evidence in such disinformation for their previously held believes. Such tactics were seen in the refugee crisis in 2015.

Similarly, we tend to follow stereotypic judgments [29] in our decision making. Assuming foreigners to be the culprit in a crime and mentally letting the "nice guy from the neighborhood" of the hook more readily. Partially, this occurs because of the ostrich effect [37], where people ignore relevant information that opposes held believes. Unwanted facts are simply ignored.

The *availability heuristic* [63] affects our decision making process in an interesting way. If we are unaware of a fact, we look for proxy knowledge to use instead. If for example, we are asked how many refugees were involved in crime accusations, we typically do not know the number. We still come up with an estimate, by trying to recall how many references are available from remembering. The more examples come to mind, the higher the estimate. Sadly, not all of these references must refer to facts. They could easily refer to political commercials or fake news posts. This manipulates decision making extensively. The mere-exposure effect accounts for the viability of anti-immigrant misinformation campaigns on social media. The user does not have to believe the misinformation, he just needs to vaguely remember to be affected.

If you as a reader feel, that knowing about biases will help you, I must disappoint you. Even knowing about biases does not reduce susceptibility to these biases, even though you will think differently—as suggested by the blind spot bias [57]. Most biases are innate and are not easily overruled by conscious thought. Babies, for example, are more likely to detect spiders in images, even if there are none [42]. This spider detection bias and our other biases helped with our survival in an uncertain world. In all cases it is safer to believe the rustle in the woods is a bear than just the wind, even though in most cases the wind is to blame. This fact endows us with the agenticity bias [25], making us believe that things that happen must have had a causing agent. This is part of many conspiracy theories, where often an influential agent (e.g., the government) is assumed to prevent the truth from revealing itself [9].

4 Algorithms as a Culprit in Spreading Misinformation

Even though we have seen that humans are partially responsible for the spread of fake news, some of the effects only become explainable when the matching algorithmic counterpart is understood. Here, we do not focus on social bots, although some research showed that social bots could play a role in election outcomes [4]. Instead, we focus on well-meaning algorithms only, which are designed to help the user to cope with the information overload—recommender systems.

4.1 Recommender Systems

Recommender systems were initially designed to help people cope with the large amounts of emails sent by email lists everyday. Tapestry [27]—the first recommender system—was used to let users decide which mails were relevant, which were not, and to then provide recommendation as to whether an email was actually interesting to the user.

This was achieved by so-called collaborative filtering [71], where the decisions of other users were used to measure an average predicted rating of each individual item. This approach was quickly extended to other domains, such as shopping, tourism [20], scholarly education [7], and web search [62].

Different algorithmic approaches were used (e.g., content-based filtering, collaborative filtering, matrix factorization), but the most promising approaches are so-called hybrid recommender systems [8], merging different techniques. More recent approaches, even use social media relationships to improve recommendations [68]. But what does improve actually mean?

4.2 Recommendation Metrics

Typically, recommender systems are evaluated using accuracy metrics. That means that a system's predictions are evaluated against the real user ratings. Assuming the recommender believes you are going to rate a movie with 5 stars, it will be 100% accurate, when you actually do rate it with 5 stars. This metric is easy to understand and seems reasonable, yet it is not very helpful in many aspects.

During the 2009 ACM RecSys conference, Netflix announced a prize of 1 Mio USD for the team that would perform best at recommending movies to viewers. Interestingly, the winning team did so by being able to accurately predict movies that users were *not* interested in. A high accuracy does not make a good recommendation. Good accuracy is not enough [48].

As additional metrics Ge et al. [21] suggested coverage and serendipity. This means that all items should get recommended at least once (i.e., coverage) and that items that are recommended should be novel to the user (i.e., serendipity). Users do want to have diversity in their recommendations, at least when it comes to movies, products, and music recommendations [14]. If this metrics are applied to misinformation, further new misinformation and all misinformation will be shown to at least some users.

In light of misinformation on social media, this also means that the underlying metric of the recommendation system must be known to understand how misinformation is spread in social media. Assuming that social media providers benefit from continued use, any metric that includes dwelling-time or increased involvement by interacting with the content, is a suitable candidate. The problem is that this also captures increased interaction that is caused by highly emotional arousal [3]. Content that angers the reader—such as misinformation—will increase engagement. This engagement is picked up as signal by the recommendation engine.

4.3 User Experience in Recommender Systems

Current research [39] focuses more on the full user experience of recommender systems [10]. Understanding the perceptions that users have about a recommender system is crucial to their user experience [58]. Trending topics in this field are explainability (i.e., showing the user how a recommendation was generated), interactive recommendation, and privacy. This addresses the fact that users have different needs with regard to recommender systems [38].

However, the effects that continued recommendation has on opinion formation still needs further investigation. It is known that some recommender system algorithms increase the exposure of individual items and cause Matthew effects (the more you have, the more you get) [18]. Understanding how to analyze such effect in real recommender systems with real users is still very hard, as it requires to understand both human and algorithmic behaviors and outcomes.

4.4   Interactive Recommender Systems

Interaction has been proposed as a means to improve the quality of recommendations for users. Interaction may come as an interactive visualization that allows for both transparency and controllability of influencing factors [69]. A large number of recommender systems have adapted this approach, which was successful in many different domains [30]. User satisfaction with recommendation increases when interaction is added to the equation [31]. A problem with misinformation in mind is that user exploration is driven by user expectations and user misconceptions as well. The *garden of forking path bias* [23] states that users that interact with visualizations, e.g., become unaware of all those paths not taken for exploration, thus overvaluing the individual items found. Naturally, this increases satisfaction, but it also increases the risk for the spread of misinformation. It allows users to follow their own confirmation bias into the path of self-deception.

4.5   Novel Approaches to Recommender Systems

Very recent approaches have been suggested to include other factors in recommendation. As one concept **trust-based** recommendation [52] incorporates explicit trust-relationships with other users, whose recommendations were successful previously. However, this does not level out the danger of confirmation bias.

Risk-aware recommender systems [5] do not only look at user and item data for their recommendation, but incorporate a model of risk that each recommendation has for the user and the population. In theory, this could be used to reduce the exposure of misinformation to susceptible individuals, however the risk must be modeled explicitly to work properly. Novel scenarios and novel threats are either unevaluated or always considered high risk scenarios.

Value-aware recommender systems [56] go a step further and attach ethical values to items and consider the ethical values for all recommendations. This should in theory lead to value-aware recommendation and ensure higher quality recommendations. Similarly, to risk-aware recommender systems, a value model must be supplied. And it is not clear who determines what is valuable and how much so?

5   Discussion

As we have seen both human and algorithm play a role in the spread of misinformation. Even more so, both parties play a role in each others "mistakes". The recommender system follows a metric, which makes it susceptible to the users confirmation biases. The more a user is interested in a single topic of misinformation, the more the recommender system will provide such misinformation. Even worse, as the most active users are most susceptible to misinformation, such content gets most ratings and thus is most likely to get recommended.

The problem here lies in the chosen *metric*. Most recommender systems are used in some kind of commercial product, which is designed to make money. Amazon recommends products that it believes the customer would buy. Facebook recommends posts that it believes will keep the user on the website to consume more commercials. The metric, which is determined by business rules, impacts the type of content predominantly recommended to users. For misinformation this will be content that is emotionally charged and polarizing. Such content causes a visceral reaction and manipulates users towards interacting with content. Fake News are more readily shared when emotionally charged with emotions like fear, anger, or disgust [70].

From a game theory perspective, the game is rigged against truthful information. It simply is a stable strategy to recommend misinformation, when users prefer such items [67]. This is not to say that users rationally prefer misinformation, but they act in accordance with preferring it.

Troubling is also that discussions about Fake News and "traditional media" have instilled a deep distrust in journalism in teens who rely on facebook and blogs for political information [44]. Confirmation bias and antagonization abound when teenagers discuss politics on social media. Yet, it still requires real life deliberative interaction to find compromise and common ground in political discourse [66].

Approaches in trying to limit these mistakes such as value-aware recommender system suffer from one key problem. Who defines the value model? Who defines what is misinformation and what is not? Who defines what fair exposure of opinions would be like? Should all opinions get the same share of exposure? Should majority opinions get majority exposure? The question of how we want public discourse to be shaped is one of the pressing issues for the digital age.

One approach to address these questions, is through simulation and modelling. Luckily, one part of the equation lends itself readily for simulation—algorithms. First frameworks are being built to simulate the outcome of recommendation in the news domain [6]. Most recommendation engines are readily available as open source and can easily be integrated in a simulation setting. The far harder part to understand is the human side of the equation [13]. Agent-based modelling has been used to understand opinion dynamics, identity formation, and the spread of information [12,64] since the early 2000s. However, further research is needed to understand the interplay of algorithms and humans in unified complex system.

References

1. Allcott, H., Gentzkow, M.: Social media and fake news in the 2016 election. Technical report, National Bureau of Economic Research (2017)
2. Bachrach, Y., Kosinski, M., Graepel, T., Kohli, P., Stillwell, D.: Personality and patterns of facebook usage. In: Proceedings of the ACM Web Science Conference, pp. 36–44. ACM New York (2012)
3. Berger, J., Milkman, K.L.: What makes online content viral? J. Mark. Res. **49**(2), 192–205 (2012)
4. Bessi, A., Ferrara, E.: Social bots distort the 2016 us presidential election online discussion. First Monday **21**(11-7) (2016)
5. Bouneffouf, D., Bouzeghoub, A., Ganarski, A.L.: Risk-aware recommender systems. In: Lee, M., Hirose, A., Hou, Z.-G., Kil, R.M. (eds.) ICONIP 2013. LNCS, vol. 8226, pp. 57–65. Springer, Heidelberg (2013). https://doi.org/10.1007/978-3-642-42054-2_8
6. Bountouridis, D., Harambam, J., Makhortykh, M., Marrero, M., Tintarev, N., Hauff, C.: Siren: A simulation framework for understanding the effects of recommender systems in online news environments. In: Proceedings of the Conference on Fairness, Accountability, and Transparency, pp. 150–159. ACM (2019)
7. Bruns, S., Valdez, A.C., Greven, C., Ziefle, M., Schroeder, U.: What Should I read next? A personalized visual publication recommender system. In: Yamamoto, S. (ed.) HCI 2015. LNCS, vol. 9173, pp. 89–100. Springer, Cham (2015). https://doi.org/10.1007/978-3-319-20618-9_9
8. Burke, R.: Hybrid recommender systems: survey and experiments. User Model. User-Adap. Inter. **12**(4), 331–370 (2002)
9. Calero Valdez, A., Kluge, J., Ziefle, M.: Elitism, trust, opinion leadership and politics in social protests in germany. Energy Res. Soc. Sci. **43**, 132–143 (2018)
10. Calero Valdez, A., Ziefle, M., Verbert, K.: HCI for recommender systems: the past, the present and the future. In: Proceedings of the 10th ACM Conference on Recommender Systems, RecSys 2016, pp. 123–126. ACM, New York (2016). https://doi.org/10.1145/2959100.2959158
11. Childers, T.L.: Assessment of the psychometric properties of an opinion leadership scale. J. Mark. Res. **23**, 184–188 (1986)
12. Deffuant, G., Neau, D., Amblard, F., Weisbuch, G.: Mixing beliefs among interacting agents. Adv. Complex Syst. **3**(01n04), 87–98 (2000)
13. DeGroot, M.H.: Reaching a consensus. J. Am. Stat. Assoc. **69**(345), 118–121 (1974)
14. Di Noia, T., Ostuni, V.C., Rosati, J., Tomeo, P., Di Sciascio, E.: An analysis of users' propensity toward diversity in recommendations. In: Proceedings of the 8th ACM Conference on Recommender Systems, pp. 285–288. ACM (2014)
15. Dimitrova, D.V., Shehata, A., Strömbäck, J., Nord, L.W.: The effects of digital media on political knowledge and participation in election campaigns: evidence from panel data. Commun. Res. **41**(1), 95–118 (2014)
16. Dretske, F.: Knowledge and the Flow of Information. MIT Press, Cambridge (1981)
17. Dylko, I., Dolgov, I., Hoffman, W., Eckhart, N., Molina, M., Aaziz, O.: The dark side of technology: an experimental investigation of the influence of customizability technology on online political selective exposure. Comput. Hum. Behav. **73**, 181–190 (2017). https://doi.org/10.1016/j.chb.2017.03.031
18. Fleder, D., Hosanagar, K.: Blockbuster culture's next rise or fall: the impact of recommender systems on sales diversity. Manag. Sci. **55**(5), 697–712 (2009)

19. Floridi, L.: Electronic Library. Brave. net. world: the internet as a disinformation superhighway? **14**(6), 509–514 (1996)
20. Gavalas, D., Konstantopoulos, C., Mastakas, K., Pantziou, G.: Mobile recommender systems in tourism. J. Netw. Comput. Appl. **39**, 319–333 (2014)
21. Ge, M., Delgado-Battenfeld, C., Jannach, D.: Beyond accuracy: evaluating recommender systems by coverage and serendipity. In: Proceedings of the Fourth ACM Conference on Recommender Systems, pp. 257–260. ACM (2010)
22. Gearhart, S., Zhang, W.: "Was it something i said?" "No, it was something you posted!" a study of the spiral of silence theory in social media contexts. Cyberpsychol. Behav. Soc. Netw. **18**(4), 208–213 (2015)
23. Gelman, A., Loken, E.: The garden of forking paths: why multiple comparisons can be a problem, even when there is no "fishing expedition" or "p-hacking" and the research hypothesis was posited ahead of time. Columbia University, Department of Statistics (2013)
24. Gerbner, G., Gross, L., Morgan, M., Signorielli, N., Shanahan, J.: Growing up with television: Cultivation processes. In: Media Effects: Advances in Theory and Research, vol. 2, pp. 43–67 (2002)
25. Gilbert, D.T., Brown, R.P., Pinel, E.C., Wilson, T.D.: The illusion of external agency. J. Pers. Soc. Psychol. **79**(5), 690 (2000)
26. Glynn, C.J., Huge, M.E.: Public opinion. In: The International Encyclopedia of Communication (2008)
27. Goldberg, D., Nichols, D., Oki, B.M., Terry, D.: Using collaborative filtering to weave an information tapestry. Commun. ACM **35**(12), 61–70 (1992)
28. González, R.J.: Hacking the citizenry?: Personality profiling, 'big data' and the election of Donald Trump. Anthropol. Today **33**(3), 9–12 (2017). https://doi.org/10.1111/1467-8322.12348
29. Hamilton, D.L., Gifford, R.K.: Illusory correlation in interpersonal perception: a cognitive basis of stereotypic judgments. J. Exp. Soc. Psychol. **12**(4), 392–407 (1976)
30. He, C., Parra, D., Verbert, K.: Interactive recommender systems: a survey of the state of the art and future research challenges and opportunities. Expert Syst. Appl. **56**, 9–27 (2016)
31. Hijikata, Y., Kai, Y., Nishida, S.: The relation between user intervention and user satisfaction for information recommendation. In: Proceedings of the 27th Annual ACM Symposium on Applied Computing, SAC 2012, pp. 2002–2007. ACM, New York (2012). https://doi.org/10.1145/2245276.2232109
32. Hmielowski, J.D., Hutchens, M.J., Cicchirillo, V.J.: Living in an age of online incivility: examining the conditional indirect effects of online discussion on political flaming. Inf. Commun. Soc. **17**(10), 1196–1211 (2014)
33. Hoff, R., Stroh, W., Zimmermann, M.: Divus augustus (2014)
34. Clemm von Hohenberg, B., Maes, M., Pradelski, B.S.: Micro influence and macro dynamics of opinion formation (2017). SSRN: https://ssrn.com/abstract=2974413 or https://doi.org/10.2139/ssrn.2974413
35. Iyengar, S., Hahn, K.S.: Red media, blue media: evidence of ideological selectivity in media use. J. Commun. **59**(1), 19–39 (2009)
36. Jonas, E., Schulz-Hardt, S., Frey, D., Thelen, N.: Confirmation bias in sequential information search after preliminary decisions: an expansion of dissonance theoretical research on selective exposure to information. J. Pers. Soc. Psychol. **80**(4), 557 (2001)
37. Karlsson, N., Loewenstein, G., Seppi, D.: The ostrich effect: selective attention to information. J. Risk Uncertainty **38**(2), 95–115 (2009)

38. Knijnenburg, B.P., Reijmer, N.J., Willemsen, M.C.: Each to his own: how different users call for different interaction methods in recommender systems. In: Proceedings of the Fifth ACM Conference on Recommender Systems, RecSys 2011, pp. 141–148. ACM, New York (2011). https://doi.org/10.1145/2043932.2043960

39. Konstan, J.A., Riedl, J.: Recommender systems: from algorithms to user experience. User Model. User-Adap. Inter. 22(1–2), 101–123 (2012)

40. Kosinski, M., Stillwell, D., Graepel, T.: Private traits and attributes are predictable from digital records of human behavior. Proc. Nat. Acad. Sci. 110(15), 5802–5805 (2013)

41. Lee, J.K., Choi, J., Kim, C., Kim, Y.: Social media, network heterogeneity, and opinion polarization. J. Commun. 64(4), 702–722 (2014)

42. LoBue, V.: And along came a spider: an attentional bias for the detection of spiders in young children and adults. J. Exp. Child Psychol. 107(1), 59–66 (2010)

43. Macy, M.W., Kitts, J.A., Flache, A., Benard, S.: Polarization in dynamic networks: a hopfield model of emergent structure. In: Dynamic Social Network Modeling and Analysis, pp. 162–173 (2003)

44. Marchi, R.: With Facebook, blogs, and fake news, teens reject journalistic "objectivity". J. Commun. Inquiry 36(3), 246–262 (2012)

45. Mark, N.: Beyond individual differences: social differentiation from first principles. Am. Soc. Rev. 63, 309–330 (1998)

46. Mäs, M., Opp, K.D.: When is ignorance bliss? Disclosing true information and cascades of norm violation in networks. Soc. Netw. 47, 116–129 (2016)

47. McCombs, M.E., Shaw, D.L.: The agenda-setting function of mass media. Public Opinion Q. 36(2), 176–187 (1972)

48. McNee, S.M., Riedl, J., Konstan, J.A.: Being accurate is not enough: how accuracy metrics have hurt recommender systems. In: CHI 2006 Extended Abstracts on Human Factors in Computing Systems, pp. 1097–1101. ACM (2006)

49. Myers, J.H., Robertson, T.S.: Dimensions of opinion leadership. J. Mark. Res. 9, 41–46 (1972)

50. Noelle-Neumann, E.: Die Schweigespirale. Piper (1980)

51. Nowak, A., Szamrej, J., Latané, B.: From private attitude to public opinion: a dynamic theory of social impact. Psychol. Rev. 97(3), 362 (1990)

52. O'Donovan, J., Smyth, B.: Trust in recommender systems. In: Proceedings of the 10th International Conference on Intelligent User Interfaces, IUI 1005, pp. 167–174. ACM, New York (2005). https://doi.org/10.1145/1040830.1040870

53. O'Hara, K., Stevens, D.: Echo chambers and online radicalism: assessing the internet's complicity in violent extremism. Policy Internet 7(4), 401–422 (2015)

54. Pariser, E.: The Filter Bubble: What the Internet is Hiding from You. Penguin, London (2011)

55. Park, B., Rothbart, M.: Perception of out-group homogeneity and levels of social categorization: memory for the subordinate attributes of in-group and out-group members. J. Pers. Soc. Psychol. 42(6), 1051 (1982)

56. Pei, C., et al.: Value-aware recommendation based on reinforcement profit maximization. In: The World Wide Web Conference, pp. 3123–3129. ACM (2019)

57. Pronin, E., Lin, D.Y., Ross, L.: The bias blind spot: perceptions of bias in self versus others. Pers. Soc. Psychol. Bull. 28(3), 369–381 (2002)

58. Pu, P., Chen, L., Hu, R.: A user-centric evaluation framework for recommender systems. In: Proceedings of the Fifth ACM Conference on Recommender Systems, pp. 157–164. ACM (2011)

59. Quandt, T., Frischlich, L., Boberg, S., Schatto-Eckrodt, T.: Fake news. The International Encyclopedia of Journalism Studies, pp. 1–6 (2019)

60. Resnick, P., Varian, H.R.: Recommender systems. Commun. ACM **40**(3), 56–58 (1997)
61. Rogers, E.M., Cartano, D.G.: Methods of measuring opinion leadership. Public Opinion Q. **26**, 435–441 (1962)
62. Santos, R.L., Macdonald, C., Ounis, I.: Selectively diversifying web search results. In: Proceedings of the 19th ACM International Conference on Information and Knowledge Management, pp. 1179–1188. ACM (2010)
63. Schwarz, N., Bless, H., Strack, F., Klumpp, G., Rittenauer-Schatka, H., Simons, A.: Ease of retrieval as information: another look at the availability heuristic. J. Pers. Soc. Psychol. **61**(2), 195 (1991)
64. Smaldino, P., Pickett, C., Sherman, J., Schank, J.: An agent-based model of social identity dynamics. J. Artif. Soc. Soc. Simul. **15**(4), 7 (2012)
65. Spohr, D.: Fake news and ideological polarization: filter bubbles and selective exposure on social media. Bus. Inf. Rev. **34**(3), 150–160 (2017)
66. Suiter, J., Farrell, D.M., O'Malley, E.: When do deliberative citizens change their opinions? Evidence from the irish citizens' assembly. Int. Polit. Sci. Rev. **37**(2), 198–212 (2016)
67. Taylor, P.D., Jonker, L.B.: Evolutionary stable strategies and game dynamics. Math. Biosci. **40**(1–2), 145–156 (1978)
68. Tinghuai, M., et al.: Social network and tag sources based augmenting collaborative recommender system. IEICE Trans. Inf. Syst. **98**(4), 902–910 (2015)
69. Verbert, K., Parra, D., Brusilovsky, P., Duval, E.: Visualizing recommendations to support exploration, transparency and controllability. In: Proceedings of the 2013 International Conference on Intelligent User Interfaces, pp. 351–362. ACM (2013)
70. Vosoughi, S., Roy, D., Aral, S.: The spread of true and false news online. Science **359**(6380), 1146–1151 (2018)
71. Yang, X., Guo, Y., Liu, Y., Steck, H.: A survey of collaborative filtering based social recommender systems. Comput. Commun. **41**, 1–10 (2014)
72. Zaller, J.: Political awareness, elite opinion leadership, and the mass survey response. Soc. Cogn. **8**(1), 125–153 (1990)

Between Overload and Indifference: Detection of Fake Accounts and Social Bots by Community Managers

Svenja Boberg[✉], Lena Frischlich, Tim Schatto-Eckrodt, Florian Wintterlin, and Thorsten Quandt

University of Muenster, 48143 Muenster, Germany
svenja.boberg@uni-muenster.de

Abstract. In addition to the increased opportunities for citizens to participate in society, participative online journalistic platforms offer opportunities for the dissemination of online propaganda through fake accounts and social bots. Community managers are expected to separate real expressions of opinion from manipulated statements through fake accounts and social bots. However, little is known about the criteria by which managers make the distinction between "real" and "fake" users. The present study addresses this gap with a series of expert interviews. The results show that community managers have widespread experience with fake accounts, but they have difficulty assessing the degree of automation. The criteria by which an account is classified as "fake" can be described along a micro-meso-macro structure, whereby recourse to indicators at the macro level is barely widespread, but is instead partly stereotyped, where impression-forming processes at the micro and meso levels predominate. We discuss the results with a view to possible long-term consequences for collective participation.

Keywords: Online journalism · Community management · Moderation · Fake accounts · Social bots

1 Introduction

The emergence of participatory journalism has fundamentally changed communication between citizens, public actors, and the mass media. The quasi-permanent stream of news on the Internet is now accompanied by a multitude of participatory offerings and often by direct feedback from readers [1]. Some articles are commented on, shared, or criticized within minutes.

Along with citizens who can expand their opportunities to participate in society through participatory offerings, strategic actors are using participatory formats to place hidden propaganda through the use of fake identities. These "pseudo users" can either be operated manually in the form of fake accounts or set up (partly) automatically as social bots.

© Springer Nature Switzerland AG 2020
C. Grimme et al. (Eds.): MISDOOM 2019, LNCS 12021, pp. 16–24, 2020.
https://doi.org/10.1007/978-3-030-39627-5_2

Community managers are expected to guard these "open gates" [1] of online newspapers and carefully separate the authentic opinions of citizens from manipulative statements. Yet this responsibility carries with it the danger of either censoring public expression or allowing propagandists to abuse the reach and credibility of their own media house.

So far there are few studies that deal with the question of what criteria journalists use to distinguish between "real" and "fake" users. It is clear that journalists feel responsible for what happens in their participative channels [2]. Users classified as "fake" will most likely be excluded from the discussion. However, the criteria on which these decisions are based are hardly known.

The present study addresses this gap. With the help of expert interviews (N = 25) with selected community managers and digital editors of German national and regional online newspapers, we examined their experiences with fake accounts and social bots as well as their criteria used to classify users as "fake".

2 Identifying Features of Social Bots and Fake Accounts

The term "social bot" has lately gained a lot of media attention. It refers to a "superordinate concept which summarizes different types of (semi-) automatic agents. These agents are designed to fulfill a specific purpose by means of one- or many-sided communication in online media" [3]. A special form are political bots, which are used to spread masses of political or even propagandistic messages. Bots pretend to be ordinary citizens in order to take advantage of the supposed trust that other users in social networks have emplaced in them. However, the level of automation is difficult to assess; thus the differentiation between social bots and fake profiles, which also pretend to be normal social media users, is almost impossible. Fake profiles are often operated manually either by highly engaged online users or even paid actors. For example, hate comments are observed to be disseminated by coordinated groups that set up a series of accounts in order to spread a certain agenda [4].

Regarding the impact of social bots, the research results are somewhat mixed. While Bastos and Mercea [5] report on a Twitter botnet during the Brexit referendum that helped to spread hyper-partisan pro-Brexit messages, Neudert, Kollanyi, and Howard [6] found moderate levels of automation in Germany. Bots are also often associated with spreading spam. Badri et al. [7] show that Twitter is only able to detect the original propagators of spam, whereas retweeted networks are not blocked.

Generally, the activity of an account serves as a key criterion to detect bots. Woolley and Howard [8] classify accounts as bots if they post more than 50 tweets a day. It can be argued that frequency as the only criterion is not sufficient, since many regular accounts post as much, or programmers give their bot networks more realistic activity patterns. The botometer project [9] takes other metrics into account, such as interaction patterns of profiles, sentiments, or the reaction rates of accounts. All of these scientific approaches have one thing in common: they rely on big data analysis to detect underlying patterns—tools and procedures that normal users and forum moderators don't necessarily have access to.

3 Guarding the Gates Against Intruders: The Journalists' Need to Defend Their Platforms

Gatekeeping is one of the most studied areas of communication research. Gatekeeping deals with the question of how editorial decisions are made and how topics, events, and interpretative patterns are arranged [10]. The emergence of user-generated content has not only changed journalistic decision-making processes but also the position of traditional media in the information flow. Now citizens are able to add their views to participatory platforms curated by journalists and thus open up the public communication processes [11]. So the traditional role of journalists as gatekeepers has changed to "gatekeeping" [12]. Despite the promise of increased user participation [13], participatory formats also allow for irrelevant or even uncivil content to be posted, such as attacks against other persons [14] or social groups [15].

The reason why news media still enable user comments is rooted in the journalistic role of the "press advocating for the public [and] serving as its voice in a mass-mediated society" [16]. In that regard, comments are seen as an additional tool to create a deliberative public sphere. The prevalence of veiled or even manipulative actors might damage the relationship between readers and media brands by putting off users who want to engage in a constructive discussion, as well as making journalists question the benefit of having comment sections.

As a consequence, community managers operate in a field of tension between their perceived moral obligation to permit fruitful discussions and keep out manipulative content. They have to balance the risk of letting undesirable comments slip through and repelling users who would prefer a focused discussion, *or* restricting the forum too much and thereby being accused of censorship. As a result, journalists need to develop strategies to recognize false actors in order to preserve the comments sections for their target readership. Yet little is known about how journalists perceive fake accounts and social bots, which detection criteria they use, und how they evaluate the problem.

Therefore, we state the following research questions:

1. How do gatekeepers detect fake accounts and social bots?
2. How do gatekeepers define fake accounts and social bots?
3. Do gatekeepers perceive fake accounts and social bots as a problem?

4 Method

We conducted a series of guided interviews (N = 25) that addressed community managers' detection strategies and experiences with fake accounts and social bots at German newspapers. In the following, the selection of participants and qualitative analysis are briefly described.

4.1 Participant Selection and Sample

Participant Selection. We selected our interview partners via a purposeful multi-level procedure. (For a detailed description see Frischlich, Boberg, and Quandt [17]. We considered only professional journalists [18] working at mainstream newspapers with their own websites, that have attracted more than 100,000 unique visitors in the first quarter of 2016. In order to create a sample that most accurately represents the different regions, reaches, and editorial lines in the German newspaper landscape, a pre-study was conducted. Newspapers were rated regarding their editorial leaning, ascribed influence, and perceived trustworthiness. On that basis, the online magazines were grouped in clusters ranging from nationwide conservative and liberal, to regional newspapers and low-trust yellow journals. To represent this variability, we interviewed 50% of the newspapers within each cluster, thus ensuring that different types of media organizations were represented in our sample.

Sample. Within each selected newspaper, we approached the person responsible for social media management—that is, the digital/social media editor or community manager. The social media staff was defined as curating user comments on the newspapers' profiles on Facebook, Twitter, Instagram and WhatsApp and/or moderating the comments sections that are hosted by the online magazine itself. A total of $N = 25$ (10 females) interviews were conducted.

Data Collection. All interviews were carried out between January and March 2017. The interviews had an average length of 42 min (range 31–70 min). Interviews were transcribed and pseudo-anonymized. The interviews followed a pilot-tested, semi-structured guideline. Two experienced interviewers asked interviewees about (a) experiences with fake accounts, (b) definition of social bots, (c) the prevalence of social bots, (d) detection strategies, and (e) the interviewees' evaluation of fake accounts and social bots as a problem.

Data Analysis. The interview transcripts were analyzed using qualitative content analysis, following Mayring [19]. This analysis combines deductively determined pre-set categories and inductively developed categories that emerged during the initial coding of a subsample. A subsample of eight interviews was coded to develop the inductive categories and check for reliability via MaxQDA12. The coders agreed on 83–89% of the assigned codes. Disagreements were solved via discussion. After coding the whole sample following the developed category system, we used the coded interviews to identify underlying types among the comment moderators.

5   Results

In the following, the characteristics that journalists use to identify fake accounts and social bots are presented *(RQ1)*. These detection strategies are largely dependent on how much prior knowledge and experience exists with such veiled actors *(RQ2)*. We also shed light on the journalistic evaluation of social bots and fake accounts as a problem or even a threat *(RQ3)*. A total of seven types of evaluators can be identified that differ in terms of their experience, their detection strategies, and their problem perceptions.

5.1 Journalistic Detection Strategies of Fake Accounts and Social Bots

Regarding *RQ1*, forum moderators rely exclusively on their personal experience and tend to review the comments manually. Only two newsrooms in the sample have experimented with machine learning algorithms to identify undesirable content, but these methods were not yet found to be satisfying. If the moderators notice something unusual, they look primarily at the individual comment or the corresponding profile. Few consider the context of the comment, such as interactions with other suspicious content or actors.

At the micro-level of the individual comment, journalists focus primarily on topics and familiar argumentation patterns (n = 16). This can also include certain buzzwords such as "thank you, Merkel" which is often used ironically to express the harm the German chancellor allegedly has done.

"The comment as such can be identified. Of course, this is also vague and a bit based on experience. The wording." (IV 10)

The language of the comment, such as spelling, syntax, or orthographic mistakes, is also used as a criterion, especially when Russian profiles are not set up in correct German.

After looking at the comment itself, forum moderators get a general overview of the profile, with regard to thematic focus or the amount of available information (n = 13). Posting behavior is often obvious here, especially if the profiles are monothematically oriented and similar posts appear in large numbers (n = 21).

"They all have a certain topic, which drives them. They also interpret this in every current topic. [...] That's something very idealistic." (IV 13)

Also, community managers take a look at the person behind the profile. They get suspicious if the profile has no picture or a picture that looks like a stock photo (n = 12), if the creation date of the profile is very recent (n = 6), if the relationship between followers and followees is unbalanced (n = 8), or if the profile is a member of suspicious or shady groups that the community managers have encountered before (n = 1).

"Then you see a weird comment without a profile picture and go to the profile and there's little information or just three friends." (IV 21)

Even though most of them only look at the profile and comment itself, some also include contextual features on the macro level. These are, for example, the so-called flooding with comments.

"There used to be one, two, kinds of hacker attacks, where we were spied [...] from a [...] account, where hundreds of comments came within a few minutes, which paralyzed our system for a short time." (IV 6)

Lack of interaction with other users (n = 4) and recurring profiles (n = 4) can be seen as a further indication.

"They'll be banned and then they'll come back […], they'll be old acquaintances. You can tell by the way they express themselves, by what they call themselves. So they're not so smart that they would somehow give themselves a new name now, instead of Anton B he's called Anton C." (IV 15)

5.2 How Do Journalists Define and Evaluate Fake Accounts and Social Bots?

With respect to *RQ2*, gatekeepers do not differentiate between human-like fake accounts or automated social bots when they reflect on suspicious user profiles. When asked directly about social bots, community managers have different ideas about what they are dealing with. While some have no deep understanding at all, other journalists argue more technically, while others associate the term with a buzzword that stands for the ongoing public debate and scaremongering about the danger posed by social bots. Regarding their prevalence, all respondents have had prior experience with fake accounts, but there is a great uncertainty as to whether they are automated accounts. Here, journalists rely primarily on their feelings, but admit that automation cannot be determined without specific tools.

"But even there, it's very difficult to determine and understand whether they're actually bots or agreed-upon people who've organized themselves somehow." (IV 14)

All in all, the respondents reported that fake accounts infiltrate public discussions, especially on political issues. On Facebook in particular, fake accounts were described as a constant phenomenon, whereas social bots were primarily attributed to Twitter. But manipulation attempts were also observed on their own forums.

In addressing fake accounts and social bots as a problem *(RQ3)*, community managers have different perceptions. Some of the respondents are not aware of the problem, or have not really thought about it yet, or are sure that the fear of social bots is exaggerated.

"It's not like we're slapping our hands over our heads and say, 'Oh, God, how are we supposed to handle this?'" (IV 5)

Other journalists simply see themselves as not influential enough to be attractive to social bots and believe that such problems only affect the big media brands. Others, however, already see the handling of fake profiles and social bots as a problem, especially with regard to future elections:

"I'm just afraid that this is an issue that will definitely occupy us. […] Or will occupy even more. Also now in the course of […] the Bundestag elections." (IV 10)

The results thus show that all journalists deal with the identification of veiled profiles on a daily basis, but differ greatly in the extent to which this is perceived as a problem. Based on the evaluations and experiences with fake accounts and social bots, seven types can be derived (see Fig. 1).

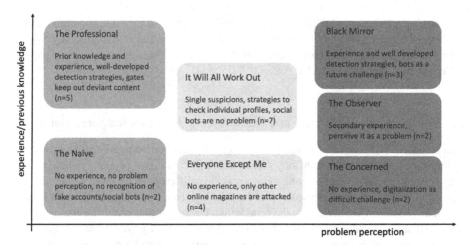

Fig. 1. Community managers' problems with perceiving fake accounts and social bots

When it comes to the detection of pseudo users, there are substantial differences in prior knowledge and competence. The two types that use the most differentiated strategies to recognize fake profiles and social bots can be contrasted by their perception of pseudo users as a problem. "The professional" have well-developed methods at their disposal, because they deal with pseudo users on a daily basis. They feel well equipped to deal with the problem. These journalists belong to large media brands that are coping with a large amount of comments and thus have institutionalized the moderation of comments to a great extent. The "black mirror" type has the same abilities, but at the same time accentuates the potential danger and the concern that the problem may be greater than is currently assumed. On the other side of the spectrum "the naïve" see no problem at all, mostly because they claim they do not have to deal with deceptive profiles apart from a few harmless fakes. They have a vague knowledge of recognition features, so it can be assumed that they also experience forms of pseudo users but simply do not recognize them. Closely related is "everyone except me" who also shows little knowledge and sees pseudo users as a problem for other magazines. The members of this type belong to smaller regional newspapers that perceive themselves as unimportant and not an attractive target for manipulation attempts. Between these extremes, the "it will all work out" type has encountered suspicious users and developed strategies to identify single profiles, but they do not fear social bot attacks and thus are confident in their ability to protect their comment sections. Lastly, "the observer" and "the concerned" both have little or no experience with pseudo users and express considerable distress. While "the observer" knows the characteristics of social bots from reports or second-hand experience and perceive them as a possible threat, "the concerned" rather refer to social bots as a buzzword and are generally skeptical about online phenomena.

6   Conclusion

The results show that experiences with fake profiles are consistent among the interviewed community managers. Without exception, all interviewees reported the prevalence of pseudo users, even though most of them were uncertain about the degree of automation of these accounts. The basis of their judgments also varied greatly and was not bound to their own professional field, but was also fed by mass media coverage and the experiences of colleagues.

The criteria by which someone was classified as a "fake user" could be described along a micro-meso-macro structure, ranging from single comments to the overall context of a comment. The features of the comments (micro-level), the account and its digital networks (meso-level) as well as the overarching patterns (macro-level) became apparent. However, most respondents based their judgment exclusively on micro- and meso-level indicators (e.g. incorrect grammar, untrustworthy user names). Characteristics at the macro level, such as the interaction between accounts, were seldom used for impression building—although the interviewees attributed the latter with the best suitability for recognizing automated manipulation attempts. The clearly recognizable recourse to stereotypes also requires a critical reflection of the filtering processes in participative journalistic offerings.

Overall, our study provided the first empirical insights into the experiences of journalists dealing with manipulation attempts by fake accounts and social bots in Germany. It contributes to the understanding of the criteria used to separate "real" from "fake" users. The results underline the need to address this issue, as the increase of manipulative attempts in comment sections could lead to a decrease of discussion quality, resulting in either biased online discourse or even the shutdown of participatory formats entirely.

References

1. Singer, J.B., et al.: Introduction. In: Singer, J.B., et al. (eds.) Participatory Journalism: Guarding Open Gates at Online Newspapers. Wiley Subscription Services, Inc., Sussex (2011)
2. Diakopoulos, N., Naaman, M.: Towards quality discourse in online news comments. In: Proceedings of the ACM 2011 Conference on Computer Supported Cooperative Work, pp. 133–142 (2011)
3. Grimme, C., Preuss, M., Adam, L., Trautmann, H.: Social bots: human-like by means of human control. Big Data 5, 279–293 (2017)
4. Erjavec, K., Kovačič, M.P.: You don't understand, this is a new war!' Analysis of hate speech in news web sites' comments. Mass Commun. Soc. 15(6), 899–920 (2012)
5. Bastos, M.T., Mercea, D.: The brexit botnet and user-generated hyperpartisan news. Soc. Sci. Comput. Rev. (2017). https://doi.org/10.1177/0894439317734157
6. Neudert, L.-M., Kollanyi, B., Howard, P.N.: Junk news and bots during the German parliamentary election: what are German voters sharing over Twitter? In: COMPROP Data Memo, vol. 7, September 2017
7. Badri Satya, P.R., Satya, B., Lee, K., Lee, D., Zhang, J.J.: Uncovering fake likers in online social networks. ACM Trans. Internet Technol. 2365–2370 (2016). https://doi.org/10.1145/2983323.2983695
8. Woolley, S.C., Howard, P.N.: Social media, revolution, and the rise of the political bot. In: Routledge Handbook of Media, Conflict, and Security, pp. 282–292. Routledge, New York (2016)
9. Davis, C.A., Varol, O., Ferrara, E., Flammini, A., Menczer, F.: BotORNot: a system to evaluate social bots. In: WWW 2016 Companion, pp. 1–11 (2016)
10. Heinderyckx, F.: Gatekeeping Theory Redux. In: Vos, T.P., Heinderyckx, F. (eds.) Gatekeeping in Transition, pp. 253–268. Routledge, New York (2015)

11. Williams, B.A., DelliCarpini, M.X.: Unchained reaction: the collapse of media gatekeeping and the Clinton-Lewinsky scandal. Journalism 1(1), 61–85 (2000)
12. Bruns, A.: Gatewatching. Collaborative Online News Production. Peter Lang, New York (2005)
13. Vos, T.P.: Revisiting gatekeeping theory during a time of transition. In: Vos, T.P., Heinderyckx, F. (eds.) Gatekeeping in Transition, pp. 3–24. Routledge, New York (2015)
14. Gagliardone, I., et al.: MECHACHAL: online debates and elections in Ethiopia - from hate speech to engagement in social media, Oxford (2016)
15. Engelin, M., De Silva, F.: Troll detection: a comparative study in detecting troll farms on Twitter using cluster analysis. KTH, Stockholm, Sweden, 11 May 2016
16. Braun, J., Gillespie, T.: Hosting the public discourse, hosting the public. J. Pract. 5(4), 383–398 (2011)
17. Frischlich, L., Boberg, S., Quandt, T., Boberg, S., Quandt, T.: Comment sections as targets of dark participation? Journalists' evaluation and moderation of deviant user comments, vol. 9699 (2019)
18. Weischenberg, S., Malik, M., Scholl, A.: Journalismus in Deutschland 2005 Zentrale Befunde der aktuellen Repräsentativbefragung deutscher journalisten. Media Perspekt. 7, 346–361 (2006)
19. Gläser, J., Laudel, G.: Experteninterviews und qualitative Inhaltsanalyse als Instrument rekonstruierender Untersuchungen, 4th edn. VS Verlag für Sozialwissenschaften/Springer, Wiesbaden (2010)

Use and Assessment of Sources in Conspiracy Theorists' Communities

Tim Schatto-Eckrodt$^{(\boxtimes)}$ (iD), Svenja Boberg, Florian Wintterlin(iD),
and Thorsten Quandt(iD)

Department of Communication, University of Münster, Münster, Germany
tim.schatto-eckrodt@uni-muenster.de

Abstract. The endemic spread of misinformation online has become a subject of study for many academic disciplines. Part of the emerging literature on this topic has shown that conspiracy theories (CTs) are closely related to this phenomenon. One of the strategies deployed to combat this online misinformation is confronting users with corrective information, often drawn from mainstream media outlets. This study tries to answer the questions (I) whether there are online-communities that exclusively consume conspiracy theorist media and (II) how these communities use information sources from the mainstream. The results of our explorative, large-scale content analysis show that even in conspiracy theorist communities, mainstream media sources are being used very similar to sources from the conspiracy theorist media spectrum, thus not reaching any of their assumed corrective potential.

Keywords: Conspiracy theory · LDA · Content analysis · Sources · Alternative media

1 Introduction

For half a decade the World Economic Forum has been listing "massive digital misinformation" as one of the biggest global risk (World Economic Forum 2018). A reason for this assessment – one that is shared by many global policy-makers – is simple: It is crucial for any society to have a certain baseline of agreement on how the world is constituted; what can be seen as real, what is fact and what is fiction. The study of misinformation, disinformation and its many related concepts thus has become a priority in many academic disciplines, including the humanities, social sciences and even some fields of computer science.

One of the aforementioned related phenomena of online mis-/disinformation are conspiracy theories (CTs). Albeit falling into the general topic of digital misinformation, research on the phenomenon itself is comparatively scarce. CTs are often just a stand-in for various examples of false information, a mere subcategory of mis-/disinformation and sometimes used synonymously with any form of false information that has some kind of narrative structure. Yet, CTs are a relevant research topic on their own. Historically, CTs were used to discredit political opponents, the formation of groups of like-minded people or the building of distrust in the political system (Soukup 2008). Nowadays conspiracy

© Springer Nature Switzerland AG 2020
C. Grimme et al. (Eds.): MISDOOM 2019, LNCS 12021, pp. 25–32, 2020.
https://doi.org/10.1007/978-3-030-39627-5_3

theories have become a part of pop-culture and the vast availability of information on the internet, gives conspiracy theorists the ability to back up every claim with (sometimes dubious) facts (Wood 2013).

Current research also suggests that CTs are being used as tool of (modern) propaganda (Broniatowski et al. 2018), that they can be found in nearly all social subsystems (e.g. politics, health, science and journalism) and that CTs could foster epistemological counter-publics, where its members view the world differently than the rest of the public (Klein et al. 2018).

One of the strategies deployed to combat online misinformation is debunking, i.e. confronting users with corrective information (in the context of fake news see Lazer et al. 2018). Often, this corrective information is drawn from mainstream media outlets or other public institutions like publicly funded research centers or the government. These sources are believed to work under certain criteria of quality and to represent the official and factually correct perspective on current events.

This conceptual differentiation between official, factual *orthodox* sources and the alternative, unscientific *heterodox* sources is also a central element in many definitions of CTs. Following Anton et al. (2014) the main distinguishing characteristic of CTs and one of their defining properties is their heterodoxy e.g. their deviation from to societal norm of what is considered the scientifically and factually correct world view. A similar distinction is made in the context of alternative media, which is conceptualized to try to set up a critical counter-public to traditional, established media (Mathes and Pfetsch 1991). CT-media falls by definition into the category of heterodox, alternative media, which is contrasted by the orthodox, legacy media. Users of CT-media, as part of a (media-)critical counter-public, thus might reject information spread by orthodox, legacy media.

The underlying assumption of the debunking-strategy is that the misinformed users, who mainly consume heterodox media, simply have to be confronted with orthodox information that corrects their misinformed word view (Chan et al. 2017). This is assumption has been supported in an experimental setting: Douglas and Sutton (2018, p. 286) show that fact- and logic-based arguments can be used to challenge the believe in conspiracy theories.

Yet, the literature also suggests, that individuals with a higher believe in conspiracy theories seem to process information differently than ones with a low believe in conspiracy theories (Leman and Cinnirella 2013) and that debunking as does not work as well for the users of CT-media, because they are rarely confronted with orthodox sources (Zollo et al. 2015). To gain a better understanding of the phenomenon of conspiracy theories and its implications for society, this explorative study tries to answer the question whether there are online-communities that exclusively consume conspiracy theorist media and whether these communities use information sources from the mainstream or only the fringes of online media. Can mainstream media outlets cross the boundary between mainstream and fringe audiences?

2   Research Questions

Following this conceptualization of heterodox vs. orthodox media/sources in the context of debunking, we try to answer two research questions.

RQ1: *Are CT-communities cut-off from the real world in terms of news consumption?*

According to the widely cited filter-bubble hypothesis by Pariser (2011), media-users tend to consume media that fits their own ideology, thus creating a skewed and biased world view. Users rarely break out of their filter-bubbles and seek out information that does not fit their established world view. Are users of CT-media only exposed to heterodox sources or are orthodox sources also used?

RQ2: *Are legacy media treated differently than fringe media?*

The core assumption of the debunking-strategy is that the confrontation with corrective information can change users' believe in false information. Following this assumption, information spread by mainstream media outlets should be seen by the conspiracy theorist online communities as opposing to their own belief.

3   Method and Data

To answer the research questions, we conducted an explorative, large-scale, automated content analysis of seven of the most popular conspiracy theorist online communities on reddit.com (i.e. subreddits). The sample used in the analysis includes 31,569 submissions and 320,193 comments, posted in a 12-month timespan (from June 2017 to May 2018). The submissions are drawn from *files.pushshift.io*, an API collection originally done by Jason Baumgartner. The corresponding comments were then crawled via the *PRAW* Python library.

In order to better understand the use and assessment of both heterodox and orthodox sources in these communities, the hyperlinks used in the submissions were extracted, reduced to the domain-subdomain-level (e.g. "bbc.com") and coded by the authors to be either heterodox or orthodox sources. A source was deemed orthodox, when falling in either of the following categories: (a) Official, governmental organizations (e.g. the United States Environmental Protection Agency), (b) large, established media organizations (e.g. bbc.com) or (c) online encyclopedias[1] (e.g. Wikipedia). Heterodox sources were coded when falling into the definition of *alternative new media* by Holt, Ustad Figenschou and Frischlich (2019), that is position themselves as a counter-part to the hegemonically interpreted heterodox media or were solely focused on a specific conspiracy theory (e.g. realclimatescience.com). Additionally, the titles and the corresponding comments were preprocessed and then analyzed with LDA topic modelling (Blei et al. 2003) and a sentiment analysis (Hu and Liu 2004). Preprocessing steps included the removal of non-word tokens (e.g. urls, numbers, etc.) and stop words (using the stop word dictionary from the *tidytext* R package (Silge and Robinson 2016)), reducing the corpus by 47.2% and removing 474 cases completely. The number of topics was estimated using different two different metrics (see Fig. 1). A total number of $k = 16$ topics was chosen.

---

[1] For reference, see https://en.wikipedia.org/wiki/List_of_online_encyclopedias, retrieved September, 2019.

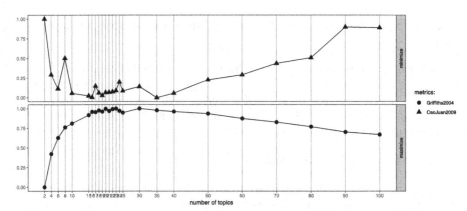

Fig. 1. Calculated metrics by Cao, Xia, Li, Zhang, & Tang 2009 and Griffiths and Steyvers 2004 for $k = 2 - 100$

To validate the results of the topic modelling human coders were used. Here, the correspondence of the human coders with the automated coding by the LDA can be understood as the quality of the topic modelling (Scharkow 2013). The odd-one-out method was used in the validation process. In this method, human coders have to identify a document or term that scores highly in one topic, from a list of documents/words that score highly on a different topic. The resulting inter-rater reliability measure between human coders and the LDA was Fleiss's Kappa > 0.8, indicating coherent and interpretable top word lists (Landis and Koch 1977).

Additionally, to gain an understanding of the emotional reaction of users confronted with a heterodox or an orthodox source, a sentiment analysis of the preprocessed comments was conducted using the sentiment dictionary by Liu et al. (2005). Sentiments were calculated on a per-comment-basis using the mean sentiment score of all words in the comment.

4   Results

In our dataset, 49% of submissions linked to an external (i.e. non-reddit) source and over 11% of all those submissions link to an orthodox, legacy media outlet. 23 of the 100 most frequently shared sources are orthodox sources (Table 1).

Over 25% of all submissions link to social media, while almost all of the linked Twitter accounts and YouTube channels are somewhat related to CT-media. The social media accounts of legacy media outlets are very uncommon. The only social media profile related to orthodox-media is *@realDonalTrump*, other politicians rarely occur.

Neither the sentiment analysis, nor a comparison of average scores (i.e. upvotes) revealed significant differences between the assessment of the heterodox and the orthodox sources ($p > 0.05$). These effects were still present when controlling for the topic of the comments under each submission. A plausible explanation for this counterintuitive result might be that users of CT-media only chose to post heterodox sources, when they fit their conspiracy theorist's narrative. The analyzed communities on reddit are overall

Table 1. Top 50% of used orthodox sources

Source	Usage (%)
dailymail.co.uk	12,7
foxnews.com	11,0
theguardian.com	7,2
thehill.com	5,6
nytimes.com	5,0
reuters.com	4,1
washingtonpost.com	4,1
bbc.com	3,8

relatively closed, attracting mainly other CT-users. The only difference in the reaction to heterodox vs. orthodox sources, was found when looking at the number of posted comments. Orthodox media submissions generated a higher number of comments than heterodox media submissions ($t = -5.5868$, $df = 406.14$, $p < 0.001$).

The extracted topics resemble the typical repertoire of conspiracy theorist issues, including topics such as US-politics, climate change and alternative health (see Table 2).

In LDA topic modelling, each document (i.e. each comment) is represented as a mixture of topics. The per-document-per-topic probabilities are called γ. These γ-values describe what percentage of words in a document were generated from (i.e. belong to) a topic. Comparing the γ-values for comments on posts with a heterodox source with those on orthodox source posts, revealed a significant difference (t-test with $p < 0.01$).

Although, due to the large number of cases in this sample, it is challenging to infer meaningful relationships from simple tests of significance. For instance, using standard nil-null hypothesis significance testing on the given sample size would most likely result in finding a significant difference between the two corpora, even though the difference might be close to non-existent (Weber and Popova 2012). To bypass this problem, the logic of the independent sample t-test is reversed: instead of testing for difference and rejecting the null hypothesis ("no difference"), the data is tested for equivalence, which means rejecting the rephrased H0 ("true effect") and supporting the alternative hypothesis ("absence of an effect that is worth examining") (Lakens 2017). Naturally, a null-effect cannot be supported, thus a maximum-no-effect (Δ) has to be predefined as a threshold. For the vast majority of the submissions, the assumption of equivalence can be supported, meaning, when applying a small maximum-no-effect of $\Delta = 0.1$, the equivalence tests for all topics are highly significant. All outliers in this analysis could be explained by a specific source dominating the topic (e.g. realclimatescience.com for the Climate Change topic or ae911truth.org for the 9/11 Truther topic). For all topics, an average of 11% of all external (i.e. non-reddit) sources were orthodox sources.

Table 2. Description of submission topics

Description	Most representative terms
Climate change	Climate, change, global, warming, science, study, scientists, earth, ice, al, sea, claims, wrong, paris, gore
Alex Jones	Qanon, conspiracy, corsi, power, dr, energy, theory, alex, live, jones, life, solar, recent, book, analysis
QAnon (Discussion)	Time, real, day, coming, storm, ve, don, death, awakening, guys, remember, love, reason, didn, isn
QAnon (Information Dumping)	Post, posts, anon, march, april, free, read, drop, chat, fire, set, board, speech, edition, night
Facebook/Zuckerberg	Red, twitter, facebook, pill, meme, google, posted, data, link, green, mark, share, zuckerberg, action, company
Pizzagate/Child Pornography	World, clinton, hillary, child, trafficking, human, children, sex, soros, police, george, trade, pope, nxivm, cult
Syria	Syria, war, attack, military, russia, israel, evidence, russian, false, uk, chemical, attacks, plane, flag, pentagon
Misc	News, deep, white, john, fake, house, security, national, black, list, mccain, fox, snowden, bolton
Holocaust Denial	People, video, truth, watch, story, history, days, holocaust, water, true, hrc, proof, ago, warning, sick
Mueller-Investigation	Mueller, bill, sessions, internet, law, justice, federal, gt, sign, court, special, questions, rights, investigation, michael
Iran	Fbi, iran, cia, obama, report, deal, comey, breaking, nuclear, memo, mccabe, page, released, documents
US-Government	Government, secret, de, youtube, la, info, https, www, ses, check, chandler, search, family, las, vegas
Alternative Health	Found, natural, health, dead, home, island, top, usa, pain, oil, related, treatment, online, support
Trump	Trump, president, america, patriots, trust, plan, china, donald, fight, god, potus, meeting, team, north, message
Media conspiracy/Censorship	Media, american, msm, cbts, link, times, reddit, saudi, article, social, intelligence, stream, foreign, narrative, election
Gun Control/School Shootings	Control, boom, money, shooting, david, past, future, school, question, don, mind, gun, stop, assange, word
9/11-Truther	Building, collapse, fire, wtc, towers, demolition, buildings, controlled, nist, fires, evidence, fall, tower

Notes: *LDA, method = Gibbs, k = 16, alpha = 5, N = 31095*

5 Limitations

The presented study has some limitations. Although the analyzed subreddits are among the most popular CT-communities on reddit and by that can give an insight into the use and assessment of sources in the general CT-community, there might be more fringe, closed-off communities that do not use orthodox sources in the same way.

Additionally, the content of links to social media or image hosting sites like imgur.com were not analyzed. It is possible that CT-users sometimes do not link to the original source of a journalistic article, but a screenshot of the article, possibly with added highlights or additional content that fits the CT-narrative. Further research is needed.

6 Conclusion

Even though it is assumed that communities that are exposed to misinformation, simply need access to corrective information provided by mainstream media outlets, to debunk false claims, our analysis shows that that might not be the case. CT online communities use a mix of mainstream and fringe media to support their claims and sources from the mainstream are assessed similarly to conspiracy theorist's sources. Thus, countering this specific form of misinformation must rely on more than simple debunking and counter-information by orthodox sources.

One of the theoretical assumptions drawn from this literature is that the believe in CTs is not necessarily based in the actual contents of the conspiracy theory, i.e. the conspiracy theorist information represented in heterodox sources, but rather a certain epistemology (Klein et al. 2018). This CT-epistemology excels at revising and match facts to support their sententia, drawn from broader CTs and are not susceptible to external information. More research on this epistemology of CT-users is needed.

References

Anton, A., Schetsche, M., Walter, M.K.: Einleitung: Wirklichkeitskonstruktion zwischen Orthodoxie und Heterodoxie – zur Wissenssoziologie von Verschwörungstheorien. In: Anton, A., Schetsche, M., Walter, Michael K. (eds.) Konspiration, pp. 9–25. Springer, Wiesbaden (2014). https://doi.org/10.1007/978-3-531-19324-3_1

Blei, D.M., Ng, A.Y., Jordan, M.I.: Latent Dirichlet allocation. J. Mach. Learn. Res. 3(4–5), 993–1022 (2003). https://doi.org/10.1162/jmlr.2003.3.4-5.993

Broniatowski, D.A., et al.: Weaponized health communication: Twitter bots and Russian trolls amplify the vaccine debate. Am. J. Public Health e1–e7 (2018). http://doi.org/10.2105/AJPH.2018.304567

Cao, J., Xia, T., Li, J., Zhang, Y., Tang, S.: A density-based method for adaptive LDA model selection. Neurocomputing 72(7–9), 1775–1781 (2009). https://doi.org/10.1016/j.neucom.2008.06.011

Chan, M.-P.S., Jones, C.R., Hall Jamieson, K., Albarracín, D.: Debunking: a meta-analysis of the psychological efficacy of messages countering misinformation. Psychol. Sci. 28(11), 1531–1546 (2017). https://doi.org/10.1177/0956797617714579

Douglas, K.M., Sutton, R.M.: Why conspiracy theories matter: a social psychological analysis. Eur. Rev. Soc. Psychol. **29**(1), 256–298 (2018). https://doi.org/10.1080/10463283.2018.1537428

Griffiths, T.L., Steyvers, M.: Finding scientific topics. Proc. Natl. Acad. Sci. **101**(Suppl. 1), 5228–5235 (2004). https://doi.org/10.1073/pnas.0307752101

Holt, K., Ustad Figenschou, T., Frischlich, L.: Key dimensions of alternative news media. Digit. J. 1–10 (2019). https://doi.org/10.1080/21670811.2019.1625715

Hu, M., Liu, B.: Mining and summarizing customer reviews. In: Proceedings of the 2004 ACM SIGKDD International Conference on Knowledge Discovery and Data Mining (KDD 2004), 168 (2004). https://doi.org/10.1145/1014052.1014073

Klein, C., Clutton, P., Polito, V.: Topic modeling reveals distinct interests within an online conspiracy forum. Front. Psychol. **9**, e0134641–e01346412 (2018). https://doi.org/10.3389/fpsyg.2018.00189

Lakens, D.: Equivalence tests: a practical primer for t tests, correlations, and meta-analyses. Soc. Psychol. Pers. Sci. **8**(4), 355–362 (2017)

Landis, J.R., Koch, G.G.: The measurement of observer agreement for categorical data. Biometrics **33**(March), 159–174 (1977)

Lazer, D.M.J., et al.: The science of fake news. Science **359**(6380), 1094–1096 (2018)

Leman, P.J., Cinnirella, M.: Beliefs in conspiracy theories and the need for cognitive closure. Front. Psychol. **4**, 1–10 (2013). https://doi.org/10.3389/fpsyg.2013.00378

Liu, B., Hu, M., Cheng, J.: Opinion observer: analyzing and comparing opinions on the web. In: Proceedings of the 14th International Conference on World Wide Web, pp. 342–351 (2005). https://doi.org/10.1145/1060745.1060797

Mathes, R., Pfetsch, B.: The role of the alternative press in the agenda-building process: spill-over effects and media opinion leadership. Eur. J. Commun. **6**(1), 33–62 (1991). https://doi.org/10.1177/0267323191006001003

Pariser, E.: The Filter Bubble. Penguin, UK (2011)

Scharkow, M.: Automatische Inhaltsanalyse. In: Möhring, W., Schlütz, D. (eds.) Handbuch standardisierte Erhebungsverfahren in der Kommunikationswissenschaft, pp. 289–306. Springer, Wiesbaden (2013). https://doi.org/10.1007/978-3-531-18776-1_16

Silge, J., Robinson, D.: tidytext: text mining and analysis using tidy data principles in R. J. Open Source Softw. **1**(3), 37 (2016). http://doi.org/10.21105/joss.00037

Soukup, C.: 9/11 conspiracy theories on the World Wide Web: digital rhetoric and alternative epistemology. J. Lit. Technol. **9**(3), 2–25 (2008)

Weber, R., Popova, L.: Testing equivalence in communication research: theory and application. Commun. Methods Meas. **6**(3), 190–213 (2012)

Wood, M.: Has the Internet been good for conspiracy theorising? PsyPAG Q. **88**, 31–34 (2013)

World Economic Forum. The Global Risks Report (2018). http://www3.weforum.org/docs/WEF_GRR18_Report.pdf

Zollo, F., et al.: Debunking in a World of Tribes. CoRR, abs/1510.04267 (2015)

Credibility Development with Knowledge Graphs

James P. Fairbanks⬤, Natalie Fitch$^{(\boxtimes)}$, Franklin Bradfield⬤,
and Erica Briscoe

Georgia Tech Research Institute, Atlanta, GA 30332, USA
`{james.fairbanks,natalie.fitch,`
`franklin.bradfield,erica.briscoe}@gtri.gatech.edu`

Abstract. Detection of misinformation online requires understanding both the sources and content of information. While a variety of supervised learning methods have been proposed for automated fact checking with respect to the information content of media, the source is usually not taken into account. To address this gap in existing methods, we describe a novel framework for validating online content based on a knowledge graph of media content and an attribution graph of media sources. This approach enables decision makers to identify factual information and supports counter disinformation operations by tracing the spread of disinformation across reliable and unreliable outlets. We have found that tracking knowledge provenance is critical to assessing the credibility of that knowledge. In addition to building a knowledge graph of fact triples *(subject, verb, object)*, we construct an attribution graph composed of links between all extracted facts and their sources on which we apply our main credibility reasoning mechanism, belief propagation. Analysis of credibility based on sources best captures reliable knowledge generation processes such as science, legal trials, and investigative reporting. In these domains there is a process for identifying experts and coming to consensus about the validity of claims to establish facts. Our method models these processes in news media by considering the relations between credible information and reliable sources.

Keywords: Knowledge graph · Belief propagation · Event extraction

1 Executive Summary

Reputable academic and journalistic institutions have traditionally operated under a peer-reviewed, expert distillation of credible editorial content. In contrast, online media creation is as rampant and unpoliced as online media consumption, which is often accompanied by unreliable judgment of content credibility by the individual consumer. Even good-intentioned and well-informed human purveyors of open online media are highly susceptible to cognitive biases that mislead their judgments about what content and sources are credible. Responsibility for verifying content is shared between readers, publishers, editors, and

© Springer Nature Switzerland AG 2020
C. Grimme et al. (Eds.): MISDOOM 2019, LNCS 12021, pp. 33–47, 2020.
https://doi.org/10.1007/978-3-030-39627-5_4

authors in online media. Denying our collective responsibility to mitigate this problem is damaging because misinformation can lead to severe political, social, and economic consequences that cannot be ignored. Technical means to aid humans in content verification are essential to protecting the utility of online media.

Verifying the integrity of information content and sources is challenging in the digital age due to the volume of data and variety of sources. We describe a unified framework of modeling human understanding of the world by distilling media content into a set of facts in a knowledge graph, which is a graph that contains real-world entities as nodes and the relations between them as edges. As it applies to event understanding, we view knowledge elements as facts derived from media sources, where they demonstrate relations between two entities, such as "France is part of the European Union".

The knowledge graph that we compose embeds two core types of knowledge: global and local. Global knowledge is composed of facts that are invariant with respect to time such as "Democracy is a form of government" and forms the background knowledge necessary for understanding the world. Local knowledge is more situational and temporally localized such as "The Foreign Minister held a press conference in Brussels", and relates to specific knowledge about an event or set of events. We distinguish these two forms of knowledge, and acquire global knowledge from open source ontologies and knowledge bases. Local knowledge is extracted from online content such as online news articles, social media, and public statements.

When humans assess the credibility of a new piece of information they naturally scrutinize the source of the information: "Do I trust where this information came from?". Along these lines, our source and fact credibility model quantifies the confidence associated with each fact and the reliability of each source[1]. When modeling the credibility of facts and sources, we evoke the intuition that facts are credible if corroborated by many credible sources, and sources are credible if they corroborate many credible facts. Prior work has demonstrated that a source centric analysis of credibility can be more effective than content based methods [3]. Our approach builds a network of facts and sources, called the *attribution graph*, and assigns a probabilistic *belief* to each vertex in this graph. By propagating these beliefs we solve for a confidence in every source and every fact. Interpreting this solution provides a quantitative measure of credibility.

2   Literature Review

The predominant approach to automated fact checking and credibility assessment in news media is that of supervised machine learning [10]. While methods in this area [7,9,11] contain unique variations, in general they frame the problem as a text classification problem, where features of specific text spans, including words, phrases, sentences, and entire documents, are extracted and utilized for

---

[1] We use *this fact is credible* as a synonym for *we have confidence in this fact.*, and a *source is reliable* if most of the facts it generates are credible.

labeling facts or claims with a discrete category such as *credible* or not credible. Another technique [5] frames the problem as a textual similarity problem, where new text spans are compared with previously seen spans that are known to be credible or not credible. In practice, both groups of approaches are hindered from the same issues that face all supervised learning problems, namely the requirement of large labeled datasets that are expensive to acquire and maintain. As applied to the specific problem of credibility assessment however, a key drawback of these approaches is that each text span is considered in an isolated context where application of background knowledge to the reasoning process is not involved. This is a critical limitation, because statements that are inherently false can be worded in a manner that appears credible [10]. Models trained on this task in this manner are able to compute a result over the shallow linguistic features that the words in the content provide, but do not consider the source from which the information originates. On the other hand, our approach described herein only requires prior credibilities assigned to source nodes in the attribution graph, bypassing the need for large quantities of labeled data. Furthermore, being a source-centric technique for credibility assessment, it is not hindered by ambiguity that arises from sole consideration of linguistic features in the content.

3   Building and Extending the Knowledge Graph

Often in the effort to ascertain whether information is credible, a person will draw upon an extensive amount of background knowledge to start the assessment. In our framework, a knowledge graph therefore serves as a surrogate for human memory, recall, and reasoning. The knowledge graph is used to organize and store information as it becomes available in media. In order to model the credibility of both data and sources we use an attribution graph to compute credibility using belief propagation. The posterior beliefs represent credibility scores that quantifies the trustworthiness of the information relative to its source(s).

3.1   Global Knowledge Resources

Humans analyze new information through the lens of personal experience but also against the backdrop of historical, cultural, and political situations, thus analysis requires inclusion of global background knowledge. We leverage BabelNet [8], which is a multi-lingual encyclopedic dictionary and semantic network of entities, concepts, and relations. BabelNet integrates knowledge of concepts and entities from 47 distinct knowledge bases such as WordNet, Wikipedia, Wikidata, Wiktionary, and OmegaWiki. It contains nearly 6.1M concepts, 9.7M entities, and 1.3B lexico-semantic relations among them. Tens of millions of entries possess various forms of multi-modal metadata as well such as images and phonetic details.

3.2 Local Knowledge Extraction

Online media content arrives in a variety of unstructured, multi-modal formats including text, image, video, and audio. Although our fact parsing methods operate on text directly, non-text elements within content could be extracted and represented as text prior to parsing and insertion into the knowledge graph. While this extension is out-of-scope in our current efforts, we propose applying object recognition and image captioning [12] to produce textual representations of images and videos, and speech to text models to address audio captures [2].

A particular challenge encountered in extracting knowledge from unstructured text is that of word sense disambiguation, or resolving discrete text spans to their correct lexical meanings. In the absence of large labeled datasets to build supervised learning models from, we apply an approach that exploits relations between named entities in BabelNet to perform these mappings. An algorithm that performs entity linking with respect to this knowledge base is accessible through a service called Babelfy [6]. To in order to extend its capability, we augmented the original Babelfy algorithm by including a number of accuracy-improving heuristics, while preserving the core algorithm.

3.3 Knowledge Representation

Global and local knowledge extractions are referred to as *facts* in the knowledge graph and are assimilated in the form of tuples. Representing information as facts in the knowledge graph enables reasoning over the knowledge that humans bring to their interpretation of a new piece of information from documents, imagery, or other media.

Figure 1 shows a notional sample of the knowledge graph and how to interpret the information in it. Each vertex represents an entity and each edge represents a relationship between two of them. Edges in this graph are labeled with probabilities representing likelihood and confidence, along with a binary label of local or global. Consider the fact tuple *(Vaccine, prevents, Polio)*. The edge weight is a numerical value between [0, 1] that quantifies the *likelihood* that the local fact *(Vaccine, prevents, polio)* is true. The edge colors denote the categorical labels of *confidence* in the likelihoods given by the edge weight, which conditions the belief a fact is true on the credibility of supporting evidence and the reputation of the source. An edge's line style indicates the type of knowledge to which the relation belongs. A dotted line denotes local knowledge that is susceptible to change such as *(Polio, is, Curable)*, and a solid line denotes global knowledge such as *(Polio, is a, Disease)*. The time the event occurred t and a decay rate μ are also affixed to each fact edge. These attributes can be used to modulate the likelihood that the event is still true given any passage of time. For events that last a long time, as is the case of global knowledge, the decay rate μ should be smaller. While temporal information is not used in our application of belief propagation, it is useful when manipulating the knowledge graph in an applied setting.

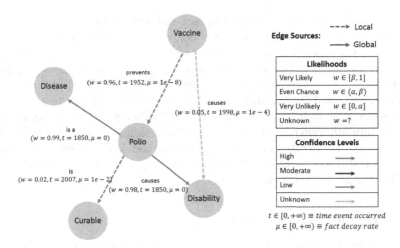

Fig. 1. Knowledge Graph representation and Edge Encoding, each vertex is an entity with facts represented as edges. Each edge has a likelihood (weight), confidence (color), type (dashed for local and solid for global), time of occurrence t, and decay rate μ. Here α, $\beta \in (0, 1)$. (Color figure online)

4 Credibility Assessment

Our approach for credibility reasoning is based on assessing information sources and facts relative to their sources. A separate representation called the attribution graph is constructed between facts and source vertices. Belief Propagation is applied to infer the credibility of all facts and sources in this graph. Sources and their credibility scores are stored in a separate database for later analysis and retrieval while fact credibility scores are encoded as edge weight attributes in the knowledge graph, which we denote as *confidences* in Fig. 1. We summarize this credibility assessment process in the following steps:

1. Process New Data: Ingest multimedia documents and extract facts
2. Update Attribution Graph: Build the graph linking facts and their sources
3. Assess Source-Fact Pairs: Run Belief Propagation on the attribution graph
4. Update Sources Database: Store sources and credibility in separate database
5. Update Knowledge Graph: Assign fact credibility scores as edge attributes.

4.1 Building the Attribution Graph

The attribution graph is bipartite with two types of vertices: sources and facts. Sources are retrieved from the database while the facts are derived from the knowledge graph. Specifically, each fact tuple *(subject, verb, object)* from the knowledge graph is encoded as a single fact vertex in the attribution graph. Edges are added connecting a fact vertex to each of the source vertices that provided that fact.

Prior to running belief propagation, fact and source vertices are assigned a prior probability of being credible and is denoted as $\phi(x)$ where x is a random variable denoting the credibility score. There are many factors that influence the prior probability. In general, when assessing the trustworthiness of a piece of information, people consider factors such as how it was collected, its level of completeness, and its age in addition to the source. When the source is a digital media asset such as an image, document, video, or audio recording, then detailed information such as metadata and hyperlink information can be used to determine a prior estimate of credibility. Our method can augment any existing credibility assessment technique by taking the output of that technique as the prior distribution for belief propagation.

4.2 Calculating on Confidence

We apply belief propagation (BP) on the attribution graph as the primary reasoning mechanism for credibility for all observed sources and facts. Belief Propagation algorithms have been developed successfully for cybersecurity problems in computer networks to classify malware and detect infected machines [1]. The applied intuition here is that if a fact is corroborated by many credible sources, then it will be credible, and if a source corroborates many credible facts then it is reliable. Beliefs are adjusted for every vertex in the graph as based on the entire history of the sources and the facts they provide.

The BP algorithm, illustrated in Fig. 2, requires that every source and fact vertex in the attribution graph is assigned a credibility value at the start, which is the prior probability of belonging to the target class label. More formally, this approach treats each fact or source vertex as a random variable $x_i \in \{0, 1\}$ and the prior probability, denoted by $\phi(x_i)$, represents the a priori belief that vertex i belongs to class x_i. Iterations of the belief propagation algorithm are interpreted as passing messages denoted by $m_{ij}(x_j)$, which is the message from vertex i to vertex j about vertex $j's$ likelihood of being in class x_j. The message update equation is given in Eq. 1 below.

$$m_{ij}(x_j) \leftarrow \sum_{x_i \epsilon X} \phi(x_i)\psi_{ij}(x_i, x_j) \prod_{k \epsilon N(i)/j} m_{ki}(x_i) \tag{1}$$

The function $\psi_{ij}(x_i, x_j)$ is a hyper-parameter that determines the conditional probability that if a neighboring node i is of class x_i, then its neighbor j will be of class x_j. Table 1 shows the 2×2 affinity matrix ψ. Smaller choices for ϵ in ψ assumes homophily of the labels.

Upon convergence, the BP algorithm solves for the posterior beliefs of credibility for each vertex in the attribution graph. Beliefs are denoted as $b(x_i)$, and the belief update equation is given in Eq. 2, where Z is a normalizing constant:

$$b_i(x_i) = Z\phi(x_i) \prod_{k \epsilon N(i)} m_{ki}(x_i) \tag{2}$$

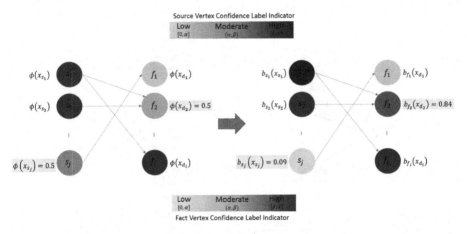

Fig. 2. Belief propagation on the attribution graph takes prior credibility estimates (left) and the links between sources and facts to solve for posterior credibility estimates (right). Credibility scores are tied back to knowledge graph edges for those facts.

Table 1. Edge potentials between neighboring nodes

$\psi_{ij}(x_i, x_j)$	x_i	x_j
x_i	$1-\epsilon$	ϵ
x_j	ϵ	$1-\epsilon$

For fact vertices, the posterior belief informs the confidence level associated with that fact in the knowledge graph. For source vertices, the posterior belief represents the overall credibility of facts supplied by that source and is stored for later retrieval and analysis but is not used in the knowledge graph.

4.3   Belief Propagation on a Toy Example

Figure 3 shows the attribution graph constructed on a synthetic dataset of 5 source nodes and 8 fact nodes with class labels color-coded according to the included legend. There are a total of 5 test nodes with credibility class labels stripped: $(s_1, s_4, f_3, f_6, f_8)$. Note, labeled nodes have a prior estimate of credibility equal to 0.9 if credible and 0.1 if not credible while unlabeled nodes are initialized with a uniform prior of 0.5 across both classes. In this simulation, $eps = 0.1$ for the edge potential function $\psi_{ij}(x_i, x_j)$ with a maximum number of iterations set to 10. Table 2 shows the resulting prior and posterior beliefs for a class label of *credible*, where a higher posterior indicates a stronger probability that the vertex is credible. The last column shows the ground truth class labels where 1 encodes *credible* and 0 encodes *notcredible*.

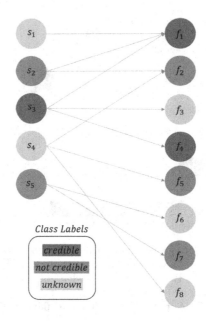

Fig. 3. Toy attribution graph demonstrating intuition of the belief propagation algorithm upon convergence

5   Experiments

Several experiments were designed in order to demonstrate theoretical and empirical performance of our proposed credibility assessment method. The first experiment creates synthetic data using graph generators to analyze the ability of belief propagation to correctly classify reliable sources. The second experiment demonstrates the performance of belief propagation to correctly classify the credibility of sources and facts using an actual news dataset and reports ROC curves using 3-fold cross-validation.

5.1   Belief Propagation Reliability on a Synthetic Dataset

The simulated experiment generates synthetic graph data with known properties and runs our algorithm on such data to measure accuracy. The simulation consists of a set of fact extractors that each generate edges from a known, distinct distribution over $(V \times V)$, each having a tunable parameter. For example, the distribution over pairs of vertices is uniform, so that each extractor is an Erdos Renyi (ER) graph generator. These generators would then be joined with a Bernoulli distribution with probability p_i to indicate the accuracy of the extractors. Each extractor would have a different probability of generating a false positive edge. Since our method cannot generate edges that the extractors failed to find, we are more concerned with eliminating spurious facts reported by the extractors than with creating edges the extractors failed to find. The goal

Table 2. Prior and posterior beliefs of credibility vs ground truth for toy example

Vertex	Prior	Posterior	Truth
s_1	0.500	0.816	1
s_2	0.010	0.114	0
s_3	0.900	0.979	1
s_4	0.500	0.044	0
s_5	0.010	0.024	0
f_1	0.900	0.894	1
f_2	0.010	0.031	0
f_3	0.500	0.883	1
f_4	0.900	0.977	1
f_5	0.010	0.034	0
f_6	0.500	0.119	0
f_7	0.010	0.024	0
f_8	0.500	0.135	0

of this simulation is to show that the attribution graph beliefs identify the least reliable extractors, ie. those with the highest probability p_i of emitting spurious facts.

Figure 4 shows that the BP method is a reliable method of recovering the source reliability ranking. Here ρ, written rho on the charts, is defined as the Spearman rank correlation between the observed BP score of the information extractor and the ground truth reliability of that extractor. Figure 4 shows that as the problem gets larger the method is able to acquire a better estimate of the reliabilities of the extractors. This makes sense because in this example there is a fixed number of extractors (6) and the number of samples is growing. This additional information per sample enables more accurate estimates of the source reliabilities.

5.2   Credibility Assessment on the Fake News Challenge Dataset

The Fake News Challenge (FNC) dataset is based on the emergent dataset [4] originally curated at Columbia's School of Journalism in order to address the task of rumor-debunking. Creators of the Fake News Challenge released this dataset for the classification task of stance detection, which they believe to be a critical milestone to mitigate the problem of fake news in media. The FNC dataset consists of 843 news articles and 958 headlines with a total of 4,518 headline-article pairs with a label of *agree*, *disagree*, *discuss*, or *unrelated*. We re-purposed the FNC dataset in order to demonstrate credibility assessment of sources and facts using real news articles. Using this dataset, we report on two such experiments below and refer to them as the *simplified* model and the *complex* model.

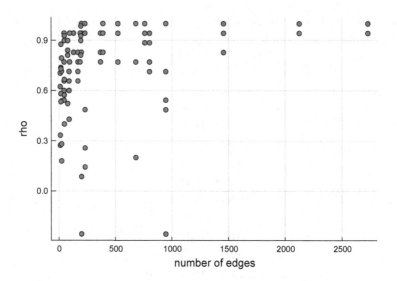

Fig. 4. Simulation correlation of source reliability as a function of the size of the graph in edges

Table 3. Publisher class metrics and reporting accuracy

Publisher label	Class percentage	Mean acc	Median acc
Credible	0.545	0.891	0.900
Not credible	0.455	0.053	0.054

Experimental Dataset. The FNC dataset was re-purposed for our experiments by first filtering the set of article-headline pairs to only include pairs labeled with a stance of *agree* or *disagree*. Next, we assigned groups of articles as being sourced from a single entity, notionally equivalent to a *publisher*. A total of 55 different publishers were created with an average of 13.163 articles per publisher, minimum of 6 and maximum of 22. In both experiments, each publisher entity represents a source vertex in the attribution graph.

In the simplified model, each headline (ie claim) represents a fact vertex and an edge occurs between a source and a fact if the publisher (source) owns at least one article that agrees with the given headline (fact). Note that each headline has a ground truth label of *credible* or *notcredible* and publishers may possess articles that agree with a headline that is not true. Therefore a priori estimates of publisher credibility are based on the accuracy of their reporting, that is an average of the number of claims they agreed with that were true. Table 3 shows publisher reporting accuracy metrics for each target class. Further, the distribution of credible and not credible headlines is 0.644 and 0.356, respectively. Note, this model does not rely on facts extracted from the articles but rather leverages the headlines as a proxy for facts present in the articles with the assumption that an article headline is a concise summary of the central claim present in an article. This model demonstrates proof-of-concept for our proposed credibility assessment methodology and reports performance on a simplified experiment with a predictable outcome.

In the complex model, a set of fact *(subject, verb, object)* tuples are extracted for each article and are represented as fact vertices in the attribution graph, in accordance with Sect. 3.1. In this model, an edge occurs between a source and a fact if the publisher owns the article that produced the extracted fact tuple. A priori estimates of publisher credibility are dervied as described above. A priori estimates of fact credibility were derived based on the given headline labels using a textual entailment prediction model. Details of this process are described in more detail below.

Simplified Model: Belief Propagation Between Sources and Headlines. In the attribution graph, each publisher entity represents a source vertex and each headline (or claim) represents a fact vertex. An edge in the attribution graph occurs between a source and a fact if the publisher (source) owns at least one article that agrees with the given headline (fact). In this setup, the attribution graph has a total of 55 source nodes and 783 fact nodes, which constitutes a majority of the 958 available headlines from the original FNC dataset.

In this experiment, 3-fold cross-validation was performed by randomly selecting 1/3 of source and fact vertices to be unlabeled (i.e. test vertices) with the remaining 2/3 of vertices retaining their credibility labels. Figure 5 shows the ROC curves for the test vertices in each of the 3 folds. Note, it is assumed that performance will degrade at the granular fact level that is used in the complex model. The next section reports on performance where the attribution graph is built between publishers (source vertices) and extracted facts from articles (fact vertices).

Complex Model: Belief Propagation Between Sources and Facts. The simplified model described above builds an attribution graph between publishers of articles and headlines, which act as a proxy for the facts contained in the articles. We view the simplified model's credibility assessment performance as a "best-case" scenario as we expect the noise generated by the fact extraction process to degrade performance. In contrast, the complex model builds the attribution graph between publishers of articles and the facts extracted from those articles. The main challenges in creating an attribution graph between sources and extracted facts is knowing (1) how to resolve fact vertices (i.e. identify facts as the same vertex in the attribution graph if they support the same claim) and (2) what the a priori class labels are for each extracted fact (*credible* or *notcredible*).

To construct the attribution graph, each article is processed through our in-house fact-extraction pipeline which leverages state-of-the-art NLP models from spaCy and AllenNLP. In order to determine a priori estimates of credibility for each extracted *(subject, verb, object)* fact tuple, we use a textual entailment

Table 4. Extracted Fact and Headline Entailment Examples

Headline: "Rare meteorite impact causes blast in Nicaragua's capital, Managua"
Fact: "a meteorite plummeting to Earth caused A blast near the Nicaraguan capital city of Managua on Saturday night"
Predictions: [Entailment: 0.957, Contradiction: 0.002, Neutral: 0.041]

––––––––––

Headline: "Texas Truck Winds Up in Syria With Islamic Militants"
Fact: "the truck had different owners since auction before ending up in the hands of Islamic terrorists"
Predictions: [Entailment: 0.619, Contradiction: 0.016, Neutral: 0.365]

––––––––––

Headline: "Dylan Thomas Finds Tropical Spider Burrowed Under Skin"
Fact: "Doctors retrieved a tropical spider from The 21 year old's abdomen"
Predictions: [Entailment: 0.561, Contradiction: 0.097, Neutral: 0.342]

––––––––––

Headline: "eBay is planning an Apple Watch app'"
Fact: "At least one of the big boys planning on developing an app for the Apple Watch"
Predictions: [Entailment: 0.954, Contradiction: 0.009, Neutral: 0.037]

––––––––––

Headline: "Breaking: Soldier shot at National War Memorial in Ottawa"
Fact: "a gunman shot A uniformed soldier at the Canadian War Memorial on Wednesday morning"
Predictions: [Entailment: 0.529, Contradiction: 0.007, Neutral: 0.464]

prediction model to generate predictions for each fact relative to their paired headlines. The model returns a probability distribution for each headline/fact pair with labels of *entailment*, *contradiction*, and *neutral* that quantifies the amount of agreement held between a headline and a fact. For each headline, all fact pairs that generate an *entailment* prediction of at least 50% are resolved to the same fact vertex in the attribution graph and assumes the given headline credibility class label. The complex model is equally a demonstration of both (1) the reliability of our fact extraction generators and (2) credibility assessment performance using a real news dataset at the fact-granular level. Table 4 shows examples of extracted facts (here joined together as a single string for readability) and headline pairs that have an entailment prediction of greater than or equal to 50%.

Similar to the simplified model, 3-fold cross-validation is executed on this new attribution graph with a randomized 1/3 of the vertices remaining unlabeled as test vertices. Figure 6 shows performance for each fold on the attribution graph composed between publishers (sources) and their extracted facts. The performance does decrease slightly, which was expected, but is still respectable.

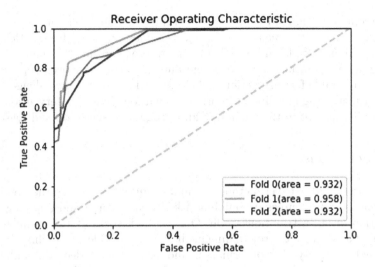

Fig. 5. ROC curve for simplified model

While this performance analyzes the extent to which extracted information is congruent with the main article claim represented by the headline, it does not provide a measure of the total quality of the facts that were extracted. Further experiments must be developed that assimilates into the attribution graph those extracted facts which are predicted to refute (*contradiction*) or are unrelated (*neutral*) to their paired headlines.

With respect to the simplified model, the attribution graph constructed for the complex model captures 53/55 original publishers but only preserves 243/783 headline claims with the facts that are extracted. This reduction of publisher and

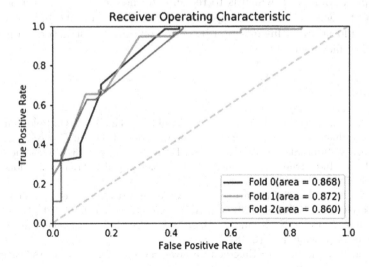

Fig. 6. ROC curve for the complex model

headline representation in the attribution graph could be a consequence of either (1) a lack of complete *(subject, verb, object)* tuples extracted from articles and (2) extracted fact tuples from articles that do not capture the main claim of the headline as quantified by textual entailment. The first reason represents a challenge in reliable fact extraction and the second represents a challenge in reliably scrutinizing the meaning of information without human intervention, both of which are inherent in the domain of knowledge representation and reasoning.

6   Conclusions

We have presented a novel method to rapidly ingest and judge the credibility of information and sources by building a knowledge graph and applying belief propagation on an attribution graph. Our method works at the granularity of individual facts extracted from online media and is capable of handling, in addition to text, a variety of data formats including imagery, video, and audio with the addition of neural processing methods. Instead of merely passing through credible data and discarding the non-credible, our system quantifies measures of data integrity and assigns weights to each fact and source. As such, our method has the advantage of being transparent and interpretable to the user in that it incorporates human readable relationships between entities and events extracted directly from data sources.

Future work should build on the experiments addressed herein to develop more holistic and larger datasets that includes both global and local knowledge sources on which to test the proposed method. In addition to questioning the source, we also aim to address another natural question that scrutinizes the content of information: "How does this new information relate to existing knowledge?". Pairwise similarity measures in graphs are traditionally used to solve the link prediction task, which is to recommend new connection in a network. Therefore, models of structural support for facts based on the link prediction problem could address this question by characterizing the structural context in which a new fact would occur.

References

1. Chau, D., Nachenberg, C., Wilhelm, J., Wright, A., Faloutsos, C.: Polonium: tera-scale graph mining and inference for malware detection. In: Proceedings of the 2011 SIAM International Conference on Data Mining, pp. 131–142. Proceedings, Society for Industrial and Applied Mathematics, April 2011. https://doi.org/10.1137/1.9781611972818.12
2. Chiu, C., et al.: State-of-the-art speech recognition with sequence-to-sequence models. CoRR abs/1712.01769 (2017). http://arxiv.org/abs/1712.01769
3. Fairbanks, J., Fitch, N., Knauf, N., Briscoe, E.: Credibility assessment in the news: do we need to read? p. 8 (2018)
4. Ferreira, W., Vlachos, A.: Emergent: a novel data-set for stance classification. In: HLT-NAACL (2016)

5. Hassan, N., Arslan, F., Li, C., Tremayne, M.: Toward automated fact-checking: detecting check-worthy factual claims by claimbuster. In: Proceedings of the 23rd ACM SIGKDD International Conference on Knowledge Discovery and Data Mining, pp. 1803–1812. ACM (2017a)

6. Moro, A., Raganato, A., Navigli, R.: Entity linking meets word sense disambiguation: a unified approach. Trans. Assoc. Comput. Linguist. (TACL) **2**, 231–244 (2014)

7. Nakashole, N., Mitchell, T.: Language-aware truth assessment of fact candidates. In: ACL, pp. 1009–1019 (2014)

8. Navigli, R., Ponzetto, S.P.: BabelNet: the automatic construction, evaluation and application of a wide-coverage multilingual semantic network. Artif. Intell. **193**, 217–250 (2012)

9. Rashkin, H., Choi, E., Jang, J.Y., Volktova, S., Choi, Y.: Truth of varying shades: analyzing language in fake news and political fact-checking. In: Proceedings of the 2017 Conference on Empirical Methods in Natural Language Processing, pp. 2931–2937. Association for Computational Linguistics (2017)

10. Thorne, J., Vlacos, A.: Automated fact checking: task formulations, methods and future directions. In: Proceedings of the 27th International Conference on Computational Linguistics, pp. 3346–3359 (2018)

11. Vlachos, A., Riedel, S.: Fact checking: task definition and dataset construction. In: Proceedings of the ACL 2014 Workshop on Language Technologies and Computational Social Science, pp. 18–22. Association for Computational Linguistics (2014)

12. Xu, K., et al.: Show, attend and tell: Neural image caption generation with visual attention. CoRR abs/1502.03044 (2015). http://arxiv.org/abs/1502.03044

Automated Detection of Nostalgic Text in the Context of Societal Pessimism

Lena Clever[1]([⊠])(iD), Lena Frischlich[2](iD), Heike Trautmann[1](iD),
and Christian Grimme[1](iD)

[1] Department of Information Systems, University of Münster,
Leonardo-Campus 3, 48149 Münster, Germany
{lena.adam,heike.trautmann,christian.grimme}@uni-muenster.de
[2] Department of Communication, University of Münster,
Bispinghof 9-14, 48149 Münster, Germany
lena.frischlich@uni-muenster.de

Abstract. In online media environments, nostalgia can be used as important ingredient of propaganda strategies, specifically, by creating societal pessimism. This work addresses the automated detection of nostalgic text as a first step towards automatically identifying nostalgia-based manipulation strategies. We compare the performance of standard machine learning approaches on this challenge and demonstrate the successful transfer of the best performing approach to real-world nostalgia detection in a case study.

Keywords: Nostalgia · Emotion · Text classification · Propaganda

1 Motivation

The term nostalgia (Greek: "nostos" = "home" and "algia" = "pain") defines "a sentimental longing or wistful affection for the past" [20] commonly refers to personal memories of the past, e.g, the house one lived in, or the media one has consumed ("personal nostalgia"). Nostalgia related to the collective identity is called group-based nostalgia or collective nostalgia and defined as "the nostalgic reverie [...] that is contingent upon thinking of oneself in terms of a particular social identity or as a member of a particular group [...] and concerns events or objects related to it." [29]

Nowadays, collective nostalgia is a prevalent phenomenon in interactive online media. Ranging from single user comments, retro-styled Instagram posts, up to Facebook groups, nostalgia can be found across platforms. Many people

The authors acknowledge support by the German Federal Ministry of Education and Research (FKZ 16KIS0495K) and the European Research Center for Information Systems (ERCIS) as well as the Digital Society research program funded by the Ministry of Culture and Science of the German State of North Rhine-Westphalia. Further, the authors thank Constantine Sedikides, Tim Wildschut, and Tim Wulf for their advice in designing the conducted data collection study.

© Springer Nature Switzerland AG 2020
C. Grimme et al. (Eds.): MISDOOM 2019, LNCS 12021, pp. 48–58, 2020.
https://doi.org/10.1007/978-3-030-39627-5_5

contribute to these posts, e.g. by liking them or linking their friends, which may have a related past on topics. The finding, that collective nostalgia solidifies a shared social identity [29] is also strategically employed by companies in online media in order to build up online brand communities [10]. Last but not least, nostalgia is part of political campaigns [27]. Slogans like "Make America great again!" used by Donald Trump's campaign imply the wish of re-establishing the "good old days". Especially right-wing populist actors refer to (collective) nostalgia to advertise their master-narrative of a glorious, ethnic homogeneous past that has been destroyed by corrupt elites and dangerous immigrants but can be restored by voting the respective populist party [27]. Therewith, the populists benefit from collective nostalgia's power to evoke societal pessimism.

On this background, nostalgia can be seen as a medium for spreading propagandistic content. In order to strengthen resilience against the misuse of nostalgic feelings in propagandistic campaigns, nostalgic content (e.g. in online discourses) has to be detected first. Besides manual classification of nostalgic texts based on so-called emotion dictionaries [9] there is no study that applies automated approaches to this problem.

The current study aims at providing an initial step in closing this gap, by applying and comparing machine learning approaches for the classification of German nostalgic texts. To this end, we set up a panel to acquire nostalgic and non-nostalgic texts for training and evaluation purposes of the machine learning approaches. For feature extraction, a dictionary-based approach was applied. For classification three established classifiers are trained and compared. Finally, the best classifier was used to analyze online user comments from a news forum. Results indicate that automatic classification of nostalgia is possible and that it is principally transferable to online discussions beyond laboratory contexts. Furthermore, it is important to mention, that nostalgic content is not exclusively spread in textual from, but also especially as pictures. Within this paper, the authors focus - as a starting point - on text based content.

2   Nostalgia as an Emotional Concept

Initially, nostalgia was described by Hofer [15] in 1688 as a synonym for homesickness, indicating a rather negative sentiment. Nowadays, the lay understanding of nostalgia has shifted to a more positive meaning. Since studies show that people categorize a nostalgic feeling as a predominantly positive and past oriented emotion [29]. However, memories of the past are often linked to missing specific persons or conditions of that time, which may lead to a longing to return that past. Further, nostalgia has been found to be a pan-cultural emotion [14] as well as a character trait, leaving specific persons more prone to nostalgia than others [5].

Although former research predominantly focused on the individual level of nostalgia (personal nostalgia), more recent studies show that nostalgia is deeply connected to sociality [13]. The analysis of nostalgic narratives implies, that nostalgia is often linked to family, friends, or group members [29]. Based on the

Intergroup Emotions Theory by Mackie et al. [18], studies show that nostalgia can be transferred from an individual-level to group-level emotion [26].

3   Nostalgia as an Instrument

Evoking nostalgic emotion is highly effective in marketing, since, "individual and collective nostalgia can inspire consumers a richer emotional experience." [8]. Nostalgic advertisement on social media platforms has a high impact on the customers purchase intentions and the positive attitude towards the brand [30]. Not surprising, multiple successful brands such as Coca Cola use nostalgia in their campaigns [8]. Techniques to use nostalgia in marketing are, for example, nostalgic packaging or advertisement campaigns [8].

If we consider political campaigns as political advertising [4], techniques from marketing may blend into strategies used for populist communication. As nostalgia can fuel anti-elitist attitudes and societal pessimism [27], right-wing populist actors might particularly benefit from nostalgic narratives [17]. The fear of losing collective roots [19] or security [11] may result in a longing for the better-believed past and in stronger feelings against foreigners or others [25].

In summary, personal and collective nostalgia are relevant emotions that are used as strategic tools both in marketing and political campaigning to manipulate public perception, emotion, and cognition.

4   Methodology

4.1   Data Collection

So far, the automated detection of nostalgia in written texts has not gained much scientific attention. As such, suitable data for classifier-development is missing. To overcome this issue, we conducted an online study to gain adequate data. Therein, participants were asked in a questionnaire to write either a short nostalgic essays or about an every day memory. During a first pre-processing step, observations containing only simply sentences like "i do not know what to write" or arbitrary character combinations, have been omitted. After this, 285 questionnaires (140 nostalgic and 145 non nostalgic condition) are used for further analysis. Analysis of Socio-demographic data between the two conditions showed, that age, gender and educational status follow similar distributions. Furthermore, the sample is comparable to the age, gender and educational distribution within the German population[1]. Participants of the study are on average of age 41, which is slightly younger, than the average age of 43 of the German population. Additionally, participants are slightly higher educated.

In terms of text structure, nostalgic essays were only slightly shorter ($med = 72$ words, range between $q_4 = 29$, and $q^4 = 147$) than non-nostalgic ones ($med = 76$ words, range between $q_4 = 28$, and $q^4 = 133$). As shown in Fig. 1, there is no significant difference between the essay length of both text types.

---

[1] https://www.destatis.de.

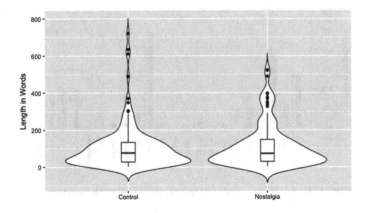

Fig. 1. Length of nostalgic and non-nostalgic essays.

4.2   Feature Extraction

For data representation and feature extraction, we followed two approaches: a bag-of word (BOW) approach [21] and a dictionary-based sentiment analysis to get a grasp on emotions [28]. For the BOW approach, features refer to the importance of terms within a specific text, without regarding grammar or semantic word order [3]. Terms are character- or word-based n-grams. For the former the text is split into character snippets of length n [6]; for the latter, existing combinations of n consecutive words define a feature [1]. Grams are simply counted within the texts (term frequencies) [12], categorized as present or absent with a Boolean representation (term presence) [21], or set into context of term frequencies within the whole data base (Term Frequency-Inverse Document Frequency, TF/IDF) [23].

For sentiment extraction, the German version of the Linguistic Inquiry and Word Count dictionary (LIWC) was used [22]. To ensure reliability, we evaluated the dictionary manually. A representative sample of all 72 categories has been re-coded by two independent coders. Based on this, 24 (for the task most important) categories have been revised completely. The resulting dictionary contains the following categories: Pronouns (I, we, self, you, other), Positive (positive emotion, positive feeling, optimism), Negative (negative emotion, anxiety, anger, sad), Social (communication, other-reference, friends, family, humans), Time (past, present, future). The exploratory analysis, shown in Fig. 2 of the dictionary analysis shows, that categories follow similar distributions within both essay types.

If we consider the Pearson correlation of features (see Figs. 3 and 4), only few interesting effects can be observed. Most notable, while "social" and "time" have similar correlation for both conditions ($cor_c(social, time) = 0.8$ and $cor_n(social, time) = 0.81$), "social" and "past" ($cor_c(social, past) = 0.66$ and $cor_n(social, past) = 0.7$) as well as "present" time ($cor_c(social, present) = 0.56$ and $cor_n(social, present) = 0.67$) are slightly stronger correlated for the

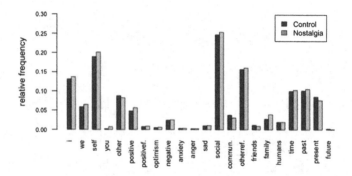

Fig. 2. Relative usage of sentiment words in both conditions.

nostalgia condition. In contrast, "social" and "future" are stronger correlated for the control condition ($cor_c(social, future) = 0.47$ and $cor_n(social, future) = 0.41$). Nevertheless, the findings suggest, that a distinction of both text types on basis of sentiment features will not lead to satisfying results. Therefore, we base the training of classifiers on BOW representations in a first experiment.

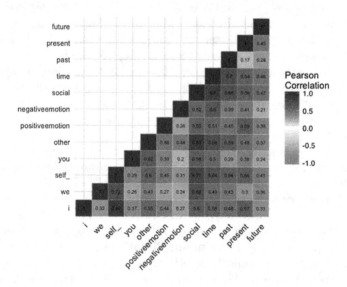

Fig. 3. Correlations of sentiments within Control condition.

4.3   Text Classification

Several researchers report on good results using the Naive Bayes classifier (NB) for text classification [21]. The NB is a probabilistic classifier, which computes

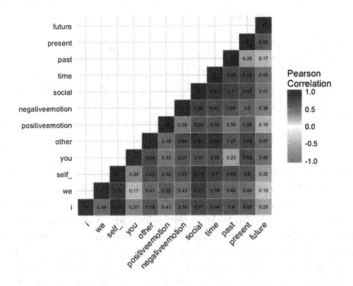

Fig. 4. Correlations of sentiments within Nostalgia condition.

the posterior-probability of a document belonging to a class, based on the distributions of terms within the document, while assuming, that features are independent of each other [2].

Secondly, the Support Vector Machine (SVM) is used [16]. The goal of a SVM is to partition the data space between different classes with the help of linear or in higher dimensional kernel space. A so-called hyper plane, which separates the two classes with the widest margin is used for assigning a discrete class label $\in \{-1; +1\}$ to the instances [24].

Furthermore, the Logistic Regression (LR) classifier is often used in terms of text classification [7]. In logistic regression, a linear combination of the input features is used to predict the probability for a specific class in contrast to other observations. The probability value is then transformed with a logistic function into a prediction value between $[0, 1]$.

For all mentioned classifiers the best performing feature set and parameter setting were extracted by parameter configuration by means of grid search and k-fold cross validation. Since the data set is limited, 70% of the data was used for training and 30 for testing.

4.4   Classifier Performance and Results

As the number of essays is similar for both conditions, performances can be compared by the accuracy metric[2], which is the relation of all correctly classified instances compared to the complete number of instances within the test set.

---

[2] As the classes of the classification problem are balanced, the accuracy metric can be used as a first indicator to compare classifier results.

Table 1. Classifier performance

Algorithm	Accuracy	Feature set	Parameter setting
MN Bayes	0.66	word 2-gram	alpha = 0.1
SVM	0.67	word 1-gram	kernel = 'linear'
LR	0.65	word 2-gram	C = 0.05
Random	0.49	all feature sets	

As displayed within Table 1, LR and MN Bayes perform best for word based 2-grams, whereas the overall best classifier SVM, works best on a feature set based on word 1-grams. For comparison: A random classifier has an average accuracy of 0.49 depending on feature representation. Considering this comparison, the findings imply that the classifiers are of only mediocre quality. However, compared to the performance of two independent coders on the same text corpus (average accuracy of 0.54), we still see a promising potential of the conducted approach. As prior research [29] reports that human coders classify nostalgic essays with an accuracy of 99%, the relatively low accuracy in our study indicates that the experimental essays were not distinct enough to allow for precise distinction.

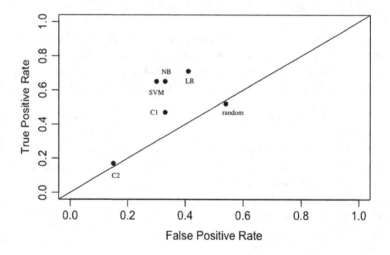

Fig. 5. Classifier results in ROC space.

This is also shown in Fig. 5, which represents the classifier and coder results (C1 and C2) in the ROC space. All classifiers and coders have problems with distinguishing between the texts and the error rates of falsely positive and falsely negative classified instances are equally distributed.

In order to get a better understanding of the classifiers decision criteria, we could have a look at the top features for the best performing classifier SVM.

Within Fig. 6, twenty most describing features are displayed for both conditions. Whereas the nostalgic condition contains mainly words related to family and greater events, such as marriage, participants of the control condition wrote about every day memories and friends. This finding goes with the results of a prior research [10], where it is stated, that nostalgic posts on Facebook are linked to special events in the past, often related to ones family.

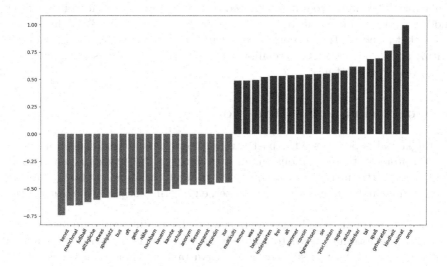

Fig. 6. Most describing Features.

Based on the above stated results, we decided to test the classifier on a more natural data set.

5   Classification of User-Comments in Online Media

In a small case study, we tested the performance of the tuned classifiers on 'real' data. Therefore, 'nostalgic comments' from an on-line newspaper article[3] were used. The article referred to childhood in former days in contrast to today, which triggered people to comment and write about their childhood memories.

24 comments were manually collected from this article and labeled 'nostalgic' (n = 12) and 'non-nostalgic' (n = 12) by three independent coders. Furthermore, another twelve comments from articles concerning sports and politics are extracted. The comments resemble the essays in terms of writing style, as well as text length[4].

---

[3] http://www.spiegel.de/wissenschaft/mensch/erziehung-lasst-eure-kinder-frei-kolumne-a-1223770.html.
[4] Median = 121 words, min = 61 words, max = 248 words.

The SVM classifier achieves an accuracy score of 0.83 on the nostalgic comment data set and somehow failed for the detection of the control comments (accuracy = 33%). In order to get a better understanding of the classifiers ability to adapt on real world scenarios, we had a closer look on the falsely classified instances of the control comments. Interestingly those comments all included words like "mother", "grandmother", etc., which are related to family. As those words are highly related to the nostalgia class, the incorrect classification is explicable. The twelve comments related to external articles concerning politics and sports is again classified correctly with an accuracy of 83%. The results show, that although the authors were not instructed on nostalgic writing or the writing style, the classifiers were able to transfer the trained nostalgia detection to the real-world setting.

6   Conclusion and Future Work

Nostalgia makes people see the past through rose-tinted glasses, which makes it easy to promote those 'glorious times' and charging the developments of time. Political advertisement or propagandistic content including nostalgic evoking elements may manipulate people and foster, e.g., voting for populist right-winged parties.

Both algorithmic models and humans were able to differentiate between non-nostalgic and nostalgic essays to some extent. The results of the analysis showed that classifiers performed slightly better than random choice. Classification on a real-world data set led to good results.

An interesting by-catch of this study is, that a number of people answered the writing task by criticizing the current (political or societal) situation, although they were not asked for political opinions. Exemplary comments are:

> At that time, there have been no problems like overpopulation because of refugees. [...] Nobody covered their faces and bodies [...].

or,

> [...] There have not been so many refugees and asylum-seekers in Berlin. One could drive home from North-town to South without being scared.[...] Oh well this have been nice times, i doubt, that it will be like this anymore.

These findings strengthen the assumption that nostalgia, as a group emotion, can be observed in nationalistic context. The writing task fosters people to express out-group prejudices and strengthen their positive in-group evaluation of their home town or country. Within the formulations of those essays, no negative issues in context of their former times are reported. Participants describe their experiences through rose-tinted glasses and dramatically shift into hateful excesses towards the current societal and political situation.

Furthermore, the findings imply the importance of further research on nostalgia as an intermediary for propagandistic content. Considering the powerful effect of evoking nostalgia even in the unproblematic context of the study, is an indication that nostalgia used in an appropriate setting can be utilized to manipulate or stir up people. Consequently, further research could address the examination of different nostalgia-evoking content types. Next to textual content, especially images are used to spread nostalgic feelings on social media platforms. The analysis of such images is an interesting starting point. From a technical point of view, the combination with state-of-the-art classifiers and a sophisticated parameter tuning are next steps.

References

1. Abbasi, A., Chen, H., Salem, A.: Sentiment analysis in multiple languages. ACM Trans. Inf. Syst. **26**(3), 1–34 (2008). https://doi.org/10.1145/1361684.1361685
2. Aggarwal, C.C., Zhai, C.X.: A survey of text classification algorithms. In: Aggarwal, C., Zhai, C. (eds.) Mining Text Data, vol. 9781461432, pp. 163–222. Springer, Boston (2012). https://doi.org/10.1007/978-1-4614-3223-4_6
3. Aggarwal, C.C., Zhai, C.: An introduction to text mining. In: Aggarwal, C., Zhai, C. (eds.) Mining Text Data, pp. 1–10. Springer, Heidelberg (2012). https://doi.org/10.1007/978-1-4614-3223-4_1
4. Baines, P.R., Worcester, R.M.: Researching political markets: market-oriented or populistic ? Int. J. Market Res. **42**(3), 339–357 (2000)
5. Barrett, F.S., Grimm, K.J., Robins, R.W., Wildschut, T., Sedikides, C., Janata, P.: Music-evoked nostalgia: affect, memory, and personality. Emotion **10**(3), 390–403 (2010). https://doi.org/10.1037/a0019006
6. Cavnar, W.B., Trenkle, J.M.: N-gram-based text categorization. Ann arbor mi (1994). https://www.osti.gov/biblio/68573
7. Cooper, W.S., Gey, F.C., Dabney, D.P.: Probabilistic retrieval based on staged logistic regression. In: Proceedings of the 15th Annual International ACM SIGIR Conference on Research and Development in Information Retrieval, pp. 198–210. ACM (1992)
8. Cui, R.: A review of nostalgic marketing. Sci. Res. Publ. 8(February), 125–131 (2015). https://doi.org/10.4236/jssm.2015.81015
9. Davalos, S., Merchant, A., Rose, G.: Using big data to study psychological constructs: Nostalgia on Facebook. Psychol. Psychother. **5**, 221–223 (2015). https://doi.org/10.4172/2161-0487.1000221
10. Davalos, S., Merchant, A., Rose, G.M., Lessley, B.J., Teredesai, A.M.: 'The good old days': an examination of nostalgia in Facebook posts. Int. J. Hum. Comput. Stud. **83**, 83–93 (2015). https://doi.org/10.1016/j.ijhcs.2015.05.009
11. Duyvendak, J.W.: The Politics of Home: Belonging and Nostalgia in Europe and the United States. Springer, Heidelberg (2011). https://doi.org/10.1057/9780230305076
12. Forman, G.: An extensive empirical study of feature selection metrics for text classification. J. Mach. Learn. Res. **3**, 1289–1305 (2003). https://doi.org/10.1162/153244303322753670
13. Hepper, E.G., Ritchie, T.D., Sedikides, C., Wildschut, T.: Odyssey's end: Lay conceptions of nostalgia reflect its original homeric meaning. Emotion **12**(1), 102 (2012)
14. Hepper, E.G., et al.: Pancultural nostalgia: prototypical conceptions across cultures. Am. Psychol. Assoc. **14**(4), 733–747 (2014)

15. Hofer, J., Harder, J.J.: Dissertatio medica de nostalgia, oder Heimwehe. J. Bertsch **2** (1688)

16. Joachims, T.: Text categorization with support vector machines: learning with many relevant features. In: Nédellec, C., Rouveirol, C. (eds.) ECML 1998. LNCS, vol. 1398, pp. 137–142. Springer, Heidelberg (1998). https://doi.org/10.1007/BFb0026683

17. Kenny, M.: Back to the populist future?: understanding nostalgia in contemporary ideological discourse. J. Polit. Ideol. **22**(3), 256–273 (2017). https://doi.org/10.1080/13569317.2017.1346773

18. Mackie, D.M., Devos, T., Smith, E.R.: Intergroup emotions: explaining offensive action tendencies in an intergroup context. J. Personal. Soc. Psychol. **79**(4), 602 (2000)

19. Mols, F., Jetten, J.: No guts, no glory: how framing the collective past paves the way for anti-immigrant sentiments. Int. J. Intercultural Relat. **43**, 74–86 (2014). https://doi.org/10.1016/j.ijintrel.2014.08.014

20. Oxford Dictionary: The Oxford Dictionary of English (1989)

21. Pang, B., Lee, L., Vaithyanathan, S.: Thumbs up? Sentiment classification using machine learning techniques. In: Proceedings of the ACL-02 Conference on Empirical Methods in Natural Language Processing - EMNLP 2002, vol. 10, pp. 79–86 (2002). https://doi.org/10.3115/1118693.1118704

22. Pennebaker, J.W., Francis, M.E., Booth, R.J.: Linguistic inquiry and word count: LIWC 2001. Lawrence Erlbaum Associates Mahway **71**(2001), 2001 (2001)

23. Salton, G., Buckley, C.: Term-weighting approaches in automatic text retrieval. Inf. Process. Manag. **24**(5), 513–523 (1988)

24. Schölkopf, B., Smola, A.J., et al.: Learning with Kernels: Support Vector Machines, Regularization, Optimization, and Beyond. MIT Press, Cambridge (2002)

25. Smeekes, A., Verkuyten, M., Martinovic, B.: Longing for the country's good old days: national nostalgia, autochthony beliefs, and opposition to Muslim expressive rights. Br. J. Soc. Psychol. **54**(3), 561–580 (2015). https://doi.org/10.1111/bjso.12097

26. Smith, E.R., Seger, C.R., Mackie, D.M.: Can emotions be truly group level? Evidence regarding four conceptual criteria. J. Pers. Soc. Psychol. **93**(3), 431 (2007)

27. Steenvoorden, E., Harteveld, E.: The appeal of nostalgia: the influence of societal pessimism on support for populist radical right parties. West Eur. Polit. **41**(1), 28–52 (2018). https://doi.org/10.1080/01402382.2017.1334138

28. Tumasjan, A., Sprenger, T., Sandner, P., Welpe, I.: Predicting elections with Twitter: what 140 characters reveal about political sentiment. In: Proceedings of the Fourth International AAAI Conference on Weblogs and Social Media, pp. 178–185 (2010). https://doi.org/10.1074/jbc.M501708200

29. Wildschut, T., Bruder, M., Robertson, S., van Tilburg, W.A., Sedikides, C.: Collective nostalgia: a group-level emotion that confers unique benefits on the group. J. Pers. Soc. Psychol. **107**(5), 844–863 (2014). https://doi.org/10.1037/a0037760

30. Youn, S., Jin, S.V.: Reconnecting with the past in social media: the moderating role of social influence in nostalgia marketing on Pinterest. J. Consumer Behav. **16**(6), 565–576 (2017). https://doi.org/10.1002/cb.1655

What Is Abusive Language?

Integrating Different Views on Abusive Language for Machine Learning

Marco Niemann[(✉)] [iD], Dennis M. Riehle[iD], Jens Brunk[iD], and Jörg Becker[iD]

University of Münster – ERCIS, Leonardo-Campus 3, 48149 Münster, Germany
{marco.niemann,dennis.riehle,jens.brunk,
joerg.becker}@ercis.uni-muenster.de
http://www.ercis.org

Abstract. Abusive language has been corrupting online conversations since the inception of the internet. Substantial research efforts have been put into the investigation and algorithmic resolution of the problem. Different aspects such as "cyberbullying", "hate speech" or "profanity" have undergone ample amounts of investigation, however, often using inconsistent vocabulary such as "offensive language" or "harassment". This led to a state of confusion within the research community. The inconsistency can be considered an inhibitor for the domain: It increases the risk of unintentional redundant work and leads to undifferentiated and thus hard to use and justifiable machine learning classifiers. To remedy this effect, this paper introduces a novel configurable, multi-view approach to define abusive language concepts.

Keywords: Abusive language · Hate speech · Offensive language · Harassment · Machine learning

1 The Issue of Abusive Online User Comments

Online debates are getting out of control. Hidden behind the anonymity of the internet, people are posting content in a style of speech, which is unlikely to be used in the offline world. The result can, for instance, be seen in a much-noted article published in The Guardian. Many comments received by The Guardian were "crude, bigoted, or just vile", showing of xenophobia, racism, sexism, and homophobia. The authors refer to these comments as "the dark side of Guardian comments" [38]. A similar observation could be made during the German refugee crisis in 2016, which triggered a national debate on hate against refugees and made German authorities build a special task force [35]. As a consequence, (German) news outlets have to do more intense filtering of user-generated content on their websites, which—when done manually—is a challenging task [69].

With methods from the domain of machine learning (ML) being on the rise, it is not surprising that researchers started to apply ML techniques to detect hateful comments or abusive language in general [e.g., 50,51]. A reliable method

© Springer Nature Switzerland AG 2020
C. Grimme et al. (Eds.): MISDOOM 2019, LNCS 12021, pp. 59–73, 2020.
https://doi.org/10.1007/978-3-030-39627-5_6

for the detection of abusive language would significantly reduce the currently required manual work for the moderation of user-generated content [see, e.g., 13, 64]. Unquestionably, news outlets need to moderate user-generated content, since having abusive content on their websites may not only reduce their amount of visitors but may also lower the income social media providers make with advertisement [51]. In an industry where advertisement marks a large percentage of the profit, (semi-)automatic detection of abusive language is crucial. Abstracting a bit further, we are currently facing a situation in which computational systems excel more and more in supporting the human need for communication, but lack the flexibility to deal with detrimental users disturbing the established online communities [39]. While it is intriguing to directly opt for computational solutions given the advances in machine learning and artificial intelligence, we argue to include human decisions in the moderation process, which also ensures no algorithmic censorship is taking place—an important factor for user acceptance of such systems [12]. Consequently, we want to approach this socio-technical problem [2, 41] from the underlying linguistic, legal, and academic perspective – plus potential instance-specific adaptations for individual platforms.

A core concept of supervised ML is that an ML algorithm learns data from a so-called training data set. Therefore, training data needs to be collected, which reflects the artifact based on which the algorithm should be trained. This, however, implies that we have a common understanding of the term abusive language. Nevertheless, even after more than 10 years of research in this area, there is no unequivocal vocabulary available. Through this paper, we want to illustrate the existing gap and will present an approach to create definitions that account for the different perspectives linked to abusive language.

2   Prior Work and Definitional Approaches

Even though online abusive language has already been around for more than 20 years, the first attempts to systematically define and identify it were conducted by [73] in 2009. At that time, their focus has been on the detection of "(online) harassment", broadly defined as the intentional annoyance of a target, including intentional offensiveness and personal insults. However, only five years later [10] picked up the term "harassment" for one of the first abusive language publications targeting the German language. Doing so they also redefined the term to refer to electronic messages causing psychological harm to a targeted victim, also including profanity and cyber-bullying (as a repeated form). Similarly, [42, 54] altered the existing term further to include "hate speech", "self-harm", "sexual violence", and "reputation damaging rumors". In the end, both [42, 54] even agree that "harassment" might be too complex to define in a format that might serve as an annotation schema.

However, "harassment" has not remained the only term used to characterize and detect abusive language. So for example, [62] and [63] put a focus on "insults" and "profanity" while, e.g., [16, 46] focus what they term "offensive language". Looking deeper into the single publications, clear-cut definitions are typically still lacking, as, e.g., [63, p. 270] rather broadly summarize the detection of "insults" and "profanity" as "identifying negative content that is offered with malicious intent". Similarly, "offensive language" according to [16,46] can contain different types of language ranging from "vulgar" over "pornographic" to "hateful". Interestingly, "hateful speech" or "hate speech" has also evolved to one of the core constructs of analysis for several authors such as [37,51,59,66,69]. While some of them [e.g., 66] still align it as a sub-concept of "offensive language", others either treat it as an independent form of abusive language [e.g., 51] whereas a third group even understands "hate speech" as the primary concept and "offensive language" just as one of its sub-concepts [59,69].

A further concept that is getting more commonly used is the term "abusive language" which has, among others, been coined by [51] as a more integrative term to summarize the already existing concepts under a larger umbrella[1]. As such, it has been accepted well by the community as can, e.g., be seen by the Workshop on Abusive Language Online [5,6] now regularly taking place[2]. Yet, even though "abusive language" is becoming an established general concept, the exact definitions of its sub-concepts are still rather unclear. As this section has shown, there is no lack of definitions for the specific concepts, however, these often either contain large amounts of ambiguity or different definitions even contradict each other.

3 A Configurable, Multi-view Approach to Abusive Language Definitions

Looking back at Sect. 2 from a purely academic perspective, there appears to be little to no problem since debate and discussion are fundamental elements of academic work. However, as we pointed out in the introduction, the underlying social problem is leading to the shut-down of public discussion fora and even the suicide of attacked individuals—with no existing wide-spread computer-supported moderation support tool available[3]. While this is partly attributed to lacking computational intelligence in the media [see, e.g., 40], the fault might not only be with the machine but also the data it learns from. Without clear, consistent and suitable definitions of what is considered abusive, it is hard to create human-made training data sets that can be used to train effective machine classifiers [cf., e.g., 36,68].

Hence, we want to present a novel, configurable, multi-view approach to elicit abusive language definitions (see Fig. 1) in a meaningful and consistent respectively highly reproducible manner. The approach is based on a careful analysis of potential views that should be part of a definition of "abusive language".

---

[1] With the term "Socially Unacceptable Discourse" [36] introduced another umbrella term, which, however, so far has not received a similar uptake as "Abusive Language".

[2] The third iteration in the year 2019 is already scheduled [7].

[3] For example, Facebook is still opening ever new moderation centers [61] and there is a growing amount of reports on how the moderation of content gets ever more unhandable [40].

A first view that comes to mind when discussing the meaning of a linguistic term is the linguistic one. It will not only help to get a deeper understanding of the meaning of the respective abusive language-related terms but also help to identify linked concepts and synonyms.

The second view of the approach has a more pragmatic background: In many countries, all web services (incl. discussion fora and comment section) are subject to certain legal restrictions concerning publishable content (cf., e.g., [36]). Hence, it will be inevitable to include a legal view to obtain an "abusive language" definition if subsequent research outcomes should ever be usable in a practice setting.

Last but not least, it will be undoubtedly helpful to reconsider prior academic work to make use of already conducted analyses and to support the alignment of a new definition with existing prior ones.

A visualization of the underlying model can be found in Fig. 1. The presented model is structured into two major parts: The first and major part describes the creation of the abusive language definitions as discussed above. In the first step (as indicated by the leftmost node) an assessment of the general linguistic notion of abusiveness will be carried out. Once a general understanding is reached, the academic literature will be assessed next to get a broader context of abusiveness notions which have been subject to academic (and practice) assessments so far. Finally, the legal perspective will be checked to identify those concepts that are justiciable and require persecution respectively deletion. However, the analysis of the three views is not conducted in a strictly iterative fashion. As indicated by the dotted arrows in Fig. 1, each view is meant to inform the other. So, for example, insights gained from the legal analysis can be double-checked against academic and dictionary sources to, e.g., account for different naming rules and conventions. To model this implicit parallelism the three views are enclosed by two AND operators.

The second part of the presented model is an extension added after the presentation at the MISDOOM 2019. It accounts for the feedback received after the presentation and subsequent talks with practitioners who outlined the need to have the ability to not rely on uniform standard definitions but to adjust them to the audiences present. The underlying issue is that the different outlets might be willing to accept different styles of language used, since, e.g., sensational outlets might go with rather loose rules whereas very traditional and sophisticated outlets might filter even beyond the legal standards (cf. also [47,54]). However, this view/step – differing from the others – is only meant to be optional since it lacks any form of generalizability given the differences in platform terms of use [54].

Furthermore, including the linguistic and the legal perspective (and also the optional platform perspective) prohibits the achievement of a single and unified abusive language definition. Not only do the different language systems (e.g., English vs. German vs. Chinese) imply different notions of "abusiveness" – also the legal requirements will differ for different nations affected. To account for this, we decided to make the model configurable (see the dark gray boxes in Fig. 1), so that even though no unified definitions will be possible, at least the approach itself can be applied consistently.

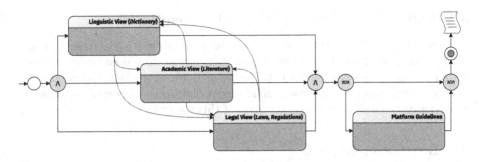

Fig. 1. Configurable, multi-view approach to abusive language definitions

3.1 Extracting Definitional Information from Dictionaries

Even though the linguistic perspective might be one of the simpler views, it still demands careful analysis. For example, one crucial point is the selection of queried dictionaries. Here, nowadays one has to choose between the reputable paper-based versions and their more regularly updated but less controlled online counterparts [1,3]. Furthermore, researchers have to decide to go for either monolingual or multi-lingual works, the language of choice (will typically be the language of the target country) as well as the depth of analysis to circumvent the symbol grounding problem [44,45].

3.2 Extracting Definitional Information from Literature

The most common view in the extant abusive language literature is the academic one. In general, researchers can follow the guidelines for a thorough literature review as postulated by [18,71] or [11]. Aside of the methodological approach to reviewing the literature, most other configurative options include the period to be analyzed, as well as the potential keywords (might be different for different languages) and outlets to be searched.

3.3 Extracting Definitional Information from Legal Texts

Another, supposedly rather straightforward view is the legal one. Here the obvious area of analysis is the respective national legislation of the target country. However, for many countries and areas worldwide this might be too limited as super-national organizations and institutions might have released further (non-)binding legislation to be taken into account. One classical example of this is the European Union which through its regulations and directives can have a direct impact on [24,57]. Furthermore, it might be necessary to go beyond restrictive legislation, since many countries also have specific laws guaranteeing free speech [e.g., 31] within certain boundaries.

3.4   Extracting Definitional Information from Guidelines

For the adaption to platform-specific needs, relevant policy documents, community guidelines, and rules regarding content moderation need to be checked. As an example, one can refer to the paper of Pater et al. [54] who conducted such a similar analysis for major social media platforms. This configuration on a per-instance level is, however, not part of this research.

4   Test-Case: Europe

The European Union (EU) with its currently 28 participating nations is one of the largest political and economic unions in the world. Both the European Commission (EC) and the Council of Europe (CoE) are important players involved in the development of laws and publication of directives and resolutions. As these documents have a significant impact on the large number of member states, this paper focuses on abusive language and hate speech in Europe. While we will be able to assess our newly developed approach and demonstrate its applicability in the domain of abusive language research, this super-national focus also enhances the relevance of this publication laying an easy to use and adjust foundation for nation-specific definitions of more than two dozen European countries.

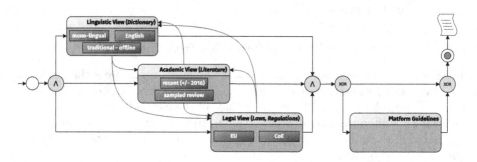

Fig. 2. Configurable, multi-view approach applied to the European case

The corresponding configuration of our model is depicted in Fig. 2. Given the European focus of our test case, the legal perspective will take into considerations official publications of the corresponding European bodies (CoE, EU, EC). For the linguistic view, we will focus on English as the most commonly spoken official language in Europe and restrict the assessment to traditional offline dictionaries given their higher credibility. Regarding the academic perspective, the focus will be on a selected sample of recent publications representing the current understanding of abusive language.

Table 1. Dictionary definitions of *Abusive* (Language)

	Coarse	Cruel	Harsh	Illegality	Injustice	Insulting	Maltreatment	Offensive	Rude	Scolding	Scurrilous	Violence
[15]		✓						✓	✓			
[17]	✓	✓	✓			✓	✓	✓	✓	✓	✓	✓
[48]		✓				✓		✓				✓
[49]		✓	✓			✓						
[52]		✓		✓	✓	✓		✓				
[55]		✓										

4.1 Dictionary-Based View

For the initial linguistic contemplation of the concept of "abusive language" six major, mono-lingual English dictionaries have been analyzed. The selection ranges from old, established (and partially academically rooted) dictionaries such as Merriam-Webster [49], Collins English Dictionary [17], Cambridge [15] and Oxford Dictionary [52] towards rather modern ones like the Macmillan Dictionary [48] and the Longman Dictionary of Contemporary English [55].

Since none of these publications defines "abusive language", the search has been restricted to the keyword "abusive"[4]. Identified synonyms and related concepts have been mapped in Table 1.

Even though the analysis shows no full consensus between dictionaries, most to all of them agree on "abusive" being related to concepts such as cruelty[5], "violence" (in terms of communicative harmfulness towards others), "insults" and offensiveness. Abstracting from these concepts, one could state that "abusive (language)" refers to language that is intentionally used to inflict harm on others. Given the presence of the less intentional concepts "coarse" and "harsh", it is debatable if "intention" is a mandatory characteristic of "abusive (language)".

To further illuminate the concept of "abusive language" from a more problem-centric perspective, the academic view will be assessed next.

4.2 Literature-Based View

Following the dictionary-based view, the literature-based view adds concepts found in state-of-the-art research. Unlike dictionaries, the existing literature knows and also defines abusive language; especially in cases where Natural Language Processing (NLP) is applied to detect abusive language through computational methods. Here, annotated data sets are necessary to train machine learning classifiers. In the annotation process, clear definitions and guidelines

---

[4] Given the context of the paper, "language" is assumed to refer to written online comments.

[5] The theoretical need to obtain a fully-grounded definition for "cruel" as postulated through [44,45]'s symbol grounding problem is acknowledged. However, a full grounding is beyond the scope of this study and is hence left for future work of a more apt linguist.

on what constitutes abusive language and possibly its sub-concepts are necessary. The following section summarizes the most used and relevant academic definitions of abusive language. Generally, there are two different ways to approach data annotations for NLP tasks. Either, the goal is a binary classification of a text, e.g., as *abusive* or *non-abusive*, or there are multiple labels that can be applied to a text. Additionally, there are also combinations of the two. Here, often a binary main classification is used, which is then subdivided on the second level into more detailed concepts (e.g., [51]).

In the early days of abusive language detection, [58] approached the task to automatically detect internet and cellular-based text messages that contain *flame*. Accordingly, they worked on binary data sets (flame/no flame). However, their understanding of *flame* also included concepts such as *attacks, abusive* or *hostile* words. This kind of a binary understanding of an okay/not okay text is one of the most used approaches in the domain. In many cases ([8,51,58,65,72]) binary data sets are applied which distinguish between *abusive/flame/inappropriate* and *non-abusive/okay/clean* texts. Similarly, [4,14,43, 59,60] focus on the distinction of whether something is *hateful, violent, offensive, sexist* or not. Additionally, there are some cases, where more than two labels are used as a scale from *okay* to *not okay* content [22,23,70]. Even though the labels might differ, many researchers have adopted this binary classification, which we from here on refer to as *abusive* or *clean*. When a data set is not annotated in a binary form, then it usually includes multiple (exclusive) labels. There are many studies that work with multiple labels in different combinations. The concepts that stand out the most in these works are labels regarding *sexism* (e.g., [9,23,66,67]), *racism* (e.g., [9,23,56,67]), *threat* (e.g., [4,9,56]), *insult* (e.g., [14,56,65]), and *profane language* (e.g., [8,51,65]).

4.3   Law-Based View

After narrowing down the concept of abusive language through a dictionary and literature analysis in the prior subsections, this part is meant to these insights with the existing regulatory framework in the European Union.

One of the first things that become apparent when assessing the different legal texts is the massive significance that is attributed to free speech by both the EU [31] and the CoE [21]. Even though not directly concerned with *abusive language* or any of its related concepts, permissive fundamental statements like these set the bar high for any valid definition since they only provide very vague statements with regard to things that may or have to be legally withheld (e.g., "subject to such formalities, conditions, restrictions or penalties [. . .] prescribed by law [. . .] for the protection of health or morals [. . .]", [21]).

Unfortunately, on this supra-national level, clear-cut definitions are rare and many of the terms, e.g., more commonly used in academic literature (e.g., *profanity, abusive language, offensive language, . . .*) find limited to no uptake in the legal domain so far. However, both the EU and the CoE are not completely "blind" with regard to abusive speech in general—and in online settings as a special form. Taking a step back, the assessment reveals several aspects and concepts exhibiting a strong legal relevance. Different from the literature-based approach, the binary distinction into acceptable and in-acceptable usually is not explicated in the legal context—even though always implicitly present, since the above-stated Article 10 and Article 11 make everything legal which is not rendered illegal by further restrictions. Given Europe's history of nationalism and racism-induced wars, the first restrictions of Articles 10 and 11 were made regarding all forms of "hatred, xenophobia, [...] or other forms of hatred" [19] which are based on for example "aggressive nationalism and ethnocentrism, discrimination and hostility against minorities, migrants and people of immigrant origin" [19]. Hence, looking at the concepts deemed problematic on the European level, the majority of relevant documents [19,20,25–29] specify *racist* and *xenophobic* utterances[6] as abusive and hence punishable offenses. In several of the stated cases, the documents give further indications on what they consider to be problematic, e.g., explicitly stating skin color, personal descent as well as the origin from a national or ethnic perspective as subsumed characteristics [29]. In recent years the gender debate and associated forms of discrimination also have found their way into legal considerations [20,29,30,32,34] making *sexism* a category that is not only present in academic considerations. Similar to academic literature, a concept that is often wrapped around and hence often present in the analyzed documents is the so-called *hate speech* [19]. It is often used as an umbrella term to subsume *racist* and *sexist* offenses following a similar style of speech but targeting a very different set of victims. Hence, we refrain from using the rather imprecise aggregate term and stick with the more precisely described concepts of *racism* and *sexism*. Aside from the denigrating talk linked to the previously stated abusiveness concepts both CoE and EU documents also repeatedly list *threats* and *insults* as further strictly prohibitive offenses [28,29,33,53], specifying them as proposed attacks on the physical integrity of the victims [53] respectively omitting further specifications. Further concepts such as *offensive language* or *profanity* only get few mentions [29], which is, however, understandable as these concepts are morally debatable but are far from being justiciable.

4.4 Synopsis

After completing the assessment of all three views, the causal reason for our undertaking is reaffirmed: Abusive language is indeed a diverse and broadly defined topic. However, the analysis of the literature and the legislative view indicate four concepts that have to be distinguished:

---

[6] We subsume *anti-semitism*, *anti-muslim*, and other *religious* utterance at this point.

sexism   Attacks on people based on their gender (identity), often with a focus on women

racism   Attacks on people based on their origin, ethnicity, nation - typically meant to incite some form of hatred

threats   Announcements of the violation of the physical integrity of the victim

insults   Denigrating, insolent or contemptuous statements (usually left without further specification)

Even though not legally required, the re-occurrence within academic texts and the high likelihood of profane content being removed at last through community guidelines [54] made us further include:

profane language   Usage of sexually explicit and inappropriate language

5   Conclusion and Outlook for the Testcase of Germany

As we outlined at the beginning of this paper, in prior work on abusive language and related constructs, there is considerable ambiguity regarding the exact definition and relationship between the used concepts. To remedy the situation, we propose a new configurable approach to abusive language definitions including a linguistic, legal and academic view. In addition, our model is capable of including a platform-specific point of view, which allows customization on a per-instance level. We think that this is an important feature to adopt platform-specific needs and to foster a common understanding of abusive language. However, as this adoption refers to concrete platforms and happens after the aggregation of the other three views (c.f. Fig. 1), we have not further discussed this process during the creation of our model.

Subsequently, we demonstrated the applicability of our newly developed model through the creation of a definition for the European level. Based on the assessment of English dictionaries, recent academic literature, and legal documents from the European level we were able to successfully elicit five abusive language concepts that need to be treated and defined. While this European approach provides an ample basis to label and categorize comments, it also provides an easy opportunity to fine-tune the definitions for a national level by re-configuring the legal and linguistic view. This may, for instance, be the case when our approach is adopted for a European country with a language other than English.

Given the design-orientation of the presented artifact, a step for future research would be the application of an abusive language definition created by our configurable model in a practice setting, to assess its suitability and to further evaluate our approach.

Acknowledgments. The research leading to these results received funding from the federal state of North Rhine-Westphalia and the European Regional Development Fund (EFRE.NRW 2014–2020), Project: **M⬤DERAT!** (No. CM-2-2-036a).

References

1. Abel, A., Meyer, C.M.: The dynamics outside the paper: user contributions to online dictionaries. In: Proceedings of the 3rd eLex Conference 'Electronic Lexicography in the 21st Century: Thinking Outside the Paper', pp. 179–194. eLex, Tallinn (2013)
2. Ackerman, M.S.: The intellectual challenge of CSCW: the gap between social requirements and technical feasibility. Hum. Comput. Interact. **15**(2–3), 179–203 (2000)
3. Al Sohibani, M., Al Osaimi, N., Al Ehaidib, R., Al Muhanna, S., Dahanayake, A.: Factors that influence the quality of crowdsourcing. In: New Trends Database Information Systems II: Selected Papers 18th East European Conference on Advances in Databases and Information Systems and Associated Satellite Events, ADBIS 2014, Ohrid, Macedonia, pp. 287–300 (2015)
4. Anzovino, M., Fersini, E., Rosso, P.: Automatic identification and classification of misogynistic language on Twitter. In: Silberztein, M., Atigui, F., Kornyshova, E., Métais, E., Meziane, F. (eds.) NLDB 2018. LNCS, vol. 10859, pp. 57–64. Springer, Cham (2018). https://doi.org/10.1007/978-3-319-91947-8_6
5. Association of Computational Linguistics: ALW1: 1st Workshop on Abusive Language Online (2017). https://sites.google.com/site/abusivelanguageworkshop2017/home
6. Association of Computational Linguistics: ALW2: 2nd Workshop on Abusive Language Online (2018). https://sites.google.com/view/alw2018
7. Association of Computational Linguistics: ALW3: 3rd Workshop on Abusive Language Online (2019). https://sites.google.com/view/alw3/home
8. Badjatiya, P., Gupta, S., Gupta, M., Varma, V.: Deep learning for hate speech detection in Tweet. In: Proceedings 26th International Conference World Wide Web Companion, WWW 2017 Companion, pp. 759–760. International World Wide Web Conferences Steering Committee, Perth, Australia (2017)
9. Bourgonje, P., Moreno-Schneider, J., Srivastava, A., Rehm, G.: Automatic classification of abusive language and personal attacks in various forms of online communication. In: Rehm, G., Declerck, T. (eds.) GSCL 2017. LNCS (LNAI), vol. 10713, pp. 180–191. Springer, Cham (2018). https://doi.org/10.1007/978-3-319-73706-5_15
10. Bretschneider, U., Wöhner, T., Peters, R.: Detecting online harassment in social networks. In: Proceedings International Conference on Information Systems - Building a Better World Through Information Systems, ICIS 2014, pp. 1–14. Association for Information Systems, Auckland, New Zealand (2014)
11. vom Brocke, J., Simons, A., Niehaves, B., Riemer, K., Plattfaut, R., Cleven, A.: Reconstructing the giant: on the importance of rigour in documenting the literature search process. In: Proceedings 17th European Conference on Information Systems, ECIS 2009, Verona, Italy, pp. 2206–2217 (2009)
12. Brunk, J., Mattern, J., Riehle, D.M.: Effect of transparency and trust on acceptance of automatic online comment moderation systems. In: Proceedings 21st IEEE Conference on Business Informatics, CBI 2019. IEEE, Moscow, Russia (2019)
13. Brunk, J., Niemann, M., Riehle, D.M.: Can analytics as a service save the media industry? - The case of online comment moderation. In: Proceedings 21st IEEE Conference on Business Informatics, CBI 2019. IEEE, Moscow (2019)
14. Burnap, P., Williams, M.L.: Us and them: identifying cyber hate on Twitter across multiple protected characteristics. EPJ Data Sci. **5**(1), 11 (2016)

15. Cambridge University Press: abusive (2017). http://dictionary.cambridge.org/dictionary/english/abusive
16. Chen, Y., Zhou, Y., Zhu, S., Xu, H.: Detecting offensive language in social media to protect adolescent online safety. In: Proceedings 2012 ASE/IEEE International Conference on Social Computing, 2012 ASE/IEEE International Conference on Privacy, Security, Risk and Trust, Amsterdam, Netherlands, pp. 71–80 (2012)
17. Collins: abusive definition and meaning (2017). https://www.collinsdictionary.com/dictionary/english/abusive
18. Cooper, H.M.: Organizing knowledge syntheses: a taxonomy of literature reviews. Knowl. Soc. 1(1), 104–126 (1988)
19. Council of Europe: Recommendation No. R (97) 20 of the Committee of Ministers to Member States on "Hate Speech" (1997)
20. Council of Europe: Recommendation No. R (97) 21 of the Committee of Ministers to Member States on the Media and the Promotion of a Culture of Tolerance (1997)
21. Council of Europe: European Convention on Human Rights (2010)
22. Davidson, T., Warmsley, D., Macy, M., Weber, I.: Automated hate speech detection and the problem of offensive language. In: Eleventh International AAAI Conference on Web and Social Media, Montreal, Canada (2017)
23. Del Vigna, F., Cimino, A., Dell'Orletta, F., Petrocchi, M., Tesconi, M.: Hate me, hate me not: hate speech detection on Facebook. In: 1st Italian Conference on Cybersecurity, Venice, Italy (2017)
24. European Commission: Applying EU law (2017). https://ec.europa.eu/info/law/law-making-process/overview-law-making-process/applying-eu-law_en
25. European Commission against Racism and Intolerance: ECRI General Policy Recommendation No. 1 on Combating Racism, Xenophobia, Antisemitism and Intolerance (1996)
26. European Commission against Racism and Intolerance: ECRI General Policy Recommendation No. 2 on Specialised Bodies to Combat Racism, Xenophobia, Antisemitism and Intolerance at National Level (1997)
27. European Commission against Racism and Intolerance: ECRI General Policy Recommendation No. 6 on Combating the Dissemination of Racist, Xenophobic and Antisemitic Material via the Internet (2000)
28. European Commission against Racism and Intolerance: ECRI General Policy Recommendation No. 7 on National Legislation to Combat Racism and Racial Discrimination (2002)
29. European Commission against Racism and Intolerance: ECRI General Policy Recommendation No. 15 on Combating Hate Speech (2015)
30. European Union: Council directive 2000/43/EC of 29 June 2000 implementing the principle of equal treatment between persons irrespective of racial or ethnic origin. Off. J. Eur. Communities L 180, 22–26 (2000)
31. European Union: The charter of fundamental rights of the European union. Off. J. Eur. Communities C 364, 1–22 (2000)
32. European Union: Treaty of Lisbon - amending the Treaty on European Union and the Treaty establishing the European community. Off. J. Eur. Union C 306, 1–271 (2007)
33. European Union: Council framework decision 2008/913/JHA of 28 November 2008 on combating certain forms and expressions of racism and xenophobia by means of criminal law. Off. J. Eur. Union L 328, 55–58 (2008)
34. European Union: Consolidated version of the treaty on the functioning of the European union. Off. J. Eur. Union C 326, 47–390 (2012)

35. Faiola, A.: Germany springs to action over hate speech against migrants (2016). https://www.washingtonpost.com/world/europe/germany-springs-to-action-over-hate-speech-against-migrants/2016/01/06/6031218e-b315-11e5-8abc-d09392edc612_story.html?utm_term=.737b4d4453d3

36. Fišer, D., Erjavec, T., Ljubešić, N.: Legal framework, dataset and annotation schema for socially unacceptable online discourse practices in Slovene. In: Proceedings First Workshop on Abusive Language Online, Vancouver, Canada, pp. 46–51 (2017)

37. Fortuna, P., Nunes, S.: A survey on automatic detection of hate speech in text. ACM Comput. Surv. **51**(4), 1–30 (2018)

38. Gardiner, B., Mansfield, M., Anderson, I., Holder, J., Louter, D., Ulmanu, M.: The dark side of Guardian comments (2016). https://www.theguardian.com/technology/2016/apr/12/the-dark-side-of-guardian-comments

39. Gilbert, E., Lampe, C., Leavitt, A., Lo, K., Yarosh, L.: Conceptualizing, creating, & controlling constructive and controversial comments. In: Companion 2017 ACM Conference Computer Supported Cooperative Work, Social Computing, Portland, OR, USA, pp. 425–430 (2017)

40. Gillespie, T.: The scale is just unfathomable (2018). https://logicmag.io/04-the-scale-is-just-unfathomable/

41. Grudin, J.: Computer-supported cooperative work: history and focus. Computer **27**(5), 19–26 (1994)

42. Guberman, J., Hemphill, L.: Challenges in modifying existing scales for detecting harassment in individual Tweets. In: Proceedings 50th Hawaii International Conference System Sciences, HICSS 2017, pp. 2203–2212. Association for Information Systems, Waikoloa Village, Hawaii, USA (2017)

43. Hammer, H.L.: Automatic detection of hateful comments in online discussion. In: Maglaras, L.A., Janicke, H., Jones, K. (eds.) INISCOM 2016. LNICST, vol. 188, pp. 164–173. Springer, Cham (2017). https://doi.org/10.1007/978-3-319-52569-3_15

44. Harnad, S.: The symbol grounding problem. Physica D **42**(1–3), 335–346 (1990)

45. Harnad, S.: Symbol-grounding problem. In: Encyclopedia of Cognitive Science, vol. 42, pp. 335–346. Wiley, Chichester (2006)

46. Jay, T., Janschewitz, K.: The pragmatics of swearing. J. Politeness Res. Lang. Behav. Cult. **4**(2), 267–288 (2008)

47. Köffer, S., Riehle, D.M., Höhenberger, S., Becker, J.: Discussing the value of automatic hate speech detection in online debates. In: Drews, P., Funk, B., Niemeyer, P., Xie, L. (eds.) MKWI 2018, Lüneburg, Germany (2018)

48. Macmillan Publishers Limited: abusive (adjective) definition and synonyms (2017). http://www.macmillandictionary.com/dictionary/british/abusive

49. Merriam-Webster: Abusive (2017). https://www.merriam-webster.com/dictionary/abusive

50. Niemann, M.: Abusiveness is non-binary: five shades of gray in German online news-comments. In: Proceedings 21st IEEE Conference Business Informatics, CBI 2019. IEEE, Moscow, Russia (2019)

51. Nobata, C., Tetreault, J., Thomas, A., Mehdad, Y., Chang, Y.: Abusive language detection in online user content. In: Proceedings 25th International Conference World Wide Web, pp. 145–153, Montreal, Canada (2016)

52. Oxford University Press: Abusive (2017). https://en.oxforddictionaries.com/definition/abusive

53. Parliamentary Assembly: Recommendation 1805 (2007): Blasphemy, religious insults and hate speech against persons on grounds of their religion (2007)

54. Pater, J.A., Kim, M.K., Mynatt, E.D., Fiesler, C.: Characterizations of online harassment: comparing policies across social media platforms. In: Proceedings 19th International Conference Supporting Group Work, GROUP 2016, pp. 369–374. ACM Press, Sanibel Island, Florida, USA (2016)

55. Pearson: Abusive (2017). http://www.ldoceonline.com/dictionary/abusive

56. Poletto, F., Stranisci, M., Sanguinetti, M., Patti, V., Bosco, C.: Hate speech annotation: analysis of an Italian Twitter corpus. In: 4th Italian Conference on Computational Linguistics, CLiC-it 2017, vol. 2006, pp. 1–6. CEUR-WS (2017)

57. Ravluševičius, P.: The enforcement of the primacy of the European Union law-legal doctrine and practice. Jurisprudence **18**(4), 1369–1388 (2011)

58. Razavi, A.H., Inkpen, D., Uritsky, S., Matwin, S.: Offensive language detection using multi-level classification. In: Farzindar, A., Kešelj, V. (eds.) AI 2010. LNCS (LNAI), vol. 6085, pp. 16–27. Springer, Heidelberg (2010). https://doi.org/10.1007/978-3-642-13059-5_5

59. Ross, B., Rist, M., Carbonell, G., Cabrera, B., Kurowsky, N., Wojatzki, M.: Measuring the reliability of hate speech annotations: the case of the European refugee crisis. In: Proceedings 3rd Workshop on Natural Language Processing for Computer-Mediated Communication, Bochum, Germany, pp. 6–9 (2016)

60. Seo, S., Cho, S.B.: Offensive sentence classification using character-level CNN and transfer learning with fake sentences. In: Liu, D., Xie, S., Li, Y., Zhao, D., El-Alfy, E.S. (eds.) International Conference on Neural Information Processing, pp. 532–539. Springer, Cham (2017)

61. Solon, O.: Underpaid and overburdened: the life of a Facebook moderator (2017). https://www.theguardian.com/news/2017/may/25/facebook-moderator-underpaid-overburdened-extreme-content

62. Sood, S.O., Antin, J., Churchill, E.F.: Using crowdsourcing to improve profanity detection. In: AAAI Spring Symposium Series, Palo Alto, CA, USA, pp. 69–74 (2012)

63. Sood, S.O., Churchill, E.F., Antin, J.: Automatic identification of personal insults on social news sites. J. Am. Soc. Inf. Sci. Technol. **63**(2), 270–285 (2012)

64. Švec, A., Pikuliak, M., Šimko, M., Bieliková, M.: Improving moderation of online discussions via interpretable neural models. In: Proceedings Second Workshop on Abusive Language Online, ALW2, Brussels, Belgium (2018)

65. Tuarob, S., Mitrpanont, J.L.: Automatic discovery of abusive thai language usages in social networks. In: Choemprayong, S., Crestani, F., Cunningham, S.J. (eds.) ICADL 2017. LNCS, vol. 10647, pp. 267–278. Springer, Cham (2017). https://doi.org/10.1007/978-3-319-70232-2_23

66. Warner, W., Hirschberg, J.: Detecting hate speech on the world wide web. In: Proceedings Second Workshop on Language in Social Media, Montreal, Canada, pp. 19–26 (2012)

67. Waseem, Z.: Are you a racist or Am I seeing things? Annotator influence on hate speech detection on Twitter. In: Proceedings First Workshop on NLP and Computational Social Science, Austin, Texas, USA, pp. 138–142 (2016)

68. Waseem, Z., Davidson, T., Warmsley, D., Weber, I.: Understanding abuse: a typology of abusive language detection subtasks. In: Proceedings First Workshop Abusive Language Online, Vancouver, Canada, pp. 78–84 (2017)

69. Waseem, Z., Hovy, D.: Hateful symbols or hateful people? Predictive features for hate speech detection on Twitter. In: Proceedings NAACL Student Research Workshop, Stroudsburg, PA, USA, pp. 88–93 (2016)

70. Watanabe, H., Bouazizi, M., Ohtsuki, T.: Hate speech on Twitter: a pragmatic approach to collect hateful and offensive expressions and perform hate speech detection. IEEE Access **6**, 13825–13835 (2018)

71. Webster, J., Watson, R.T.: Analyzing the past to prepare for the future: writing a literature review. MIS Q. **26**(2), xiii–xxiii (2002)

72. Yenala, H., Jhanwar, A., Chinnakotla, M.K., Goyal, J.: Deep learning for detecting inappropriate content in text. Int. J. Data Sci. Anal. **6**(4), 273–286 (2018)

73. Yin, D., Xue, Z., Hong, L., Davison, B.D., Kontostathis, A., Edwards, L.: Detection of harassment on Web 2.0. In: Proceedings Content Analysis WEB, CAW2.0, Madrid, Spain, pp. 1–7 (2009)

Automation and Disinformation

Detecting Malicious Social Bots:
Story of a Never-Ending Clash

Stefano Cresci$^{(\boxtimes)}$

Institute for Informatics and Telematics (IIT-CNR), Pisa, Italy
stefano.cresci@iit.cnr.it

Abstract. Recently, studies on the characterization and detection of
social bots were published at an impressive rate. By looking back at
over ten years of research and experimentation on social bots detection, in this paper we aim at understanding past, present, and future
research trends in this crucial field. In doing so, we discuss about one of
the nastiest features of social bots – that is, their *evolutionary* nature.
Then, we highlight the switch from supervised bot detection techniques
– focusing on feature engineering and on the analysis of one account at a
time – to unsupervised ones, where the focus is on proposing new detection algorithms and on the analysis of groups of accounts that behave
in a coordinated and synchronized fashion. These unsupervised, group-
analyses techniques currently represent the state-of-the-art in social bot
detection. Going forward, we analyze the latest research trend in social
bot detection in order to highlight a promising new development of this
crucial field.

Keywords: Social bots · Bot evolution · Reactive detection ·
Proactive detection · Adversarial machine learning · Generalizability

1 Introduction

Social media and Online Social Networks (OSNs) are having a profound impact
on our everyday life, giving voice to the crowds and reshaping the information
landscape. Indeed, the deluge of real-time data spontaneously shared in OSNs
already proved valuable in many different domains, spanning tourism [7], safety
and security [3,4], transportation and politics [14,23], to name but a few notable
cases.

However, the democratizing effect of OSNs does not come without costs [6].
In 2016, "post-truth" was selected by the Oxford dictionary as the word of the
year, and in 2017 "fake news" was selected for the same purpose by Collins
dictionary. Still in 2017, the World Economic Forum raised a warning on the
potential distortion effect of OSNs on user perceptions of reality[1]. Moreover,
the same openness of OSNs that favored the democratization of information

---

[1] http://reports.weforum.org/global-risks-2017.

© Springer Nature Switzerland AG 2020
C. Grimme et al. (Eds.): MISDOOM 2019, LNCS 12021, pp. 77–88, 2020.
https://doi.org/10.1007/978-3-030-39627-5_7

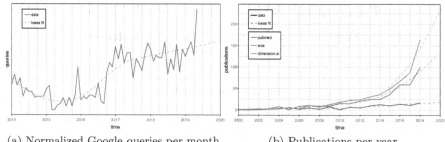

(a) Normalized Google queries per month.   (b) Publications per year.

Fig. 1. Trends in search queries and publications regarding social bots.

(e.g., the support for programmatic access via APIs and the support for anonymity), also inevitably favored the proliferation of *social bots*. Indeed, previous studies report that social bots are as old as OSNs themselves [18]. With the term social bot, we broadly refer to computer programs capable of automatically producing, re-sharing, and liking content in OSNs, or even capable of establishing and maintaining social relations. In fact, any of our supposedly online friends may instead be a fake, automated account, part of large coordinated groups [18].

Not all social bots are malicious and dangerous, and some of them also serve beneficial purposes, such as contributing to gather accurate information in the aftermath of emergencies [2,25]. Unfortunately, however, the vast majority actually pursue malicious goals. These malicious bots try to hide their automated nature by imitating the behaviors of legitimate users. Moreover, they often act in a synchronized and coordinated fashion – a strategy that collectively allows them to increase their impact. Many recent studies concluded that social bots played a role in strategic information operations orchestrated in the run up to several major political elections, both in western and eastern countries [32,33]. As additional evidence for this claim, Twitter recently banned several thousands accounts, linked to many different malicious information operations perpetrated between 2016 and 2019[2]. Other recent studies also suggested that social bots were used to exacerbate online social discussions about controversial topics (e.g., vaccination and immigration debates), thus increasing polarization and fueling abusive and hateful speech [34]. Across the whole Twittersphere, it is reported that social bots account for 9 to 15% of total active platform users [35]. Even more worryingly however, when strong political or economical incentives are at stake, the presence of bots exponentially increases. As an example, a recent study reported that 71% of all users mentioning stocks traded in US financial markets, are likely to be bots [10].

Since social bots have a central role in the diffusion of disinformation, spam, and malware, both scholars and practitioners devoted much effort to the development of detection techniques. Nowadays, new studies on the characterization and detection of social bots are published at an impressive rate, as shown in

---

[2] https://about.twitter.com/en_us/values/elections-integrity.html.

Fig. 1. An analysis of a subset of publications from 2018 reports that more than 3 new papers were published (on average) every week on the topic of social bots[3]. The rapidly growing publication trend suggests that in the near future there will be one new paper published every day, which poses a heavy burden on researchers trying to keep pace with the evolution of this field. This issue is also emphasized by the lack of a thorough survey. Perhaps more importantly, the rate at which new studies on this topic are published implies that a huge effort is taking place worldwide in order to overcome the diffusion of social bots. Given this picture, an important question arises: *where is all this effort leading?*

In the remainder of this paper we try to answer this crucial question via a longitudinal analysis of ten years of research in the field of social bot detection.

2 Traditional Social Bot Detection

The first work that focused on the detection of misbehaving accounts in OSNs dates back to January 2010 [38]. Since then and until present days, the vast majority of attempts at bot detection have been based on heuristics (i.e., rule-based) or on supervised machine learning [9]. An important implication of the adoption of supervised machine learning is that each account is analyzed singularly. In other words, given a group of accounts to investigate (e.g., an OSN community), the detection technique is separately applied to each account of the group, to which it assigns a label (either bot or legitimate). In fact, the key assumption of this large body of work is that each bot/fake/spammer has peculiar features that make it clearly distinguishable from legitimate accounts. This approach to the task of social bot detection, which we call "traditional", thus revolves around the application of off-the-shelf machine learning algorithms on the accounts under investigation, rather than on developing new algorithms. Indeed, most of the works in this branch are focused on designing machine learning features – that is, they are focused on the task of feature engineering – capable of maximizing detection performances of well-known algorithms, such as SVM, decision trees, random forests, and more [9].

Regarding features to exploit for the detection, 3 classes have been mainly considered: (i) profile features [8,15]; (ii) features extracted from the posts, such as posting behavior and content of posted messages [5,28]; and (iii) features derived from the social or interaction graph of the accounts [22,26]. The classes of features exploited by the detection technique have a strong impact on both the performances of the detector as well as its efficiency. For instance, in Twitter it has been demonstrated that those features that mostly contribute towards the predictive power of bot detectors (e.g., graph-based features such as measures of centrality in the social graph), are also the most costly ones, in terms of needed data and computation [8].

Despite achieving promising initial results, the traditional approach – which still comprises the majority of papers published nowadays – has a number of drawbacks. The first challenge in developing a supervised detector is related

---

[3] Source: https://www.dimensions.ai/.

to the availability of a ground truth (i.e., labeled) dataset, to be used in the learning phase of the classifier. In most cases, a real ground truth is lacking and the labels are simply given by human operators that manually analyze the data. Critical issues arise since, as of 2019, we still lack a "standard" definition of what a social bot is [21,37]. Moreover, humans have been proven to suffer from several biases [29] and to largely fail at spotting modern, sophisticated bots, with only $\simeq 24\%$ bots correctly labeled as such by humans [9].

The biggest drawback of traditional approaches, however, is due to the evolutionary nature of social bots, which we discuss in the following section.

3   The Issue of Bot Evolution

Early success at social bot detection, in turn, inevitably inspired countermeasures by bot developers. Because of this, newer bots often feature advanced characteristics that make them way harder to detect with respect to older ones. This iterative process, that leads to the development of always more sophisticated social bots, is commonly referred to as *bot evolution*.

A noteworthy work published in 2011, and later extended in 2013 [36], provided the first evidence and the theoretical foundations to study social bot evolution. The first wave of social bots that populated OSNs until around 2011 was made of rather simplistic bots – mainly accounts with very low perceived reputation (e.g., few social connections and posted messages) and featuring clear signs of automation (e.g., repeated spam of the same URLs). On the contrary, the social bots studied in [36] appeared as more popular and credible, given the relatively large number of their social connections. In addition, they were no longer spamming the same messages over and over again, but they were instead posting several messages with the same meaning but with different words, in order to avoid detection techniques based on content analysis. Starting from these findings, authors of [36] also proposed a supervised machine learning classifier that was specifically designed for detecting *evolving* bots. Their classifier simultaneously leveraged features computed from the content of posted messages, social connections, and tweeting behaviors, and initially proved capable of accurately detecting the sophisticated bots. More recently, new studies provided evidence of a third generation of social bots that spread through OSNs from 2016 onwards [9,18]. Unfortunately, the classifier originally developed in [36] was no longer successful at detecting the third wave of social bots, as shown in [9].

The previous example serves as anecdotal evidence of bot evolution, and of the detrimental effect it has on bot detectors. Additional evidence is reported in [9], where authors evaluated the *survivability* of different bots, and the ability of humans in spotting bots in the wild. Specifically, authors of [9] showed that only $\simeq 5\%$ of evolved bots are removed from social platforms (i.e., high survivability), whilst "old" social bots are removed $\simeq 60\%$ of the times (i.e., low/moderate survivability). Moreover, in a large-scale crowdsourcing experiment, tech-savvy social media users proved unable to tell apart evolved bots and legitimate users, 76% of the times (i.e., 3 out of 4 evade detection by humans).

The same users were instead unable of spotting "old" social bots only 9% of the times (i.e., only 1 out of 10 evades detection) [9].

What results reported in [9,18] ultimately tell us, is that current sophisticated bots are practically indistinguishable from legitimate accounts, if analyzed one at a time. In other words, the results about bot evolution tell us that the assumption of traditional (i.e., supervised) bot detection approaches, according to which bots have features that allow to distinguish them from legitimate accounts, is no longer true.

4   Modern Social Bot Detection

The difficulties in detecting sophisticated bots with supervised approaches that are based on the analysis of individual accounts, recently gave rise to a new research trend that aims to analyze groups of accounts as a whole. This new research trend is also motivated by the interest of platform administrators in detecting what they typically refer to as "coordinated inauthentic behavior"[4,5].

Since 2013, several different research teams independently started to propose new techniques for social bot detection. Despite being based on different key concepts, all these new techniques – that collectively represent the "modern" approach to social bot detection – included important contributions also from the algorithmic point of view, thus shifting from general-purpose machine learning algorithms such as SVMs and decision trees, to ad-hoc algorithms that were specifically designed for detecting bots. Furthermore, the majority of these new algorithms considered groups of accounts as a whole, rather than single accounts, thus moving in the direction of detecting the coordinated and synchronized behavior that characterizes malicious botnets [9].

As a consequence of this paradigm-shift, modern bot detectors are particularly effective at detecting evolving, coordinated, and synchronized bots. For instance, the technique discussed in [13] associates each account to a sequence of characters that encodes its behavioral information. Such sequences are then compared between one another to find anomalous similarities among sequences of a subgroup of accounts. The similarity is computed by measuring the longest common subsequence shared by all the accounts of the group. Accounts that share a suspiciously long subsequence are then labeled as bots. Instead, the family of systems described in [22,26] build a bipartite graph of accounts and their interactions with content (e.g., retweets to some other tweets) or with other accounts (e.g., becoming followers of other accounts). Then, they aim to detect anomalously dense blocks in the graph, which might be representative of coordinated and synchronized attacks. Another recent example of an unsupervised, group-based technique is RTBUST [27], which is tailored for detecting mass-retweeting bots. The technique leverages unsupervised feature extraction and clustering. An LSTM autoencoder converts the retweet time series of accounts

---

[4] https://newsroom.fb.com/news/2018/12/inside-feed-coordinated-inauthentic-behavior/.

[5] https://help.twitter.com/en/rules-and-policies/platform-manipulation.

into compact and informative latent feature vectors, which are then clustered by a hierarchical density-based algorithm. Accounts belonging to large clusters characterized by malicious retweeting patterns are labeled as bots, since they are likely to represent retweeting botnets.

Given that bot detection techniques belonging to this modern approach still represent the minority of all published papers on social bot detection, we still lack a through and systematic study of the improvement brought by the modern approach to social bot detection. However, the first preliminary results that compared the detection performances of traditional and modern detectors on the same datasets, seem to support the increased effectiveness of the latter. In particular, the technique introduced in [13] outperformed several traditional detectors on two datasets, yielding an average $F1$ improvement of $+0.37$. Similarly, RTBUST [27] improved on a widely used traditional bot detector by increasing $F1$ of $+0.44$. The promising results with modern bot detectors tell us that focusing on groups is advantageous. In fact, large groups of coordinated bots are more likely to leave traces of automation than a single bot, independently of how sophisticated the individual bots are [9]. By performing analyses at group level, this modern approach appears to be able to raise the bar for bot developers to evade detection. Furthermore, the majority of modern bot detectors are semi-supervised or unsupervised, which gives higher guarantees on the generalizability of the detector and mitigates challenges related to the acquisition of a reliable ground-truth.

5   The Way Ahead

So far, we highlighted that a shift is taking place in the development of bot detectors, in order to counter the evolutionary nature of social bots. Now, by looking at the latest advances in this thriving field, we aim at gaining some insights into the future of social bot detection.

Notably, both the traditional and the modern approach to social bot detection have always followed a *reactive* schema. Quite naturally, the driving factor for the development of new and better bot detectors have been bot mischiefs themselves. As soon as scholars and OSN administrators identified a new group of bots, possibly featuring new and advanced characteristics, they started the development of detectors capable of spotting them. A major implication of this reactive approach is that improvements in bot detection are possible only after having collected evidence of new bot mischiefs. In turn, this means that scholars and OSN administrators are constantly one step behind of bot developers, and that bots have a significant time span (i.e., the time needed to design, develop, and deploy a new detector) during which they are essentially free to tamper with our online environments.

However, another – radically different – approach to social bot detection is possible, and has just started being investigated by several researchers. This trailblazing direction of research involves the application of adversarial machine learning [19] to bot detection. Adversarial machine learning has already been applied to a number of fields such as computer vision [24] and speech recognition [30], with exceptional results. In general, it is considered as a machine learning paradigm that can be profitably applied to all scenarios that are intrinsically adversarial (i.e., with adversaries interested in fooling machine learning models) [19], with social bots detection clearly being one of such scenarios [17]. In the so-called *adversarial social bot detection*, scholars try to find meaningful adversarial examples with which to test current bot detectors [11]. In other words, this branch of research aims at studying possible attacks to existing bot detectors, with the goal of building more robust and more secure detectors. In this context, adversarial examples might be sophisticated types of existing bots that manage to evade detection by current techniques [1], or even bots that do not exist yet, but whose behaviors and characteristics are simulated [12], or bots developed ad-hoc for the sake of experimentation [20]. Finding good adversarial examples can, in turn, help scholars understand the weaknesses of existing bot detection systems, before such weaknesses are effectively exploited by bot developers. As a result, bot hunters need not wait anymore for new bot mischiefs in order to adapt their techniques, but instead they can *proactively* test them, in an effort that could quickly make them more robust. Among the positive outcomes of adversarial approaches to bot detection, is a more rapid understanding of the drawbacks of current detectors and the opportunity to gain insights into new features for achieving more robust and more reliable detectors.

Despite the high hopes placed on adversarial social bot detection, this research direction is still in its infancy. The very first works in this field have in fact been published just in 2018 and 2019. Adversarial approaches to social bot detection thus represent a promising new development of this field. However, efforts at adversarial social bot detection can only be successful if the scientific community decides to rise to the many open challenges. Among the challenges opened up by proactive and adversarial approaches is the development of techniques for creating many different kinds of *adversarial examples*, with which to test existing bot detectors. A task that, to date, was only tackled by relying on the creativity of some researchers and only for a few limited cases [11,12,20]. Moreover, adversarial approaches have proved computationally and data intensive in some of the early tasks to which they were applied, with only few solutions proposed to date to boost their efficiency [31]. Another challenge thus revolves around assessing the *efficiency* of adversarial social bot detection, as well as its *coverage* of the possible types of attacks (i.e., how likely it is with the adversarial approach to anticipate a real future attack or a real future evolution of bots).

6   Conclusions

Our longitudinal analysis of the first decade of research in social bot detection revealed some interesting trends in the development of bot detectors. In particular, we identified 3 ages of bot detection: (i) the *traditional age*, characterized by the study of account features and by the adoption of off-the-shelf supervised machine learning algorithms; (ii) the *modern age*, characterized by the development of ad-hoc unsupervised algorithms for detecting groups of colluding bots;

Table 1. The analysis of more than a decade of research and experimentation in social bot detection allows to identify 3 main directions of research, corresponding to 3 different ages: the traditional, the modern, and the adversarial age. In turn, each age is characterized by a few distinctive features reported above. Furthermore, an analysis of recently published papers on social bot detection, positions current endeavors somewhere in between the traditional and the modern ages.

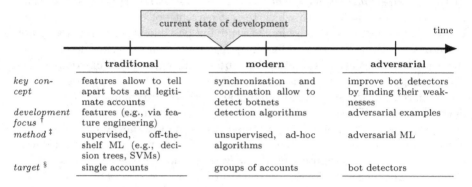

	traditional	modern	adversarial
key concept	features allow to tell apart bots and legitimate accounts	synchronization and coordination allow to detect botnets	improve bot detectors by finding their weaknesses
development focus †	features (e.g., via feature engineering)	detection algorithms	adversarial examples
method ‡	supervised, off-the-shelf ML (e.g., decision trees, SVMs)	unsupervised, ad-hoc algorithms	adversarial ML
target §	single accounts	groups of accounts	bot detectors

†: what scholars aim to optimize
‡: which machine learning (ML) paradigm scholars adopt
§: to what scholars apply their method

and (iii) the newborn *adversarial age*, whose promise is to apply the paradigm of adversarial machine learning to the task of bot detection. Given the considerable amount of work still needed to lay the foundations of adversarial social bot detection, the adversarial age has not really sparked yet. However, if it lives up to its expectations, it might blossom soon with a tremendous impact. Apart from the adversarial age, the characteristics of currently published works in social bot detection still highlight a majority of traditional detectors. However, the gap between newly proposed traditional and modern detectors is narrowing. Hence we can conclude that the peak of the traditional age is probably over, and that we are moving towards the peak of the modern age, as pictorially shown in Table 1.

The exponentially growing body of work on social bot detection shown in Fig. 1, somehow reassures us that much effort is bound to be devoted to the fight of this critical issue. However, at the same time it also poses some new challenges. Firstly, it is becoming more and more important to be able to organize this large body of work. Doing so would not only contribute to a better exploitation of this knowledge, but would also allow researchers in bot detection to more effectively and more efficiently provide new solutions (e.g., avoid wasting time and effort on solutions that have already proved unsuccessful). Unfortunately, thorough and comprehensive surveys on bot detection are still few and far between. To this regard, this paper aims to provide a contribution to the critical review and analysis of the vast literature in this field. Secondly, more papers on this topic inevitably imply that more bot detectors will

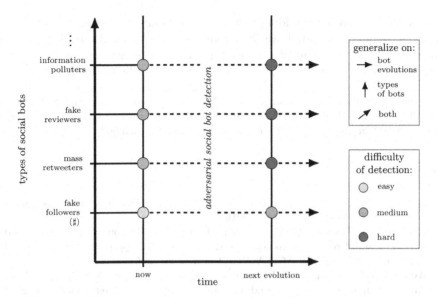

Fig. 2. A bi-dimensional theory of generalizability for social bot detectors. Let us consider a detector developed for a specific kind of bots (marked with ♯). The detector will likely achieve its best performances when used against the same bots it was developed for (green-colored scenario). However, it would be useful to also evaluate its detection performances against different kinds of bots, thus moving along the y axis. Furthermore, by exploiting adversarial social bot detection, it could also be possible to estimate its detection performances against evolved bots, thus moving along the x axis of the generalizability space. The hardest foreseeable evaluation scenario is the one where a detector is tested against evolved versions of bots for which it was not originally designed (red-colored). The vast majority of newly proposed bot detectors are only evaluated in the easiest scenario. (Color figure online)

be proposed. With the growing number of disparate detection techniques, it is thus becoming increasingly important to have standard tools (e.g., frameworks, reference datasets, methodologies) to evaluate and compare them. In particular, one facet of bot detectors that is often overlook is their *generalizability* – that is, their capability in maintaining good detection results also for types of bots that have not been originally considered. To this regard, the analyses carried out in this study lay the foundations for a bi-dimensional theory of generalizability, as shown in Fig. 2. A desirable scenario for the near future would involve the possibility to easily evaluate any new bot detector against many different types of social bots in order to assess its strengths and weaknesses, for instance by following the approach laid out in [16]. It would also be profitable to be able to evaluate detectors against possible evolved versions of current bots, by applying the adversarial approach previously described. In order to reach this ambitious goal, we must first create reference datasets that comprise several different kinds of bots, thus significantly adding to the sparse resources existing as of today[6]. Then, as already anticipated, we should also devise additional ways for creating a broad array of diverse adversarial examples. These challenges currently stand as unsolved, and call for the highest effort of our scientific community.

Acknowledgments. This research is supported in part by the EU H2020 Program under the scheme `INFRAIA-1-2014-2015: Research Infrastructures` grant agreement #654024 *SoBigData: Social Mining & Big Data Ecosystem.*

References

1. Assenmacher, D., Adam, L., Frischlich, L., Trautmann, H., Grimme, C.: Openbots. arXiv preprint arXiv:1902.06691 (2019)
2. Avvenuti, M., Bellomo, S., Cresci, S., La Polla, M.N., Tesconi, M.: Hybrid crowdsensing: a novel paradigm to combine the strengths of opportunistic and participatory crowdsensing. In: ACM WWW Companion (2017)
3. Avvenuti, M., Cresci, S., Del Vigna, F., Fagni, T., Tesconi, M.: CrisMap: a big data crisis mapping system based on damage detection and geoparsing. Inf. Syst. Front. **20**(5), 993–1011 (2018)
4. Avvenuti, M., Cresci, S., Marchetti, A., Meletti, C., Tesconi, M.: Predictability or early warning: using social media in modern emergency response. IEEE Internet Comput. **20**(6) (2016)
5. Chavoshi, N., Hamooni, H., Mueen, A.: DeBot: Twitter bot detection via warped correlation. In: IEEE ICDM (2016)
6. Cresci, S.: Harnessing the social sensing revolution: challenges and opportunities. Ph.D. dissertation, University of Pisa (2018)
7. Cresci, S., D'Errico, A., Gazzé, D., Lo Duca, A., Marchetti, A., Tesconi, M.: Towards a DBpedia of tourism: the case of Tourpedia. In: ISWC (2014)
8. Cresci, S., Di Pietro, R., Petrocchi, M., Spognardi, A., Tesconi, M.: Fame for sale: efficient detection of fake Twitter followers. Decis. Support Syst. **80** (2015)
9. Cresci, S., Di Pietro, R., Petrocchi, M., Spognardi, A., Tesconi, M.: The paradigm-shift of social spambots: evidence, theories, and tools for the arms race. In: ACM WWW Companion (2017)
10. Cresci, S., Lillo, F., Regoli, D., Tardelli, S., Tesconi, M.: Cashtag piggybacking: uncovering spam and bot activity in stock microblogs on Twitter. ACM Trans. Web **13**(2), 11 (2019)
11. Cresci, S., Petrocchi, M., Spognardi, A., Tognazzi, S.: From reaction to proaction: unexplored ways to the detection of evolving spambots. In: ACM WWW Companion (2018)
12. Cresci, S., Petrocchi, M., Spognardi, A., Tognazzi, S.: Better safe than sorry: an adversarial approach to improve social bot detection. In: ACM WebSci (2019)
13. Cresci, S., Pietro, R.D., Petrocchi, M., Spognardi, A., Tesconi, M.: Social fingerprinting: detection of spambot groups through DNA-inspired behavioral modeling. IEEE Trans. Dependable Secure Comput. **15**(4), 561–576 (2018)
14. D'Andrea, E., Ducange, P., Lazzerini, B., Marcelloni, F.: Real-time detection of traffic from Twitter stream analysis. IEEE Trans. Intell. Transp. Syst. **16**(4), 2269–2283 (2015)

---

[6] https://botometer.iuni.iu.edu/bot-repository/datasets.html.

15. Davis, C.A., Varol, O., Ferrara, E., Flammini, A., Menczer, F.: BotOrNot: a system to evaluate social bots. In: ACM WWW Companion (2016)
16. De Cristofaro, E., Kourtellis, N., Leontiadis, I., Stringhini, G., Zhou, S., et al.: LOBO: evaluation of generalization deficiencies in Twitter bot classifiers. In: ACM ACSAC (2018)
17. Ferrara, E.: The history of digital spam. Commun. ACM **62**(8), 82–91 (2019)
18. Ferrara, E., Varol, O., Davis, C., Menczer, F., Flammini, A.: The rise of social bots. Communun. ACM **59**(7) (2016)
19. Goodfellow, I.J., McDaniel, P.D., Papernot, N.: Making machine learning robust against adversarial inputs. Communun. ACM **61**(7), 56–66 (2018)
20. Grimme, C., Assenmacher, D., Adam, L.: Changing perspectives: is it sufficient to detect social bots? In: Meiselwitz, G. (ed.) SCSM 2018. LNCS, vol. 10913, pp. 445–461. Springer, Cham (2018). https://doi.org/10.1007/978-3-319-91521-0_32
21. Grimme, C., Preuss, M., Adam, L., Trautmann, H.: Social bots: human-like by means of human control? Big Data **5**(4) (2017)
22. Jiang, M., Cui, P., Beutel, A., Faloutsos, C., Yang, S.: Catching synchronized behaviors in large networks: a graph mining approach. ACM Trans. Knowl. Discov. From Data **10**(4) (2016)
23. Kavanaugh, A.L., et al.: Social media use by government: from the routine to the critical. Gov. Inf. Q. **29**(4), 480–491 (2012)
24. Ledig, C., et al.: Photo-realistic single image super-resolution using a generative adversarial network. In: IEEE ICCV (2017)
25. de Lima Salge, C.A., Berente, N.: Is that social bot behaving unethically? Commun. ACM **60**(9), 29–31 (2017)
26. Liu, S., Hooi, B., Faloutsos, C.: HoloScope: topology-and-spike aware fraud detection. In: ACM CIKM (2017)
27. Mazza, M., Cresci, S., Avvenuti, M., Quattrociocchi, W., Tesconi, M.: RTbust: exploiting temporal patterns for botnet detection on Twitter. In: ACM WebSci (2019)
28. Miller, Z., Dickinson, B., Deitrick, W., Hu, W., Wang, A.H.: Twitter spammer detection using data stream clustering. Inf. Sci. **260**, 64–73 (2014)
29. Pandey, R., Castillo, C., Purohit, H.: Modeling human annotation errors to design bias-aware systems for social stream processing. In: IEEE/ACM ASONAM (2019)
30. Pascual, S., Bonafonte, A., Serrà, J.: SEGAN: speech enhancement generative adversarial network. In: Interspeech (2017)
31. Sahay, R., Mahfuz, R., Gamal, A.E.: A computationally efficient method for defending adversarial deep learning attacks. arXiv preprint arXiv:1906.05599 (2019)
32. Shao, C., Ciampaglia, G.L., Varol, O., Yang, K.C., Flammini, A., Menczer, F.: The spread of low-credibility content by social bots. Nat. Commun. **9**(1) (2018)
33. Starbird, K., Arif, A., Wilson, T.: Disinformation as collaborative work: surfacing the participatory nature of strategic information operations. In: ACM CSCW (2019)
34. Stella, M., Ferrara, E., De Domenico, M.: Bots increase exposure to negative and inflammatory content in online social systems. Proc. Nat. Acad. Sci. **115**(49) (2018)
35. Varol, O., Ferrara, E., Davis, C.A., Menczer, F., Flammini, A.: Online human-bot interactions: detection, estimation, and characterization. In: AAAI ICWSM (2017)
36. Yang, C., Harkreader, R., Gu, G.: Empirical evaluation and new design for fighting evolving Twitter spammers. IEEE Trans. Inf. Forensics Secur. **8**(8), 1280–1293 (2013)

37. Yang, K.C., Varol, O., Davis, C.A., Ferrara, E., Flammini, A., Menczer, F.: Arming the public with artificial intelligence to counter social bots. Hum. Behav. Emerg. Technol. **1**(1), 48–61 (2019)
38. Yardi, S., Romero, D., Schoenebeck, G., et al.: Detecting spam in a Twitter network. First Monday **15**(1) (2010)

The Markets of Manipulation: The Trading of Social Bots on Clearnet and Darknet Markets

Lena Frischlich[1]([⊠]) [iD], Niels Göran Mede[2], and Thorsten Quandt[1] [iD]

[1] University of Münster, 48143 Münster, Germany
{lena.frischlich,thorsten.quandt}@uni-muenster.de
[2] University of Zürich, Zürich, Switzerland
n.mede@ikmz.uzh.ch

Abstract. Since the Brexit vote and the 2016 U.S. election, much has been speculated about the use of so-called social bots, (semi-)automatized pseudo-users in online media, as political manipulation tools. Accumulating global evidence shows that pseudo-users are used for different purposes, such as the amplification of political topics or the simulation of large numbers of followers. Social bots, as a (semi-)automated pseudo-user type, are part of a larger infrastructure, among others, entailing network access, fake accounts, and hosting services. Users and providers of social bots and their infrastructure can differ. Thus, it is plausible that a digital goods market has emerged for the exchange of social bots and infrastructure components. The present study used an ethnographic approach to study the accessibility, availability, and prices for pseudo-users and social bots on markets in the (German- and English-language) Clearnet and Darknet. The results show that an infrastructure for digital manipulation is widely available online, and that the tools for artificial content or connectedness amplification are easily accessible for lay users and are cheap on Clearnet and Darknet markets.

Keywords: Social bots · Darknet · Clearnet · Trading · Market

1 Motivation

Especially in the aftermath of the Brexit vote and the U.S. election in 2016, reports about so-called *social bots*, (semi-)automatized user accounts employed to influence political debates [1], have raised global concerns and calls for regulation [2]. The term social bots (short for "social robot") is an umbrella term that describes different (semi-)automatized account types on social media that mimic human behavior [3, 4]. Although not all social bots serve malicious aims, they are often understood as manipulative pseudo-users employed for "computational propaganda" [5, p. 3]. For instance, Oxford Internet Institute researchers argue that social bots are a valuable tool for computational propaganda because they are "cheap and easy to deploy" [5, p. 38]. Despite these concerns, systematic examinations of the availability of and access to pseudo-users are rare. The present study narrowed this gap via a systematic ethnographic analysis of pseudo-user trading on online markets.

© Springer Nature Switzerland AG 2020
C. Grimme et al. (Eds.): MISDOOM 2019, LNCS 12021, pp. 89–100, 2020.
https://doi.org/10.1007/978-3-030-39627-5_8

2 The Manipulation Infrastructure

The success of the participatory web 2.0 [6] has fundamentally altered the digital public sphere—for example, by extending opportunity structures for manipulation and covert propaganda dissemination [7], a transition we have described as the transformation from mass-mediated propaganda, traditionally directed toward a large dispersed audience, to modern multi-level "propaganda[3]"—manipulative communication produced, directed, and consumed by actors on the macro-level of the digital society, the meso-level of virtual groups, and the micro-level of the digitally networked individual [8]. Furthermore, although propaganda is not new but has been used for thousands of years of human history [9], it has never been so easy to disguise one's identity and to simulate broad support for even the most extreme ideas.

For instance, Berger and Morgan [10] showed that the self-declared "Islamic State" used Twitter apps to simulate thousands of retweets. Danish right-wing extremists disguised themselves as jihadists by setting up fake propaganda sites seemingly providing evidence for the "Islamic threat" [11], and German right-wing activists used strategically launched tweets to simulate their physical presence at a recent cyber-conference [12].

There is accumulating evidence that such pseudo-user strategies have been employed across the globe. Case reports included the promotion of political candidates [13], comment section flooding to drown voices of protest [14], as well as personal attacks [15]. In a well-known case, the electoral campaign of South Korean President Park Geun-hye was supported by millions of fake tweets [16]. The automation level of these pseudo-users can vary considerably, while the observable outcome (e.g., a massive increase in tweets about a certain topic) can remain similar. In recent analyses of national and state-level elections in Germany, Grimme et al. [17] found artificially inflated Twitter activity by right-wing activists (for an investigative media report about the coordination, see Schmehl [18]) as well as by the son of a Bavarian candidate for Parliament who run a bot army to support his father's campaign [19].

2.1 Pseudo-Users and Social Bots

For effective functioning, pseudo-users need a modular infrastructure (see Fig. 1), entailing multiple elements: (a) the account's user (i.e., the individual, group, organization, or state steering the action); (b) the orchestration level [17], broadly ranging from no automation (e.g., human "trolls") to relatively[1] fully automated "social bots" in a narrower sense; and (c) the online identity or account itself (i.e., whether it is a true, compromised, or fake account).

Pseudo-users can further execute different (d) actions, such as amplifying certain content (e.g., via liking or sharing), connecting to other accounts, or creating own content. The automation level and the accounts' abilities crucially depend on access to the environment in which the account operates via the application programming interface (API).

---

[1] For an overview of social bots' intelligence and the availability of automation tools for different platforms as indicated by the available bot-code, see Assenmacher et al. in this volume.

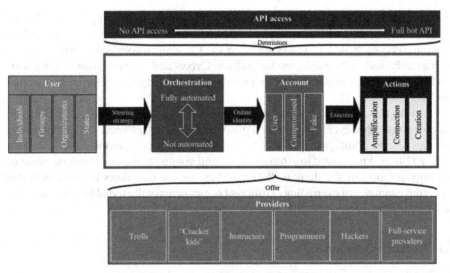

Fig. 1. The infrastructure of social bots.

Pseudo-user use can be conceptualized as an advancement of so-called black-hat marketing strategies such as search engine optimization (SEO). SEO has been discussed primarily in the context of increasing one's Google ranking, for instance, by inflating the number of links to one's website [20]. *Forbes* magazine reported that in the aftermath of the global success of social networks, black-hat marketing strategically aiming at social media optimization (SMO) have gained relevance [21], including strategies employing pseudo-users. Against this background, it is not surprising that pseudo-user providers and employers are not always the same person.

Case reports across the globe demonstrated that pseudo-user providers can range from motivated trolls [17] to programmers to cracker kids who combine code snippets, (malicious) black-hat hackers [22], and "full-service" providers offering, for example, distributed denial of service (DDoS)-ready botnets [23], in which the perpetrator seeks to block access to a network or service by flooding the target with superfluous requests from many different sources. As implied in the propaganda[3] concept, users can be individuals, groups, as well as governments [1], raising new challenges for those monitoring malicious social media activities, such as security agencies or institutions struggling with finding best practices for regulation [24].

2.2 Underground Markets for Social Bots

The present paper is particularly interested in technology-based pseudo-users, that is, social bots and their infrastructure. Reports from security agencies [25] indicate that these kinds of goods are traded in online spaces that are part of the so-called Clearnet, as well as in the Darknet [26]. The Darknet describes websites that are not indexed by search engines and need a special, anonymity-oriented browser to open them [27].

In both virtual spheres, different trading venues can be distinguished: (a) forums (e.g., black-hat marketing), where customers can scan various products, potentially stumbling over interesting offers in a discussion thread; (b) vendor shops offering a selected product range (e.g., the vendor shop cryptohackers.com offered hacking services); and (c) cybermarkets, such as Amazon or eBay on the Clearnet, respectively crypto-markets such as SilkRoad or Alphabay on the Darknet. Cyber- and crypto markets offer a wide product range, often accompanied by user reviews allowing for preferred trustworthy products and sellers [28].

Thus far, descriptions of social bots as commodities have been provided mostly in the context of other cybercrime-related overviews (see, for instance, the reports by the German federal crime police in this context [25]), or general reports about Darknet trading [29], making it hard to estimate the overall volume of the manipulation markets. Recently, a report by the think tank Trend Micro on the fake news machine provided numerous examples of the trading of different components of the social bot infrastructure on Chinese, Russian, and Middle Eastern "underground-sites" [26].

2.3 Research Questions

Against this background, in the present study, we sought to examine pseudo-users and social bots' trading in the Clearnet and Darknet focusing on English- and German-language markets.

We asked the following research questions:

RQ 1.   Where are social bots and their infrastructure traded online?
RQ 2.   What commodities are available?

3   Data Acquisition

To answer these questions, we conducted a systematic ethnographic exploration of German- and English-language online markets during August 2017. In one part of the investigation, we focused on the Clearnet, identifying access points via public accessible forums and search engines; in the other part, we inspected Darknet markets.

The procedure had multiple steps. First, we examined the scientific and publicly available "grey" literature (government and civic reports, mass media) and special online resources (e.g., Reddit and DeepDotWeb) to identify potential trading venues (such as specific crypto markets). Second, we checked (a) the venue's online status, (b) whether the venue was discussed as fraud, and (c) whether at least one relevant commodity was traded there. Most still running Darknet markets were identified via the DeepDotWeb; however, specific websites (e.g., Darknetmarkets.info) and wikis (e.g., the Hidden Wiki) were also useful as entry points. Published lists, in contrast, were often outdated only one or two years later.

To identify relevant commodities within the Darknet database and in the Clearnet, we used a set of theoretically deducted keywords describing the entire social bot infrastructure (see Table 1). Each term was entered in the anonymous search engine Duckduck.go to identify Clearnet venues, and on each of the Darknet websites to examine the trading of the corresponding commodity there. For each trading venue identified, commodities were inspected regarding the promised actions and the prices associated with these actions.

Table 1. Keywords for the identification of social bots.

Orchestration	Platform	Account	Abilities		
Bot	Facebook bot	Fake identity	Amplification	Like bot
Social Bot	Twitter bot	Fake user		Share bot
Cyborg Bot	YouTube bot	Fake profile		Fake likes
Spam Bot	Instagram bot	Fake account		Fake tweets
Bot Army	Reddit bot			Fake posts
Bot Net	WhatsApp bot			Post bot
Remote Bot/Remote Botnet	Telegram bot			Broadcasting bot
Political Bot	Social media bot			Tweet bot
Propaganda Bot			Connection	Fake follower
			Creation	Chat bot
			Other	DDoS bot
				Phishing bot

4 Results

4.1 Trading Venues

Overall, we identified 97 relevant Clearnet venues. Most were forums ($n = 81$), ranging from general discussion forums (e.g., BlackHatWorld) to specific hacker forums (such as toolba) to scam forums (e.g., cardmafia). In addition to forums, we found formalized vendor shops ($n = 15$), mostly offering ready-to-use solutions, such as social bots for amplification tasks (e.g., views, likes, or fake followers). Cyber markets such as Amazon did not really trade social bots. Only one offering on eBay promised "1700 manual social signals" for SEO marketing, claiming that these were "no bots," However, it remained unclear whether this was a scam.

The overall number of online shops in the Clearnet is unknown and—most likely—changing rapidly. A study by the EHI retail institute—relying on annual financial statements (i.e., official, legal firms), web-traffic analyses, and statistical models—recently suggested that at least 120,000 official online shops were active in Germany (for a summary, see [30]). Against this number, the identified share of underground markets and trading venues for pseudo-users is, of course, minor. Nevertheless, the underground economy is a constant concern to German security forces [26]).

The number of Darknet trading venues was nearly as large as the number of Clearnet markets ($N = 90$). However, more than half had already gone offline or went offline during the present analysis (e.g., Alphabay was shut down during that period [31]), matching previous reports about Darknet markets' short lifetimes [27]. Of the remaining 43 venues, 13 crypto markets were excluded because they traded only drugs (e.g., "stoned 100," "Dutchdrugz," or "Europills"). Thus, a final sample of 25 markets on 21 distinct platforms was used for the analysis (see the appendix, Table B). In this sample, vendor shops ($n = 13$) were the most frequent trading venue, followed by crypto markets ($n = 9$) and forums ($n = 4$). Similar to Clearnet forums, some Darknet markets required some form of a priori engagement. For instance, during the data collection period, the crypto market Valhalla required invitation codes obtained via another discussion forum.

Overall, the number of examined trading venues on the Darknet corresponds to previous reports about Western underground markets. For instance, Paoli et al. [28] reported that they had identified 18 English- or French-speaking crypto markets on which illegal weapons were traded. Although the Darknet's fluid nature impairs direct comparisons between the data Paoli et al. collected in 2016 and the present analyses one year later, the sheer number of pseudo-user trading venues was lower than the number of venues for illegal weapons.

4.2 Commodities

To account for the larger number of Clearnet markets, we compared commodities on all Darknet markets ($N = 31$) with a random sample of 30% of the Clearnet markets ($n = 30$). A table with all examined trading venues is provided in the appendix.

To gauge the commodities' quality and quantity, we created a database with (a) all relevant threads in the forums (e.g., "YouTube likes: 500 for 1$"), as well as all commodities on the first 10 result pages within (b) each cyber- or crypto market, and (c) vendor shop. Three trained coders then coded the commodity descriptions qualitatively. The codes represented different levels of orchestration, ranging from human pseudo-users, which were explicitly declared "no-bots," to source code, such as source files and builders (programs that need some additional implementation to execute the required actions) to (semi-)automated (social) bots, allowing for the automated execution of behavior such as liking or following, and botnets, as a coordinated number of such programs (e.g., "1000 followers"). We also coded different account types, namely offers for fake or compromised accounts. Finally, we coded actions such as amplification, and social media search engine optimization (e.g., "1k YouTube views"), as well as criminal aims, such as hacking tools and DDoS attacks. Ambiguities were discussed in coding conferences. Figure 2 shows the different actions offered in both spheres.

A total of 849 relevant commodities were identified on the Clearnet. A substantial number (815) were sold via vendor shops or forums. Notably, the number of commodities was much smaller on Darknet trading venues: Only 287 entries were related to social bots. Considering that we analyzed only 30% of the sample, the estimated number of manipulation tools on the Clearnet (2829.97) was nearly ten times higher compared to the Darknet (factor 9.86).

Qualitative coding of each commodity's description showed that tools for manipulation were available for nearly every larger social media platform or online service. Social networking sites (SNSs) with a large reach clearly dominated the picture. Of the 452 Clearnet descriptions that clearly mentioned a specific platform, 71% referred to

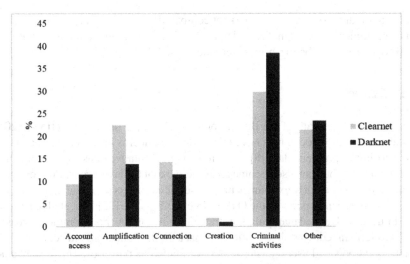

Fig. 2. Relative share of different actions. Account access entailed, for instance, fake accounts or account hacking, amplification, the liking or sharing of content, connection to the provision of fake followers, creation, the offering of comments or chat bots. Criminal activities encompassed DDoS attacks or trojans. Calculated as the share of certain actions of the total actions. One commodity could promise different actions (e.g., liking and sharing).

Facebook, Instagram, YouTube, or (much more seldom) Twitter. Similarly, 80% of the Darknet commodities that referred to a specific online platform referred to one of these four, with Twitter the least frequently mentioned.

In addition to targeting different platforms, the advertised commodities allowed for different actions. As expected, these actions ranged from access to accounts, amplification and connection, and creation of content. Moreover, a substantial part described criminal services, such as DDoS attacks, trojans, or ransomware.

4.3 Price Levels

The orchestration level and the action complexity desired influenced the prices. Technically simple and fully automated amplification tasks on platforms with a relatively open API, such as YouTube, were available for less than a euro (e.g., 100 views for 85 ct. in a Clearnet forum, i.e., 9 ct. per view).

Non-automated fake followers, simulating only social support and digital connections were comparably cheap (e.g. 3,000 Instagram followers for €18.24 on a crypto market, i.e., roughly 1 ct. per follower). Active creation of content, in contrast, was very rare and more expensive. A hundred random Instagram comments were traded for 62 ct. per comment on a Darknet crypto market. Among a pseudo-user campaign's expensive component were credible fake accounts on Facebook or Twitter, which were traded for €5 to €9 on the Clearnet and the Darknet. The highest prices were observed for full-service botnets able to conduct DDoS attacks. For instance, access to a botnet with two "live bots" for one week was sold for €424,35 in a Clearnet forum, and a three-day DDoS full botnet was offered for €578,99 on a Darknet cyber-market. However, we were able to obtain more prices for Darknet compared to Clearnet commodities. On the Clearnet, customers were often directed to more private communication platforms, such as Skype or Messenger, before prices were mentioned.

5 Discussion

Especially in the aftermath of the Brexit vote, and jarred by the U.S. election in 2016, reports about so-called social bots have raised global concerns by government and civic actors. In a digital "propaganda[3]" [8] environment, manipulative tools are no longer used by state actors only but can also become an attractive tool for laypersons. Previous cases have shown that particularly extremists might use pseudo-users to inflate their perceived online success. Recent reports by the Oxford Internet Institute [32] indicated that the use of pseudo-users and related manipulation strategies is becoming more common across the globe. The German federal police caution against a digital "underground economy" [25] in which social bots and user data are traded for malicious purposes. The present study provides an initial attempt to enlighten this digital abyss via a systematic ethnographic exploration of German- and English-language pseudo-user trading venues.

Overall, we identified four times as many trading venues for social bots on the Clearnet as on the Darknet. Although this number might be affected by the relative short lifetimes of Darknet markets [16, 17], we think that this reflects the easy access to manipulation tools by simply Googling. Clearnet venues were further characterized more strongly by forums, leaving users at a higher risk of stumbling over tools for manipulation, whereas venues on the Darknet were mostly crypto markets and vendor shops, and were characterized more strongly by user-friendly crypto-market structures.

The estimated number of pseudo-user-based manipulation commodities on the Clearnet was nearly ten times higher than for Darknet commodities. The targeted social networks sites and offered services, however, remained roughly the same across the Internet.

Although similar pseudo-user activities were available in both virtual spheres, we witnessed small qualitative differences regarding the relative shares of the activities. A relatively larger proportion of Clearnet commodities aimed at amplification, and a slightly larger proportion of Darknet commodities tackled criminal activities.

Nevertheless, the absolute number of commodities was larger on the Clearnet, including the absolute number of tools for criminal activities. In contrast to moral panics about intelligent social bots (such as those that inspired numerous German headlines about "opinion machines"), tools for automatically creating content were rare, and most of the services offering content creation seemed to be human-steered.

A price inspection showed that API access and human curation level affected price levels. In particular, relatively small-scale amplifications (e.g., 1,000 fake followers) were cheap, implying that even lay users without a large budget could use digital pseudo-users to manipulate their online success.

Although these numbers might lie well beyond what is necessary to affect state elections, and there is evidence that the large-scale success of such campaigns requires financial and social resources [1] most likely beyond a single individual's or a small-scale extremist group's means, this availability might affect democratic elections far beyond the large national context under global scrutiny. Single cases like the Bavarian candidate's son hosting a bot army to support his father's campaign [17] indicate that there might be a market for this type of manipulation even in small, state-level elections. Furthermore, although we addressed the phenomenon from the perspective of political implications and "propaganda[3]", the same techniques are used for economic manipulations. For a media report about Instagram closing fake follower apps, see DRF [33].

5.1 Limitations and Future Research Directions

The present study had several limitations. First, we focused on German- and English-language markets. Thus, the results cannot be easily generalized to global markets. An analysis of Chinese-, Russian-, and Arabic language markets for disinformation [26] reported similar commodities but different prices: One hundred views on a Chinese market are sold for about a third of the price (roughly 30 ct., see p. 16). Future research on cross-cultural differences is necessary to understand these global markets better. Second, our study had a cross-sectional design. Thus, future research on the long-term development of these markets is needed. Third, distinguishing real offers from honeypots (fake offers aimed at attracting criminals for legal investigations) and scams in the case of underground trading was a constant challenge [28], as such price levels and absolute numbers should be interpreted carefully.

5.2 Conclusion

Despite the limitations, this study contributes to the literature by showing that in contrast to common dystopic concerns, social bots with the ability to create own content are not very accessible for lay users. However, we also showed that tools for amplifying one's content and perceived popularity on large social networking sites are cheap and easily available to average online users. Thus, aggregated user responses' credibility seems questionable. This is particularly relevant in the current attention economy in which trending topics on online media are often set equal to trending topics among citizens (see also the data society reports on this issue [34–36].

In addition, our study emphasized the necessity to study the pseudo-user phenomenon beyond the Twitter realm and the famous "bot or not" question. Although most studies thus far examined Twitter (e.g., [1, 14, 15, 17]), the present study results emphasized Facebook and Instagram as top targets for traded pseudo-users. In addition, we found partially comparable price levels for human and (semi-)automated pseudo-users, depending on a given platform's technological accessibility (or API). Therefore, calls for closing APIs to prevent pseudo-user engagement might impair the employment of fully automated pseudo-users, but will be limited in erasing inflated online appearances *per se*. In sum, our work provides an initial step to understand the markets of manipulation in German and English, providing estimates for the trading venues and the volume of these new propaganda tools for a wide array of users.

Appendix

Table A. Overview of the study trading venues.

	Clearnet	Darknet
1	Altenen	0day*
2	BAE Applied Intelligence Systems	Berlusconi Market*
3	Binary Revolutions Forum	Cerberus
4	Black Hat Russia	Charlieuk*
5	Black Web Forum	Dream Market (PGP)*
6	Breach Forums	Exodu$
7	Cardmafia	FB Hack Tool
8	Cryptohackers	Fight Club*
9	Dark Pid	Free Hacking Tools
10	Devil Group	Gammagoblin*
11	Followlike	Hack Canada*
12	Free-Hack	Hackerplace
13	Hack a day	jRAT
14	Hack Forums	Mr. Robot Shop*
15	Hacker's List	Ostrich Hackers Hunters
16	Hackerthreads	Pushing Taboo*
17	Hackervoice	Quality King*
18	Hitb	Ranion
19	Malwr	Rent-A-Hacker
20	Nulled (Forum)	RsClub Market
21	Nulled (Marketplace)	Stoned100
22	Offensive Community	Sourcery*
23	Quora	The French Connection*
24	Safe Sky Hacks	The Hack Liar
25	Smart Hackerz	Tochka
26	Social Engineering	Torum
27	Team Corrupt	ToYouTeam*
28	Toolbase	Trade Route
29	Topsocialbot	Valhalla
30	Vigilante Tech	Wall Street Market
		Zion

Notes. *The market did not sell a relevant commodity.

References

1. Woolley, S.C., Howard, P.N.: Computational Propaganda Worldwide: Executive Summary. Oxford Internet Institute, Oxford (2017)
2. Commission, E.: Corporate Social Responsibility: Commission Launches European Multi-Stakeholder Forum. European Commission, Brussels (2018)
3. Frischlich, L.: Fake News und Social Bots - Erkennung, Wirkung, Bekämpfung [Fake news and social bots. Detection, effect, combating]. In: Holznagel, B., Steul, W. (eds.) Öffentlich-rechtlicher Rundfunk in Zeiten des Populismus [Public broadcast in times of populism], pp. 28–59. VISTAS, Leipzig (2018)
4. Grimme, C., Preuss, M., Adam, L., Trautmann, H.: Social bots: human-like by means of human control. Big Data 5, 279–293 (2017)
5. Woolley, S.C., Howard, P.: Computational Propaganda. Computational Propaganda Memo. Oxford Internet Institute, Oxford (2017)
6. Schmidt, J.H.: Das neue Netz: Merkmale, Praktiken und Folgen des Web 2.0 [The new net: Characteristics, practices, and consequences of the Web 2.0]. UVK, Konstanz (2009)
7. Jack, C.: What's propaganda got to do with it? Data Society Points (2017)
8. Frischlich, L.: Propaganda³: Einblicke in die Inszenierung und Wirkung von Online-Propaganda auf der Makro-Meso-Mikro Ebene [Propaganda³: Insights into the staging and effects of online-propaganda on the macro-meso-micro level]. In: Aktivismus, B.Z., Sachs-Hombach, K. (eds.) Fake news und Social Bots - Neue Mechanismen populistischer Propaganda [Fake news and social bots – populist propagandas' new mechanisms], pp. 133–170. Springer Fachmedien VS, Wiesbaden (2018)
9. Taylor, P.M.: Munitions of the Mind: A History of Propaganda from the Ancient World to the Present Day, 3rd edn. Manchester University Press, Manchester (2003)
10. Berger, J.M., Morgan, J.: The ISIS Twitter Census. Washington, DC (2015)
11. Farkas, J., Schou, J., Neumayer, C.: Cloaked Facebook pages: exploring fake Islamist propaganda in social media. New Med. Soc. 20(5), 1850–1867 (2018)
12. Schatto-Eckrodt, T., Boberg, S., Wintterlin, F., Frischlich, L., Quandt, T.: Bedrohte Deliberation. Information Warfare und Desinformation als Bedrohung digitaler Öffentlichkeiten [Threatened deliberation: Information warfare and desinformation as threat to digital public spheres]. Communicatio Socialis 52(2), 147–158 (2019)
13. Howard, P.N., Bolsover, G., Kollanyi, B., Bradshaw, S., Neudert, L.-M.: Junk news and bots during the U.S. election: what were Michigan voters sharing over Twitter? Oxford Internet Institute, Oxford (2017)
14. Verkamp, J.-P., Gupta, M.: Five incidents, one theme: Twitter spam as a weapon to drown voices of protest. In: 3rd USENIX Workshop on Free and Open Communications on the Internet, pp. 1–7. Indiana University, Indiana (2013)
15. Nimmo, B., Czuperski, M., Brookie, G.: #BotSpot: the intimidators. Twitter bots unleashed in a social media disruption tactic. https://medium.com/dfrlab/botspot-the-intimidators-135244bfe46b. Accessed 19 Oct 2019
16. McCurry, J.: South Korea spy agency admits trying to rig 2012 presidential election. The Guardian, London (2017)
17. Grimme, C., Assenmacher, D., Adam, L.: Changing perspectives: is it sufficient to detect social bots? Lect. Notes Comput. Sci. (including its subseries Lect. Notes Artif. Intell. Lect. Notes Bioinf.) 10913, 445–461 (2018)
18. Schmehl, K.: Diese geheimen Chats zeigen, wer hinter dem Meme-Angriff #Verräterduell aufs TV-Duell steckt [This secret chats show who's behind the meme attack #traitorduel on the TV-duel]. BuzzFeed News, pp. 1–9 (2017)
19. BR24: Social Bots im Wahlkampf [Social bots in the campaign] (2018)

20. Swati, P.P., Pawar, B., Ajay, S.P.: Search engine optimization: a study. Res. J. Comput. Inf. Technol. Sci. 1(1), 10–13 (2013)
21. Rampton, J.: Social media is the new black hat. Forbes Magazine, 21 July 2014
22. O'Brien, J.A., Marakas, G.M.: Management Information Systems, 10th edn. McGraw-Hill, New York (2010)
23. DRF: # ElectionWatch: Russian botnet boosts German far-right posts. medium.com/drflab, pp. 1–8 (2017)
24. Safferling, C., Rücker, C.: Das Strafrecht und die underground economy [The criminal law and the underground economy]. In: Konrad-Adenauer Stiftung: Analysen und Argumente [Analysis and arguments]. Konrad-Adenauer Stiftung, Berlin (2018)
25. Bundeskriminalamt: Cybercrime - Bundeslagebild 2017 [Cybercrime – federal overview of the situation 2017]. Federal Crime Police, Wiesbaden (2018)
26. Gu, L., Kropotov, V., Yarochkin, F.: The fake news machine: how propagandists abuse the Internet and manipulate the public, Trend Labs Report, Texas (2017)
27. Mey, S.: Darknet - Waffen, Drogen, Whistleblower. Wie die digitale Unterwelt funktioniert [Darknet- firearms, drugs, whisleblower. How the digital underground works]. Ch Beck, München (2017)
28. Paoli, G.P., Aldridge, J., Ryan, N., Warnes, R.: Behind the curtain: the illicit trade of firearms, explosives and ammunition on the dark web (2017)
29. Biryukov, A., Pustogarov, I., Thill, F., Weinmann, R.P.: Content and popularity analysis of tor hidden services. In: Proceedings of the International Conference Distributed Computing Systems, pp. 188–193 (2014)
30. Schwarz Consulting GmbH: E-Commerce-Markt Deutschland 2018. https://schwarze-consulting.de/e-commerce/2018/11/02/Studie-Top1000-Onlineshops.html. Accessed 14 Oct 2019
31. Lince, T.: Biggest marketplace on the Darknet taken down by authorities; illicit goods and counterfeits still rampant. World Trade Market Review, 18 July 2017
32. Bradshaw, S., Howard, P.N.: The Global Disinformation Order 2019 Global Inventory of Organised Social Media Manipulation. Oxford Internet Institute, Oxford (2019)
33. Firsching, J.: Who's next? Instagram greift weiter durch und schließt Follower Bot Mass-planner [Instagram takes vigorous action and closes folllower bot massplaner]. futurebiz (2017)
34. Marwick, A., Lewis, R.: Media manipulation and disinformation online. Data Soc. Res. Inst. 1–104 (2017). https://datasociety.net/output/media-manipulation-and-disinfo-online/
35. Donovan, J., Friedberg, B.: Source Hacking: Media Manipulation in Practice. Data & Society, New York (2019)
36. Phillips, W.: The oxygen of amplification: better practices for reporting on extremists, antagonists, and manipulators online. Data & Society, New York (2018)

Inside the Tool Set of Automation: Free Social Bot Code Revisited

Dennis Assenmacher[1]📷, Lena Adam[1]📷, Lena Frischlich[2]📷,
Heike Trautmann[1]📷, and Christian Grimme[1(✉)]📷

[1] Department of Information Systems, University of Münster, Leonardo-Campus 3,
48149 Münster, Germany
{dennis.assenmacher,lena.adam,heike.trautmann,
christian.grimme}@uni-muenster.de
[2] Department of Communication, University of Münster, Bispinghof 9-14,
48149 Münster, Germany
lena.frischlich@uni-muenster.de

Abstract. Social bots have recently gained attention in the context of public opinion manipulation on social media platforms. While a lot of research effort has been put into the classification and detection of such automated programs, it is still unclear how technically sophisticated those bots are, which platforms they target, and where they originate from. To answer these questions, we gathered repository data from open source collaboration platforms to identify the status-quo of social bot development as well as first insights into the overall skills of publicly available bot code.

Keywords: Social bots · Implementation · Code sharing · Data analysis

1 Introduction

These days, the usage, rise, and influence of so-called social bots – automated accounts in social media that can spread disinformation, manipulate societies, or even influence elections – is a major topic in societal discussion as well as in research [7]. Clearly, as these automatons seem to be omnipresent in political campaigns, in online discussions, and comment sections, many people fear the power of social bots in terms of opinion forming [16]. Although many researchers deal with detection of social bots in open online media, there seems to be no deeper understanding of their technical characteristics and abilities [4]. Interestingly, there is still little evidence on the capabilities and usage of social bots,

The authors acknowledge support by the German Federal Ministry of Education and Research (FKZ 16KIS0495K) and the European Research Center for Information Systems (ERCIS) as well as the Digital Society research program funded by the Ministry of Culture and Science of the German State of North Rhine-Westphalia.

C. Grimme et al. (Eds.): MISDOOM 2019, LNCS 12021, pp. 101–114, 2020.
https://doi.org/10.1007/978-3-030-39627-5_9

especially, because almost no research on the social bot software ecosystem is available.

This work opens the 'black box of social bots' and provides new technical insights based on knowledge discovery from shared bot code in open software repositories. Inspired by Kollanyi's research "Where do bots come from? An analysis of bot codes shared on GitHub." from 2016 [18], we rigorously investigate the current situation of freely available social bot code by extending Kollanyi's pioneering research in multiple aspects regarding the analyzed data as well as the used methodology. Specifically, we consider

1. multiple code repository platforms for data acquisition,
2. broaden the search for bot code towards current social media platforms, and
3. investigate the type of social bots in an automated way.

The paper is structured as follows: Sect. 2 briefly addresses the background of social bot research and Kollanyi's work, while Sect. 3 details our data acquisition process. In Sect. 4 we detail the descriptive data analysis, which is complemented by a topic analysis in Sect. 5 for identifying social bot capabilities from repository descriptions. Section 6 concludes the work and provides perspectives for next steps in research.

2 Related Work

The term 'social bot' has received more and more attention over the last years. Ten years ago, social bots were still considered a curiosity of new social networking infrastructures like 'Second Life' [29] or as a new form of spam [19]. Today, the massive spamming and broadcasting activity of automated programs in social networks during election campaigns is considered a real danger for open discourse and attributed to propaganda activities [1,2,7,8,16,20]. In the wider context, social bots are also potent vehicles for the distribution of cyberhate and fake news [9,24,27]. As a consequence, a lot of effort has been put into the automatic (sometimes learning- and thus data-based) detection of social bots [3,5–7,10,22,28], and with these detection mechanisms, several social bot taxonomies have been proposed. As an early and rough classification Wooley [32] proposed to differentiate between classical bots for pure automation purposes and those that influence "public opinion or disrupt organizational communication". He defines such bots as "political bots". Hegelich [14] distinguishes between "assistants" (these also include chat bots) and "social bots", where the latter are hidden actors in the political context. Stieglitz's classification is more fine grained [26]: the authors suggest "imitation of human behaviour" and "intent" as two nominal scales, where the first discriminates low/none and high degree of imitation while the latter distinguishes malicious, neutral and benign intent. Under these scales, social bots are represented as automated actors, which imitate human behavior with malicious intent. To integrate the variety of perspectives, Grimme et al. [13] propose a taxonomy that distinguishes social and non-social bots (the latter corresponds to assistants mentioned by [14] or [10]) while splitting the class of social bots into three sub-classes: simple, advanced, and hypothetically "intelligent" social bots. For simple bots, the authors provide source code, which is able to perform very simple tasks like posting, sharing, or liking content. The second class is considered to imitate human behavior (in the sense of Stieglitz [26]) by acting in human speed, mimicking human inactivity, and simulating off-topic interests. Here, the authors report on experiments they performed with this kind of bots (but do not provide source code). For intelligent bots, which act on their own and virtually human-like, the authors cannot provide a representative set of instances, as none has been detected or published, yet.

Interestingly, apart from the works of Grimme et al. [12,13], mostly gray literature[1] or technology reports[2] provide insights into the development processes and technical challenges of social bot creation. As a consequence, empirical evidence of social bots as well as founded insight into the degree of development of such codes are very scarce.

In a notable exception, Kollanyi [18] has examined the availability of open-source code for Twitter bots on Github. He shows that the number of repositories providing Twitter bot code has been steadily increasing since the launch of the social media platform, with the majority of repositories being provided by actors from the United State or Japan. In light of the changing media system and the global success of platforms besides Twitter, it is, however, highly plausible that Twitter bots only form a small share of the overall social bots available. As such the study by Kollanyi is certainly limited, when it comes to understanding the availability of social bots in a more general way. With this study, we continue and extend the work of Kollanyi by applying a set of data analytic tools as well as a topic modelling technique to provide an up-to-date and more general view on available social bot software and its skills related to the taxonomy by Grimme et al. [13].

3   Data Acquisition

As we are interested in available social bots codes, we focus on open development platforms that allowed for collaboration and identification of specific codes via search terms. At these platforms we searched for projects related to social bot development considering all major social media platforms that can be targeted by social bots. In the following, we describe the data acquisition process. In a first step, we detail the selection of queried open development platforms. In the second step, we detail the construction of search queries with respect to the selection of considered social media platforms.

---

[1] e.g. BotWiki https://botwiki.org/resources/twitterbots/, Fredheim http://quantifyingmemory.blogspot.co.uk/2013/06/putins-bots-part-one-bit-about-bots.html, Grossmann https://medium.freecodecamp.org/my-open-source-instagram-bot-got-me-2-500-real-followers-for-5-in-server-costs-e40491358340.

[2] e.g. https://github.com/eggheads/eggdrop/, https://dev.botframework.com/.

Data Sources: A total of eight code sharing websites fulfilled these criteria and allowed for (a) version control via Git or Apache subversion (SVN); (b) collaboration between users; (c) public access (i.e. they are accessible via the clear web); and (d) searching for specific terms. We used Alexa global usage statistics to identify the five most relevant repositories. The Alexa rank, is a metric, which can be used to evaluate the importance of a website[3]. The metric combines calculations of internal homepage traffic such as page callings, and their development over time. Web sites are ranked by their importance. The following platforms are used as data source: *Github, Sourceforge, Bitbucktet, GitLab,* and *Launchpad.*

Social Media Platforms: In order to describe the availability of different types of social bots, we focused on social media platforms, micro-blogging services, chat or Voice over IP-services, and instant messengers with the largest global reach. Reach was determined by a triangulation of (a) the number of active users (see [25]), (b) global traffic rank based on Alexa, and (c) the downloads of the accordant application (e.g. via Google's Play Store or Apple's App Store). Based on the criteria, mentioned above, the following social media platforms are used within the data-acquisition process: *Telegram, Twitter, Facebook, Reddit, Skype, Instagram, Youtube, Whatsapp, Linkedin, Tumblr, vKontakte, Snapchat and Pinterest.*

Since the collaboration platforms are differently structured, it is not feasible to establish a common and comparable procedure for searching for specific bot programs. The largest platform, `Github`, offers a detailed search engine, other services are more restricted. We selected the search terms as generic as possible. Specifically, we combined the name of each Social Platform with the term `bot` via a logical AND operator. For `Github`, `Gitlab` and `Bitbucket` a proprietary crawler was programmed that automatically gathered the repositories information for all search term combinations. While `Github` and `Gitlab` explicitly provide an external application programming interface (API) for searching, `Bitbucket` is not easily accessible. Therefore we utilized `Scrapy`, a python-based web scraping framework, for collecting the relevant information. The remaining platforms, Sourceforge and Launchpad were manually queried via the provided web interface because of the low number of matching repositories for those platforms. The scraped information was persisted within Elasticsearch[4], a document-based search engine.

4   Descriptive Analysis

In total the data of 40,301 code-repositories was gathered for the time interval from April 2008 until October 2018. The largest number of repositories was provided by `Github`(38,600), followed by `Gitlab`(1,293) and `Bitbucket`(408). Despite its high Alexa score, only 25 repositories were found on Sourceforge for

---

[3] see: Alexa Rank: https://www.alexa.com/.

[4] https://www.elastic.co.

all search term combinations. Moreover, 10 of these repositories were maintained on `Github` in parallel. We explain this observation by the fact that Sourceforge is considered as one of the oldest collaboration platforms, with a lack of sophisticated functionality. Therefore, most developers move to a different platform, which is able to fulfill their requirements. Also in 2013 and 2015 the platform was criticized for offering adware and bundled malware. As a result it was reported that users switched to other code-hosting platforms [30]. For Launchpad, only 10 repositories were found. This is not a surprising result, since the platform is of small scale. In total the platform hosts only 13,000 repositories laying the focus on big, open source software projects such as MySQL, Inkscape or Unity.

The largest competitors of `Github`, namely `Gitlab` and `Bitbucket`, provide only a small fraction of the total number of bot repositories (4%) and are thus considered as niche platforms. Furthermore, we are able to observe the impact of Microsoft's recent announcement of acquiring the `Github` platform for 7.5 billion US dollars [21]. While the average number of new repositories on the `Gitlab` platform per month was 13.97 before the announcement, it drastically increased to 234 repositories in June and 117 in July 2018. As it was reported in various news reports, the announcement was negatively perceived by many open source developers, who publicly encouraged other developers to migrate to `Gitlab` [30]. Obviously this affected the community of bot programmers as well.

4.1   Data Overview

Over all collaboration platforms, we observe a similar distribution regarding the number of repositories for a specific social-media platform (Fig. 1). Most of the identified programs are produced for Telegram, followed by Twitter, Facebook and Reddit. At first sight this is a surprising result since Telegram is not considered as one of the big social-media players and the platform only exists since 2013. A detailed inspection of the creation date for Telegram oriented repositories reveals that until 2015 the platform did not receive a lot of attention. This changed in June and July 2015, when a significant increase in the number of related projects can be observed. We can explain this sudden increase by the fact that on June 24, 2015, Telegram officially launched its open bot platform, making it easy for programmers to create automated bot programs via an external API. Furthermore, the functionality of creating inline bots (bots that can be addressed in any chat) led to a second raise of newly created applications in January 2016. Hence the social platform itself seems to directly impact the community of social-bot code. Figure 2 shows, among others, the number of newly created Telegram repositories over time.

In a second step we analyze different lifespans of repositories. We define the lifespan of one single repository as the time between the creation date and the last activity. Moreover an activity is characterized by any repository interaction such as a new contribution, a fork, or a newly assigned issue. We observe that more than 50% of the crawled Repositories (18,000) have a lifespan of 0 days (Fig. 3). This means that such repositories were created on a specific date and did not receive any further update after publication day. As indicated in [18],

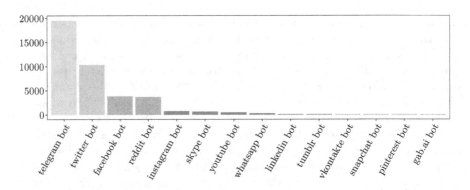

Fig. 1. Search term distribution for all social-media platforms

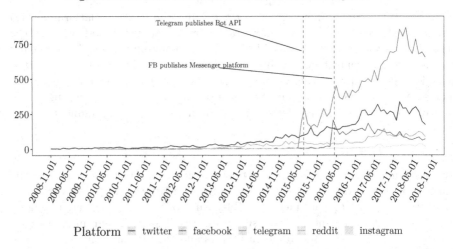

Fig. 2. Number of repositories for different platforms over time

some developers use the `Github` platform only as a medium for sharing or storing their code rather than collaborating with other users.

API Support and Programming Languages: Due to the heterogeneous structure and conflicting goals between different social media platforms, companies handle third party access to the service they provide in a different manner. Whilst some platforms actively encourage developers to create external applications by providing dedicated interfaces (application programming interface, API) for accessing their data and functionality, some platforms do not offer such information. Within this work, we differentiate between four distinct classes of third party access.

- Platforms with a `BotAPI` do not only offer API's for third party institutions, but also dedicated services and functionality for bot programs. Within our

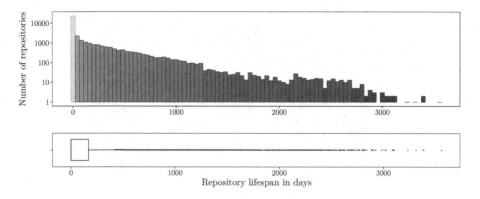

Fig. 3. Lifespan of the crawled repositories

study Telegram was the only platform that provided such sophisticated interface.

- Platforms that offer an `API` to perform all the common tasks of the corresponding web-interface in an automated way e.g. following, creating comments.
- Platforms that offer a `limited API access`. Although an interface for third parties exists, the range of functionality is limited. Platforms that are assigned to this class, for example only allow to access private user data.
- Platforms that offer `no API` and no other means of interface for external parties.

Most of the social media platforms of interest offer some kind of API to third parties. Only WhatsApp and Snapchat do not provide any official API interface. Not surprising, those platforms are situated on the lower ranks regarding the number of repositories found for the specific search term. Most of the platforms with a higher rank do offer a more sophisticated API. In general we observed a positive rank correlation between the number of repositories found for a specific social platform and the corresponding level of API support ($\rho = 0.78$). Overall, the `limited API` was the most prominent class to which social platforms are assigned. This can be explained by strict privacy policies of some bigger social-media platforms. Because of recent incidents, where private data was used for manipulation purposes (e.g. Cambridge Analytica), those companies were widely criticized by the public for providing unrestricted data-access [31].

Most of the social media platforms which provide a dedicated API, offer some additional interfaces to access their service. These interfaces can be accessed by specific programming languages. The most common programming language over all platforms is Python. Interestingly JavaScript is also frequently utilized. While Facebook explicitly provides a Java Script Toolkit, this is not the case for the other platforms. In cases where the API is restricted (e.g. companies privacy policy), programmers often directly access the web interface with JavaScript code

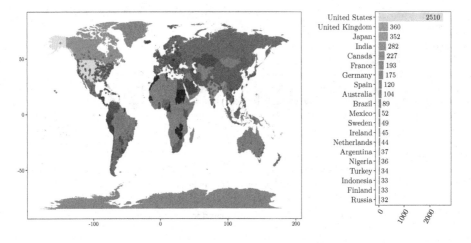

Fig. 4. Origin of Twitter repositories

to circumvent the official API. In other cases, wrappers for the web interface (in terms of remote controlling them) are provided.

4.2 Geospatial Analysis

Github and Gitlab allow users to specify their respective geo-location. We utilized Google's geo-coding API to receive longitude/latitude pairs that are approximately close to the location that was specified by the user. In total, we gathered information of 46,900 unique contributors, where geo-location information was present in 22,688 cases.

Corresponding to Kollanyi [18], we present an updated version of the origins of Twitter repositories that was already observed in 2016. It is clear from the world map in Fig. 4 that the main part of the repositories belong to ten countries. Having a look at the top five most contributing countries and comparing them to the findings of [18] shows that the distribution basically stays the same. Most of the Twitter repositories originate from the United States. In [18] the United States were directly followed by Japan. Our updated version reveals that the United Kingdom caught up to Japan and follows the U.S. by providing the second largest number of bot related repositories for Twitter. In contrast to Kollanyi's study we also have access to location data of different social-media platforms. Directly compared to the distribution of Twitter, we observe some inherent dissimilarities between the platforms. While Russia does not play an important role in the context of Twitter bots, most of the Telegram bot code contributors are from Russia (Fig. 5). A reason for this could be the popularity of Telegram within the Russian population [17].

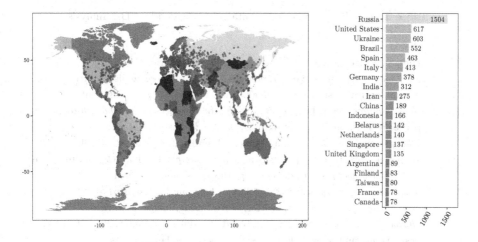

Fig. 5. Origin of Telegram repositories

5 Topic Modeling

To get an intuition about the realized functionality of the bot programs, we applied Latent Dirichlet Allocation (LDA) on the descriptions of the different repositories. LDA is a generative statistical model that is used to describe documents as a set of latent topics. Each topic follows a unique word distribution, which is generated by maximizing the conditional probability for a word occurring in a given topic. In order to achieve meaningful results, incoming data (repository descriptions) have to be pre-processed. First, we select all repositories that have English descriptions with more than one word. Additionally, we remove all occurrences of social-media platform names from the documents and therefore prevent the creation of platform-related topics. Next, we execute tokenization, stop word removal and lemmatization. We create uni- and bi-grams to account for close relationships between words within one document and word combinations. Based on the pre-processed data, we execute a LDA analysis [23]. Manual inspection of the results shows that about 15 topics are well suited to reveal existing repository types. Allowing a larger number of clusters leads to artificial separation of topics, while a smaller number of allowed clusters leads to overarching topics that contain multiple, semantically rather different repository types.

Table 1 lists the resulting fifteen topics, returned by our LDA analysis. Most of the topics represent repositories that provide simple functionality (italic) or user action such as posting random content (e.g. images or predefined messages), linking videos, or following other users (5, 6, 7, 8, 9). Further, some clusters describe more sophisticated functionality (bold italic), which enables interaction between different accounts like chatting with other users (0, 3, 10). In this context, we observe that Markov chains play an important role. However, the top representatives of the resulting topics do not indicate that state of the art

Table 1. Top fifteen topic representatives provided by LDA analysis.

Topic	Words
0	*chat* , message, group, **send**, user, app, via, google, friend, bot
1	*API*, using, written, python, *framework*, *library*, php, create, use, written_python
2	python, **script**, first, learning, small, price, twitterbot, bot, reddit, tutorial
3	tweet, *random*, reply, test, **markov**, text, chain, generates, **markov_chain**, given
4	platform, slack, implementation, ruby, language, answer, question, messenger
5	manage, aws, telegrambot, play, game, url, notification, lambda, world, live
6	*simple*, bot, weather, people, creating, thing, *sample*, heroku, program, template
7	tweet, word, *every*, *sends*, day, info, picture, give, hour, *random*
8	news, game, user, service, *follow*, follower, help, automated, card, profile
9	post, nodejs, tweet, account, twitter, *search*, using, image, user, made
10	**chatbot**, example, quote, personal, based, schedule, assistant, daily, bot, working
11	basic, node, built, apis, following, stream, access, golang, j, stats
12	code, source, track, inline, source_code, keep, stuff, information, movie, bot
13	work, created, bot, server, control, pi, raspberry, status, github, fun
14	*link*, *post*, discord, video, bot, comment, page, music, website, top

machine learning algorithms are utilized. Cluster one represents repositories that provide frameworks or use existing platform APIs.

Sophisticated machine learning techniques such as deep neuronal nets received increased attention during the last years since they significantly out-perform existing state-of-the art classification/regression algorithms. To validate whether those algorithms are actively employed within the bot creation community, we manually filtered for repositories, which apply machine learning techniques in their projects (according to their description). Within Fig. 6 the most frequent terms among all corresponding descriptions are displayed as a word cloud. Most of the repositories use machine learning algorithms for implementing chat bots. Recurrent Neural Networks (RNNs) as well as Long Short-Term Memory (LSTMs) [15] architectures are predominantly utilized for that purpose. Since text documents can be considered as sequences of words or characters, the mentioned models try to reflect a conditional probability distribution for the next word or character (x_{t+1}) given an already existing sequence of words $(x_1, ..., x_t)$: $P(x_{t+1}|x_1, ..., x_t)$ [11]. In contrast to traditional Markov chains, the probability of the next token does not depend only upon the present state, but also on the (intermediate) sequence of events that preceded it. We found that projects that employed RNN/LSTMs tried to create models that are able to imitate specific writing styles (e.g. Donald Trump). To train their models, programmers usually utilized text-corpora as ground-truth (e.g. tweets or whole novels). None of the mentioned projects' software was able to imitate human text content. Often the repository creators stated that they merely tested those new machine learning techniques as a private project.

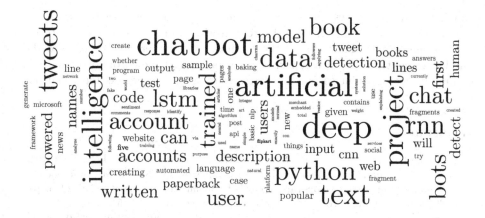

Fig. 6. Word cloud of repositories that use `machine learning` techniques.

6 Conclusion and Future Work

With this work, we provide a comprehensive study on the availability of open program code, which can be utilized for realizing the automation of accounts in social media. Based on developer repositories in the worldwide most relevant open collaboration platforms, we analyzed software development for a broad spectrum of social media platforms. The analysis proves overall availability of projects dealing with the development of social bots. The partition of data with respect to social media platforms provided additional insights into the importance and accessibility of these platforms for simple automation of accounts. The performed geo-spatial analysis offers insights into regional importance of platforms and may point to main targets for social bot application at these locations. This results in different levels of potential "threat" in the world for different platforms as a consequence of user preferences. A specific view on programming languages, however, indirectly tells us some details on the operators and programmers of social bots. The overwhelmingly dominant usage of interpreted programming languages (Python and Java Script) allows simple and rapid development of code also for inexperienced developers. This suggests that a large proportion of the observed projects is developed to enable or simplify usage of social bots or the realization of data acquisition from social media platforms at a prototype level. Additionally, the availability of simple API frameworks for specific social media platforms implies the use of simple programming languages like Python, while Java Script is presumably used to access data and functionality, which is not reachable via APIs.

For future research it is interesting to gain more insights from the content of the crawled repositories. Here, we could extend our text analysis techniques and additionally look into the actual implementations on code level to get an impression on specific purposes of the social bot scripts. As social bot functionality may change over time (e.g. the replacement of existing methods with more sophisticated approaches), it is certainly informative to track trends within the bot development cycle. Further, the repositories could be examined in terms of their importance. For instance the lifetime, the number of updates, and the number of contributors of a repository can be seen as indicators of its success or importance and hint to popular software tools or frameworks for social bot development.

References

1. Abokhodair, N., Yoo, D., McDonald, D.W.: Dissecting a social botnet: growth, content and influence in Twitter. In: Proceedings of the 18th ACM Conference on Computer Supported Cooperative Work & Social Computing, CSCW 2015, pp. 839–851. ACM, New York (2015). https://doi.org/10.1145/2675133.2675208
2. Bessi, A., Ferrara, E.: Social bots distort the 2016 US presidential election online discussion. First Monday **21**(11) (2016). https://doi.org/10.5210/fm.v21i11.7090
3. Cao, Q., Yang, X., Yu, J., Palow, C.: Uncovering large groups of active malicious accounts in online social networks. In: Proceedings of the 2014 ACM SIGSAC Conference on Computer and Communications Security, CCS 2014, pp. 477–488. ACM, New York (2014). https://doi.org/10.1145/2660267.2660269
4. Chu, Z., Gianvecchio, S., Wang, H., Jajodia, S.: Who is tweeting on Twitter: human, bot, or cyborg? In: ACSAC 2010 Proceedings of the 26th Annual Computer Security Applications Conference, Austin, Texas, USA, 6–10 December 2010, pp. 21–30 (2010). https://doi.org/10.1145/1920261.1920265. http://portal.acm.org/citation.cfm?doid=1920261.1920265
5. Clark, E.M., Williams, J.R., Galbraith, R.A., Jones, C.A., Danforth, C.M., Dodds, P.S.: Sifting robotic from organic text: a natural language approach for detecting automation on Twitter. J. Comput. Sci. **16**, 1–7 (2016)
6. Cornelissen, L.A., Barnett, R.J., Schoonwinkel, P., Eichstadt, B.D., Magodla, H.B.: A network topology approach to bot classification. CoRR abs/1809.06190 (2018)
7. Ferrara, E., Varol, O., Davis, C., Menczer, F., Flammini, A.: The rise of social bots. Commun. ACM **59**(7), 96–104 (2016). https://doi.org/10.1145/2818717
8. Fredheim, R.: Putin's bot army - part one: a bit about bots (2013). http://quantifyingmemory.blogspot.co.uk/2013/06/putins-bots-part-one-bit-about-bots.html
9. Frischlich, L., Boberg, S., Schatto-Eckrodt, T., Quandt, T.: Would the real reader please stand up? Erkennung von Fake Accounts und Social Bots in partizipativen journalistischen Angeboten. In: DGPUK, Mannheim, Germany (2018)
10. Gorwa, R., Guilbeault, D.: Unpacking the social media bot: a typology to guide research and policy. Policy Internet, 1–24. https://doi.org/10.1002/poi3.184
11. Graves, A.: Generating sequences with recurrent neural networks. CoRR abs/1308.0850 (2013). http://arxiv.org/abs/1308.0850
12. Grimme, C., Assenmacher, D., Adam, L.: Changing perspectives: is it sufficient to detect social bots? In: Meiselwitz, G. (ed.) SCSM 2018. LNCS, vol. 10913, pp. 445–461. Springer, Cham (2018). https://doi.org/10.1007/978-3-319-91521-0_32
13. Grimme, C., Preuss, M., Adam, L., Trautmann, H.: Social bots: human-like by means of human control (2017). https://arxiv.org/pdf/1706.07624.pdf
14. Hegelich, S., Janetzko, D.: Are social bots on Twitter political actors? Empirical evidence from a Ukrainian social botnet. In: International AAAI Conference on Web and Social Media, pp. 579–582 (2016). https://www.aaai.org/ocs/index.php/ICWSM/ICWSM16/paper/view/13015

15. Hochreiter, S., Schmidhuber, J.: Long short-term memory. Neural Comput. **9**(8), 1735–1780 (1997)
16. Howard, P.N., Kollanyi, B.: Bots, #Strongerin, and #Brexit: computational propaganda during the UK-EU referendum. SSRN (2016). https://ssrn.com/abstract=2798311
17. Karasz, P.: What is telegram, and why are Iran and Russia trying to ban it? (2018). https://www.nytimes.com/2018/05/02/world/europe/telegram-iran-russia.html
18. Kollanyi, B.: Where do bots come from? An analysis of bot codes shared on GitHub. Int. J. Commun. **10**(June), 4932–4951 (2016)
19. Lee, K., Caverlee, J., Webb, S.: Uncovering social spammers: social honeypots + machine learning. In: Proceedings of the 33rd International ACM SIGIR Conference on Research and Development in Information Retrieval, SIGIR 2010, pp. 435–442. ACM, New York (2010). https://doi.org/10.1145/1835449.1835522
20. Maréchal, N.: Automation, algorithms, and politics— when bots Tweet: toward a normative framework for bots on social networking sites (feature). Int. J. Commun. **10** (2016)
21. Microsoft News Center: Microsoft to acquire GitHub for $7.5 billion (2018). https://news.microsoft.com/2018/06/04/microsoft-to-acquire-github-for-7-5-billion/
22. Paradise, A., Puzis, R., Shabtai, A.: Anti-reconnaissance tools: detecting targeted socialbots. IEEE Internet Comput. **18**(5), 11–19 (2014). https://doi.org/10.1109/MIC.2014.81
23. Řehůřek, R., Sojka, P.: Software framework for topic modelling with large corpora. In: Proceedings of the LREC 2010 Workshop on New Challenges for NLP Frameworks, pp. 45–50. ELRA, Valletta, May 2010. http://is.muni.cz/publication/884893/en
24. Shin, J., Jian, L., Driscoll, K., Bar, F.: The diffusion of misinformation on social media. Comput. Hum. Behav. **83**(C), 278–287 (2018). https://doi.org/10.1016/j.chb.2018.02.008
25. Statista: We Are Social (2018). Most famous social network sites worldwide as of October 2018, ranked by number of active users (in millions) (2018). https://www.statista.com/statistics/272014/global-social-networks-ranked-by-number-of-users/
26. Stieglitz, S., Brachten, F., Ross, B., Jung, A.K.: Do social bots dream of electric sheep? A categorisation of social media bot accounts. CoRR abs/1710.04044 (2017)
27. Vargo, C.J., Guo, L., Amazeen, M.A.: The agenda-setting power of fake news: a big data analysis of the online media landscape from 2014 to 2016. New Media Soc. **20**(5), 2028–2049 (2018). https://doi.org/10.1177/1461444817712086
28. Varol, O., Ferrara, E., Davis, C.A., Menczer, F., Flammini, A.: Online human-bot interactions: detection, estimation, and characterization. In: Proceedings of the Eleventh International AAAI Conference on Web and Social Media (ICWSM 2017) Online, pp. 280–289 (2017). http://arxiv.org/abs/1703.03107
29. Varvello, M., Voelker, G.M.: Second life: a social network of humans and bots. In: Proceedings of the 20th International Workshop on Network and Operating Systems Support for Digital Audio and Video, NOSSDAV 2010, pp. 9–14. ACM, New York (2010). https://doi.org/10.1145/1806565.1806570
30. Vibhuti Sharma, S.M.: GitLab gains developers after Microsoft buys rival GitHub (2018). https://www.reuters.com/article/us-github-microsoft-gitlab/gitlab-gains-developers-after-microsoft-buys-rival-github-idUSKCN1J12BR

31. Volpicelli, G.: Can Instagram keep its nose clean? (2019). https://www.
theguardian.com/technology/2018/apr/28/instagram-at-the-crossroads-profits-
facebook-data-scandal-politics-influencers-mental-health
32. Woolley, S.: Automating power: social bot interference in global politics. First
Monday **21**(4) (2016)

Analysis of Account Engagement in Onsetting Twitter Message Cascades

Philipp Kessling[1] and Christian Grimme[2(✉)]

[1] Hamburg University of Applied Sciences, 22081 Hamburg, Germany
philipp.kessling@haw-hamburg.de
[2] University of Münster, 48149 Münster, Germany
christian.grimme@wi.uni-muenster.de

Abstract. In this work we investigate the engagement of Twitter accounts in the starting phase of reaction cascades, i.e., in the follow-up stream of an original tweet. In a first case study, we focus on a selection of very popular Twitter users from politics and society. We find a small but constantly active set of seemingly automated accounts in the onset of cascades that may contribute to the multiplication of content–especially for well-known populist politicians.

Keywords: Retweet cascades · Social bots · Engagement analysis

1 Introduction

Automation in Online Social Networks (OSN) has recently become a central point of research, as it is considered a capable vehicle for disinformation or propaganda distribution [24]. Many works report on social bots, which are defined as automated accounts in OSN plattforms [8,13]. Specific focus has been put on proving their existence [3,9] and action during election campaigns [2,11] as well as on their detection [6,20]. Although coordinated manipulation and disinformation are certainly considered as main threats for society, strategic considerations of automation have not been in the main focus of research, so far. Interestingly, many detection mechanisms try to classify single accounts concentrating on behavioral aspects and neglecting the context of social bot application.

In this work, we take an application-driven point of view on social bots and investigate whether automation can be identified in the onset of a classical message distribution in Twitter. For popular accounts, we regularly observe distinct message cascades, which are the replication-based reaction (retweets) on an original message. Figure 1 exemplarily shows multiple cascades of retweets,

The authors acknowledge support by the German Federal Ministry of Education and Research (FKZ 16KIS0752, FKZ 16KIS0495K) and the European Research Center for Information Systems (ERCIS). The authors also thank the anonymous reviewers for their valuable suggestions for improvement of this work.

C. Grimme et al. (Eds.): MISDOOM 2019, LNCS 12021, pp. 115–126, 2020.
https://doi.org/10.1007/978-3-030-39627-5_10

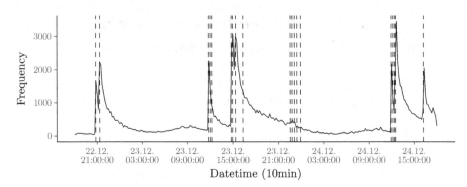

Fig. 1. Examples of information cascades launched by *@realDonaldTrump*. Dotted lines are tweets posted by the root user, plotted tweet frequency is cummulated traffic of the active cascades. Timezone is UTC-5.

quotes and replies as reactions to tweets that were originally sent out by @real-DonaldTrump. Almost every time this account tweets, an instant reaction of retweets appears that finally reaches a peak and drops over time until the next post.

In this study, we consider cascades launched by very active Twitter users from politics and society and compare the observed patterns in order to infer possible multiplication infrastuctures (MI), which support the spread of content in the onset phase of a cascade. A simple model of such a multiplication infrastructure may be few (semi-)automated accounts (e.g. simple social bots [8] or mainly human steered accounts with additional automation) that work as initial distributors instantly after publication of the original message. These accounts may monitor the Twitter stream[1] regarding the respective account's activity and (almost) instantly react on original content posted by the account by repetition (retweet or quoting). Depending on the amount of followers to the multiplicator account the original tweet may reach a larger audience than the original author could have reached by his or her own network.

In the following, we briefly review literature related to retweet cascades and automated multiplication. Then, we state our research questions in Sect. 3 and present our experimental design in Sect. 4, as well as the results of the experiments in Sect. 5. The paper is concluded by a discussion of our findings in Sect. 6.

2   Related Work

The discussion of retweet cascades is a traditional subject of information diffusion research. It aims for prediction of cascades and their size over time, as well as the potential of messages to gain attention in OSNs like Twitter [12]. While the common assumption is that Twitter cascades follow an epidemological model,

---

[1] Open access to the Twitter stream is provided via the developer account of each profile, see https://developer.twitter.com/en/docs/api-reference-index.

Goel et al. [7] find, that this model does not adequately explains observed cascades. Moreover they find that diffusion of information depends on interest. This means that cascades are no common phenomena but mainly influenced by recipient interest. Pramanik et al. [17] support this by another perspective: they find that pure retweet strategies are less effective than strategies that include mentions of users (preferably multiplicators) to gain their interest and thus increase probability of diffusion. On the other hand Myers and Leskovec [15] find that, while Twitter's social graph itself is highly dynamic, bursts like retweet cascades cause changes on the social graph during cascades traversal: specifically, retweet cascades may increase the number of followers of an account. As such, an MI may contribute to the reach of a root account in a two-step approach by first reaching out for a larger audience and successively by extending the follower network of the root account.

This general and functional view on retweet cascades is complemented by the investigation of automation in the context of retweet activity. While Bastos and Mercea [1] report on the general mechanism of replication by simple social bots in context of the Brexit vote, Stella et al. [19] find that bots are usually used to bring content (context of that work: "inflamatory" content from the Catalan vote in 2017) to humans via retweets, replies, and mentions. However, in most cases, bots and humans have similar temporal behavior (e.g. low rate of activity or daily cycle). Nasim et al. [16] find that message cascades in orchestrated bot campaigns ("content polluters" in their words) are temporally correlated, i.e. they can be detected by observing their collective actions over time. Vosoughi et al. [21] consider retweet cascades in the light of spread of true and false stories. The authors find that bot-spreaded stories are accelerated at the same rate, while humans spread false (often fear generating) stories faster. They conclude that emotion in humans is the deciding factor of spread. The finding, which is most related to this paper (but anectdotal), is published by Cresci et al. [4], who report on a data set of bots they used for different analysis. This data set was acquired by observing a very specific behavioral patter of social bots, namely the automated retweets within minutes after postings of original messages. They consider these bots as multiplicators of content provided by a central hub in the context of the Mayoral election of Rome in 2014.

3   Research Questions

The above mentioned findings of Cresci et al. [4] suggest that automation is an essential factor in gaining reach for posts by replicating content. This implies that an important indicator for replication mechanisms (MI) can be found in the onset of cascades, namely in the first minutes after the original post. The shorter the time interval between original message and retweet, the more probable is the automation of a replicating account.

In a more detailed investigation of this mechanism, we explore (for an exemplary set of very active accounts on Twitter and for a set of multiple cascades in a given timeframe) four questions:

1. *Is there a constant set of participants (accounts) in cascades?* This question aims at a quantification of multiplicators in retweet cascades compared to occasional users.
2. *How active are the constant accounts?* This question relates to observed properties of social bots [1], which suggests that few very active accounts spread most of the content.
3. *When do constant accounts act?* This question relates to the core of the observation of Cresci et al. [4] that automation tends to happen early in cascades.
4. *Are constant accouts more likely automated accounts?* This question is strongly related to the context of the previous question and asks for a possible strong dependency between early reactions, activity, and automation.

4   Data Acquisition and Evaluation Methods

If MIs are active in the cascades of a given root account, a signature of these activities must be observable in the cascades temporal features, e.g. in the time of reaction to original tweets or in the frequency of involvement in multiple retweet cascades. This signatures may only be generated by a small number of hyper-active accounts, which can suffice for creating high visibility and increase a message's reach such that other users engage in this thread as well. Not only retweet cascades are under consideration, but also replies and quotes of the original tweet, as they similarly increase the initial message's reach and contribute to the impact of tweets and popularity of accounts.

4.1   Selection of Observed Root Accounts

From a larger set of observed accounts (see Table 1), we determine a small set of investigated root accounts (see Table 2) – these are the accounts we observe in this paper for analyzing cascades – by qualitatively maximizing three properties. These properties are (1) the average cascade size (i.e. the number of messages sent out by this account), (2) cascade frequency (i.e., the frequency by which a tweet of the root account results in a cascade), and (3) the subjectively assumed potential for the application of manipulative measures. In addition, we divide our considered account set into two subsets to address international political and populist actors as well as international artists. Both sets contains prominent accounts with high engagements on almost every tweet (either from political supporters and opponents or fans, respectively). We restrict our current investigation to this small set of accounts to (1) only use account data from people of public interest and (2) to limit data collection via Twitter in order to avoid running into rate limitations or filtering mechanisms of the openly available Twitter stream API. As a consequence of the latter aspect, we expect the collected data on observed cascades for all six root accounts to be complete.

Table 1. Overview over root accounts in alphabetic order. Number of retrieved cascades and their respective average size.

Screen name	# of cascades	avg. cascade size
@Alice_Weidel	128	1,394.689
@BarackObama	14	97,823.151
@Beatrix_vStorch	84	787.374
@BolsonaroSP	625	5,416.600
@CarlosBolsonaro	516	5,933.324
@jairbolsonaro	478	18,942.620
@Joerg_Meuthen	61	1,434.419
@justinbieber	11	109,506.302
@kanyewest	87	40,372.109
@katyperry	36	5,066.429
@realDonaldTrump	659	107,895.757

Table 2. Selected and analyzed Twitter accounts of international populists (INTL_P) and international artists (ART).

Set I (INTL_P)	Set 2 (ART)
@realDonaldTrump	@kanyewest
@jaribolsonaro	@justinbieber
@BolsonaroSP	@katyperry

4.2 Technical Aspects of Data Collection

As retrieving entire cascades by means of the Twitter Search API proved infeasible due to rate, result size, and completeness limits, we persisted the Twitter stream and specifically track the root accounts and reactions on original tweets via the Twitter Streaming API[2]. In the timeframe between December 22nd, 2018 and January 31st, 2019 we gathered the mentioning tweets for the root accounts. After storing the data stream, we extracted a sequence of interactions for every tweet of the root accounts for further analysis. Mentions that were unrelated to original tweets of the root accounts were removed from the collected data.

The data storage and access infrastructure was comprised of an Elasticsearch instance. Data was ingested by a logstash instance and data retrieval was accomplished by the Elasticsearch SQL interface. Analysis was executed with Microsoft R Open 3.5.1 using the following packages: `dplyr`, `ggplot2`, `purrr`, as well as `disk.frame` [5,10,14,18,22,23].

---

[2] https://www.twitter.com.

4.3   Notation and Measures

For the analysis of our data, we apply several indicators. We first give a brief introduction in our notation and then state our indicators and their interpretation in this context.

Let a cascade $C_i^r \in C^r$ be the ordered set[3] containing all tweets linked to a single original tweet t_i^r by root account r. All cascades C_i^r for $i = 1, \ldots, n$ are contained in the overall cascade set C^r for root account r. The size of a single cascade is simply denoted by the cardinality $|C_i^r|$. The set A_i^r comprises all accounts that participate in a cascade $C_i^r \in C^r$. Let an element of C_i^r be denoted by a tuple $(\Delta t, a)$, where Δt is the time elapsed since the original tweet was posted and a is the replicating (retweeing/mentioning/replying) account.

In order to answer RQ1, we calculate the frequency of engagement for all accounts $a \in \bigcup_i^n A_i^r$:

$$F^r(a) = |\{i \in \{1, \ldots, n\} \mid a \in A_i^r\}|$$

Then, the relative frequency of participation is clearly given by:

$$f^r(a) = \frac{F^r(a)}{n}.$$

Using the determined frequency of participation of an account $F^r(a)$, we can easily determine the number of accounts that participated exactly ℓ times in cascades for a given root account r. For those accounts clearly holds $F^r(a) \overset{!}{=} \ell$. We denote this number by $N_{acc}(\ell)$, $\ell \in \mathbb{N}$. In an analogous way, we define the number of tweets $N_{tweet}(\ell)$: for a given $\ell \in \mathbb{N}$ the value of $N_{tweets}(\ell)$ denotes the number of tweets posted by those accounts for which $F^r(a) \overset{!}{=} \ell$.

We commence to modify our above metrics N_{acc} and N_{tweet} to take into account the elapsed time since the beginning of the cascade. Thus we calculate the number of tweets per time and F^r bin.

Furthermore, we calculate for N_{Acc} and N_{tweet} the CDF over $F^r(a)$ in regards of engaged accounts and the tweets these accounts have disseminated.

5   Results and Observation

In this section, we first provide an overview on the collected data from the Twitter stream and then provide observations and results from evaluation.

5.1   Data Description

The considered data set is comprised of 78,768,112 tweets and structured by root accounts, root tweets, participating accounts and their tweets. We further divide the data set in two cases, which we are going to discuss separately. This

---

[3] The set is ordered with respect to time.

separation is necessary, as the sets expose extreme differences in the tweet frequency of the root accounts. The most active accounts resemble the populist politicians' set. The second case is congruent with the set of international artist accounts, which tweet significantly less than the politicians. Set 1 exhibits an average number of cascades of $\overline{n} = 587.34$, while the second set exhibits an average number of $\overline{n} = 44.67$ cascades. Figure 2 gives a comprehensive summary of the dataset and the distribution of cascade number size for the considered six root accounts.

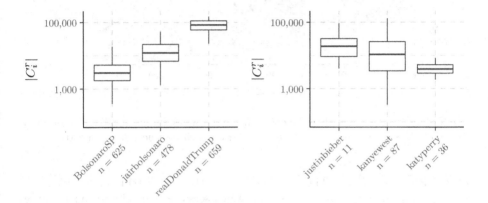

Fig. 2. An overview of the cascade frequency and cascade sizes in the retrieved dataset. The box plot on the left hand side shows the analysis of cascade size for root accounts in set 1 (politicians), the box plot on the right hand side details cascade size for account set 2 (artists). Outliers are not included.

5.2   Data Analysis

A first investigation of account (see Fig. 3) and tweet (see Fig. 4) activity shows widely consistent behavior over all cascades: most users are only active for few times over all cascades. Interestingly, a majority of users is active exactly once for all observed cascades. Only few accounts participate in most cascades (i.e., they produce a high f^r score). The most active users are found during the first 120 s of cascades' onset. As shown in Fig. 4, the maximum in tweet count n_{Tweet} is roughly consistent for all root accounts and cases.

Directly comparing user activity and tweeting behavior in Fig. 5, we observe a discrepancy in the tweet frequency of participating accounts. Accounts with higher participation f^r-score (i.e., accounts that participate in a higher percentage of cascades) seem to be more active tweeters. They contribute more tweets to a single cascade than low f^r-scored users. This discrepancy is smaller for ART set root account cascades.

An interesting artefact is visible in the evaluation of the cascades of @realDonaldTrump. For this root account, a majority of sporadic users becomes active

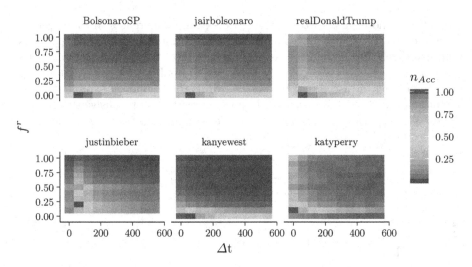

Fig. 3. Cascades gradient displayed with a temporal resolution of 60 s, f^r-score and the count of users per bin n_{Acc} are normalized for each root account, respectively.

after a first onset phase. The onset phase (i.e. the bin starting at $t = 0$), however, contains some one-time-users, almost no users that participate on a medium basis, but surprisingly also a significant amount of users that participate in all cascades directly at onset. Note, that a similar effect can be observed for the account of @katyperry, however, as the amount of cascades for that account is far smaller than for @realDonaldTrump, we will concentrate on the latter for a deeper analysis.

5.3   Analysis of Possible Automation Artefacts

In order to analyze the observed artefacts of Figs. 3 and 4 for the account of @realDonaldTrump, we (1) increase the resolution of the respective plot for user participation, see Fig. 6 (lefthand side) and (2) acquire additional data on the users that are part of the most and permanent active group.

In detail, we gather two datasets, containing the timelines of the following users: validation data set 1 (VD1) contains the tweets of the accounts that act in cascades of @realDonaldTrump with an $F^r(a) > 620$ (i.e. taking part in more than 94% of all cascades); validation dataset 2 (VD2) contains the tweets of the top 10,000 accounts sorted by N_{tweet}.

This way we collected 130,201 tweets from 1,303 accounts in VD1 and 918,105 tweets from 9,213 accounts in VD2. To decide, whether an account in these data sets can be considered automated, we applied a simple, but very conservative heuristic classifier approach that fits the assumption of a replication and multiplication infrastructure: if an account exposed a retweet-ratio of at least 80% over the last 100 tweets in the timeline we considered it automated. Using this

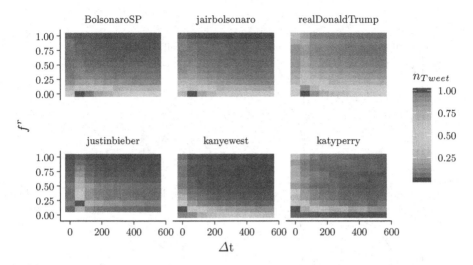

Fig. 4. Cascades gradient displayed with a temporal resultion of 60 s, f^r-score and the count of tweets per bin n_{Tweet} are normalized for each root account, respectively.

simple approach, we found 86% automated accounts in VD1 and classified 64% of the accounts in VD2 as automated.

Based on these classifications with the näive classifier we removed the tweets posted by the potentially automated accounts from the commulated cascades of @realDonaldTrump. As expected the removal of these accounts impacted solely the onset phase of the cascade - and specifically the artefact (left upper corner) of most to permanent participating users. Figure 6(b) and (c) demonstrates the effect of the stepwise account removal considering identified bot accounts from VD1 and VD2 successively.

6   Discussion

Our observations discussed before provide first interesting answers to the research questions. As expected, we find a set of continuously active users. However, this set – especially accounts that participate in almost all cascades – is rather small. Surprisingly, the overwhelming majority of accounts only participates once for *all* cascades. Especially for populist root accounts this is to some extent contradicting the assumption that there are loyal groups that form an echo chamber. Still, for the continuously active accounts specifically appearing in cascades of political populists, we can confirm that these few accounts produce a large share of the overall messages. These very active accounts are either ideologically strongly attached to the root account or automated replicators. The engagement of constantly active accounts is concentrating in the onset of the cascade, with peaks for all root account in $t < 60$ s, with $f^r(a)$ strongly correlating to Δt. A detailed investigation of these early and (almost) always

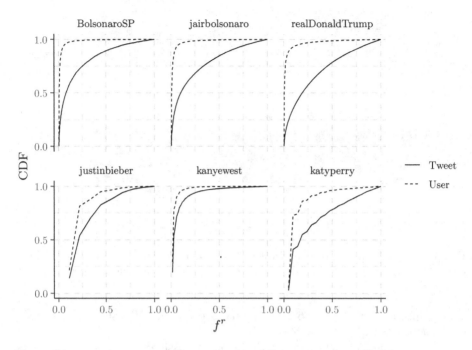

Fig. 5. Plots on the tweet and account accumulation regarding f^r. The upper row shows set 1 root accounts, while the lower row shows set 2 root accounts.

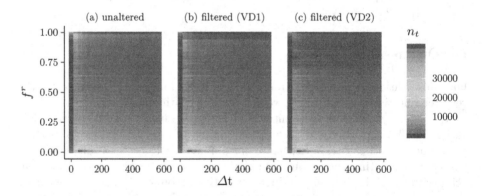

Fig. 6. (a) The onset phase of the cascades of @realDonaldTrump with an increased resolution in comparison to Fig. 4. (b) The same data but tweets from automated accounts in VD1 removed. (c) The same data as in (b) but automated accounts from VD2 removed.

acting accounts for the certainly most popular root account @realDonaldTrump showed that a majority of the accounts can be classified as automated accounts.

7 Conclusion

A large corpus of message cascades is retrieved and persisted, the data set contains nearly 80 million tweets in over 1,900 cascade from six root accounts, which belong the prominent persons from politics and arts. This first study of the corpus suggest that MIs leave a signature in cascades and the signature is detectable. The detected participating accounts showed replication-based automation behavior when using a simple and conservative classification method. This conclusion is also encouraged by the short time span between the initial message and reaction message onset, which is in most cases no longer than 120 s.

Future Work: This work is certainly only the beginning of a larger investigation. Although we found first indications for the existence of possibly automated MIs in cascades of populist root accounts and presented a first effective data analytic toolset, we do not provide a broad investigation of a large set of accounts. For generalization of the proposed approach, a larger set of very active and popular accounts has to be investigated. Additionally, the results can be strengthend by deeper insight into the diffusion structure of the multiplication network to judge on the impact of MIs on message distribution.

References

1. Bastos, M.T., Mercea, D.: The brexit botnet and user-generated hyperpartisan news. Soc. Sci. Comput. Rev. **37**(1), 38–54 (2019). https://doi.org/10.1177/0894439317734157
2. Bessi, A., Ferrara, E.: Social bots distort the 2016 us presidential election online discussion. First Monday **21**(11) (2016). https://doi.org/10.5210/fm.v21i11.7090
3. Cao, Q., Yang, X., Yu, J., Palow, C.: Uncovering large groups of active malicious accounts in online social networks. In: Proceedings of the 2014 ACM SIGSAC Conference on Computer and Communications Security, CCS 2014, pp. 477–488. ACM, New York (2014). https://doi.org/10.1145/2660267.2660269
4. Cresci, S., Petrocchi, M., Spognardi, A., Tognazzi, S.: On the capability of evolved spambots to evade detection via genetic engineering. Online Soc. Netw. Med. **9**, 1–16 (2019). https://doi.org/10.1016/j.osnem.2018.10.005
5. Dai, Z.: disk.frame: fast disk-based data manipulation framework for larger-than-RAM structured tabular data (2018). http://daizj.me/disk.frame/, r package version 0.1.0
6. Ferrara, E., Varol, O., Davis, C., Menczer, F., Flammini, A.: The rise of social bots. Commun. ACM **59**(7), 96–104 (2016). https://doi.org/10.1145/2818717
7. Goel, A., Munagala, K., Sharma, A., Zhang, H.: A note on modeling retweet cascades on Twitter. In: Gleich, D.F., Komjáthy, J., Litvak, N. (eds.) WAW 2015. LNCS, vol. 9479, pp. 119–131. Springer, Cham (2015). https://doi.org/10.1007/978-3-319-26784-5_10

8. Grimme, C., Preuss, M., Adam, L., Trautmann, H.: Social bots: human-like by means of human control. Big Data **5**, 279–293 (2017)
9. Hegelich, S., Janetzko, D.: Are social bots on Twitter political actors? Empirical evidence from a Ukrainian social BotNet. In: International AAAI Conference on Web and Social Media, pp. 579–582 (2016). https://www.aaai.org/ocs/index.php/ICWSM/ICWSM16/paper/view/13015
10. Henry, L., Wickham, H.: purrr: Functional Programming Tools (2019). https://CRAN.R-project.org/package=purrr, r package version 0.3.0
11. Kollanyi, B., Howard, P.N., Woolley, S.C.: Bots and automation over twitter during the U.S. election. Technival report, Data Memo 2016.4, Project on Computational Propaganda, Oxford, UK (2016). www.politicalbots.org
12. Kupavskii, A., et al.: Prediction of retweet cascade size over time. In: 21st ACM International Conference on Information and Knowledge Management, CIKM 2012. ACM, Maui (2012)
13. Maréchal, N.: Automation, algorithms, and politics— when bots tweet: toward a normative framework for bots on social networking sites (feature). Int. J. Commun. **10**, 10 (2016)
14. Microsoft, R Core Team: Microsoft R Open. Microsoft, Redmond, Washington (2017). https://mran.microsoft.com/
15. Myers, S.A., Leskovec, J.: The bursty dynamics of the Twitter information network. In: Proceedings of the 23rd International Conference on World Wide Web - WWW 2014, pp. 913–924. ACM Press, Seoul (2014). https://doi.org/10.1145/2566486.2568043
16. Nasim, M., Nguyen, A., Lothian, N., Cope, R., Mitchell, L.: Real-time detection of content polluters in partially observable Twitter networks, pp. 1331–1339, April 2018. https://doi.org/10.1145/3184558.3191574
17. Pramanik, S., Wang, Q., Danisch, M., Guillaume, J.L., Mitra, B.: Modeling cascade formation in Twitter amidst mentions and retweets. Soc. Netw. Anal. Min. **7**, 1–18 (2017)
18. R Core Team: R: A Lanaguage and Environment for Statistical Computing. R Foundataion for Stastical Computing, Vienna, Austria (2018). https://www.R-project.org/
19. Stella, M., Ferrara, E., De Domenico, M.: Bots increase exposure to negative and inflammatory content in online social systems. Proc. Natl. Acad. Sci. **115**(49), 12435–12440 (2018). https://doi.org/10.1073/pnas.1803470115, https://www.pnas.org/content/115/49/12435
20. Varol, O., Ferrara, E., Davis, C.A., Menczer, F., Flammini, A.: Online human-bot interactions: detection, estimation, and characterization. In: Proceedings of the Eleventh International AAAI Conference on Web and Social Media (ICWSM 2017), pp. 280–289 (2017). http://arxiv.org/abs/1703.03107
21. Vosoughi, S., Roy, D., Aral, S.: The spread of true and false news online. Science **359**(6380), 1146–1151 (2018). https://doi.org/10.1126/science.aap9559, http://science.sciencemag.org/content/359/6380/1146
22. Wickham, H.: ggplot2: Elegant Graphics for Data Analysis. Springer, New York (2016). http://ggplot2.org
23. Wickham, H., François, R., Henry, L., Müller, K.: dplyr: A Grammar of Data Manipulation (2019). https://CRAN.R-project.org/package=dplyr, r package version 0.8.0.1
24. Woolley, S.: Automating power: social bot interference in global politics. First Monday **21**(4) (2016)

Media and Disinformation

How Facebook and Google Accidentally Created a Perfect Ecosystem for Targeted Disinformation

Christian Stöcker[✉]

University of Applied Sciences (HAW) Hamburg, Finkenau 35, 22081 Hamburg, Germany
Christian.stoecker@haw-hamburg.de

Abstract. Online platforms providing information and media content follow certain goals and optimize for certain metrics when deploying automated decision making systems to recommend pieces of content from the vast amount of media items uploaded to or indexed by their platforms every day. These optimization metrics differ markedly from, for example, the so-called news factors journalists traditionally use to make editorial decisions. Social networks, video platforms and search engines thus create content hierarchies that reflect not only user interest but also their own monetization goals. This sometimes has unintended, societally highly problematic effects: Optimizing for metrics like dwell time, watch time or "engagement" can promote disinformation and propaganda content. This chapter provides examples and discusses relevant mechanisms and interactions.

Keywords: Disinformation · Online recommendation systems · Media content

1 Introduction: Online Media Curation and Disinformation

1.1 Conceptual Overview: The New Gatekeepers or - What's Considered Relevant Content These Days?

The interaction of commercially and politically motivated disinformation, propaganda and misinformation as well as the role online platforms and social media sites play in the dissemination of such content have been a focus of research for years. The dissemination of what has been called "fake news" during the US presidential campaign of 2016 (see e.g. [1, 2]) has been discussed as a potential factor in the outcome of the election. Even though the debate about the impact of such content on actual voting behavior is still in progress [3, 4], it seems clear that this kind of content now reaches audiences that could not have been reached before the advent of the internet as a mass medium (see e.g. [5–7]). There is ample evidence that various radical and extremist groups use the new means of reaching an audience to recruit members and sympathizers (see e.g. [8]). Social media platforms have even been called "the perfect platform for the radical voice" [9].

One important aspect of this new media ecosystem are the recommendation systems that search engines as well as social media platforms use to personalize results and content streams and, and this is the focus of this chapter: to optimize their own monetization

© Springer Nature Switzerland AG 2020
C. Grimme et al. (Eds.): MISDOOM 2019, LNCS 12021, pp. 129–149, 2020.
https://doi.org/10.1007/978-3-030-39627-5_11

opportunities. These recommendation systems or recommender systems (for a comprehensive overview see [10]) can rely of on a variety of different methods, e.g. so-called collaborative filtering, based on the notion that the behavior of users who consumed similar content in the past may be a good basis for new content suggestions, or content based systems that rely on information about the profile of a specific user and properties of the item of content in question (***for more on this see Calero-Valdez, this volume***). Increasingly, recommender systems rely on machine learning for optimization (see e.g. [11]).

The focus of this chapter is the question what role the optimization goals and the metrics used as proxies for those goals by a variety of online content curation platforms play in the context of online disinformation. The chapter will be drawing on examples from the world's three most visited websites [12]: The most widely used search engine, Google (over 3,5 billion searches per day [13], 2019 market share 90% or more, depending on the method used, see [14, 15]), the world's largest social network, Facebook (about 2,2 billion monthly active users, 2019 market share over 71%, see [16]) and the world's largest video platform YouTube (over 2 billion monthly active users in 2019 [17], estimated market share in 2019 over 73% [18]), a subsidiary of Google LLC. Together, these three platforms alone are thus responsible for a substantial part of the time and attention that internet users spend online every day. The way they filter and sort content is thus relevant to the way the public perception, framing and discussion of issues ranging from politics to, for example, attitudes towards medical treatments like vaccinations.

Philip Napoli has called these new gatekeepers "automated media" [19] and stressed that news production [20] as well as news selection [21] are now increasingly relying on tools of automated decision making (ADM systems), which often involve a machine learning component and are constantly tweaked.

The examples in this chapter will show that the metrics and signals these companies employ to make ranking decisions and content recommendations on their websites and in their apps can contribute to surfacing content that is inflammatory, misleading or created and published as targeted propaganda. The analysis thus focuses on what is known about the systems used for ranking and recommendation decisions and the interactions of these systems with other factors like the likelihood of certain types of users to engage with online media content, cognitive mechanisms on the user side and user interface design.

To start off, let's look at a recent example from Germany.

1.2   A Stabbing in Chemnitz and a Social Media Storm

On August 26 of 2018, in the early hours of the morning, a 35 year old man was fatally stabbed in Chemnitz in the east German state of Saxony. A 22 year old man from Iraq and a 23 year old Syrian were subsequently arrested. The man from Syria was sentenced to nine and a half years in prison in the August of 2019, a sentence that drew a fair amount of criticism from media commentators and the defense lawyer [22–26]. Many criticized, the proof presented at trial had been insufficient, some insinuated the judges had been influenced by the political climate and the debate about the case.

Right after the stabbing itself, a number of false rumors about the case had started circulating on social media sites [22]. Some users claimed the victim had tried to protect a woman from a rape attempt, others that the fight had been about cigarettes. A common false claim was that the fatal stabbing had involved dozens of stab wounds, another that there had been two casualties, not one.

In the following days, growing groups of people, some wearing right wing paraphernalia, some displaying the so-called Hitler salute, gathered in the city. Police, journalists, counter-protesters and people who their attackers though looked like migrants were attacked. TV crews and private citizens filmed scenes later described as "manhunts" by journalists. Some of these scenes were filmed with smartphones or by news crews and went viral on social media [27].

While right wing protesters were rioting in the streets of Chemnitz, a likeminded man from Bavaria published a very simple YouTube Video. In the clip, the man going by the pen name Chris Ares declares that he "has no choice but to comment on the things going on in Chemnitz" and "report on them objectively".

He then goes on to repeat a number of the false claims circulating about the crime that had occurred two days previously. "The people are waking up", he declares, "they are getting more and more angry" because "you are turning victims into perpetrators and perpetrators into victims". He also claims there are "daily disembowelments, daily rapes" perpetrated by migrants of refugees, allegedly occurring without the government taking notice.

The clip ended up being the second most viewed about the situation in Chemnitz on YouTube, as the social media analyst Ray Serrato [28] determined using his YouTube API account. By September 2, 2018, the video had accumulated way more than 400.000 views and had even briefly topped the list of YouTube trends.

How could this happen? Why did more balanced content adhering to journalistic standards of reporting not reach a larger audience in this case? To approach an answer to these questions, a brief look back is necessary: How was the relevance of media content judged in the past? How do journalists decide what is front page news and what isn't news at all?

2   What Is Relevance?

2.1   What's Relevant? News Factors then and Now

Walter Lippman published his first list of news factors in 1922 in his seminal book "Public Opinion" [29]. In the coming decades, a whole host of catalogues of criteria that journalists use to make relevancy decisions was put forward by a number of researchers. The most widely cited conceptual framework to describe the gatekeeping practices of news media is probably Galtung and Ruge's 1965 version [30]: They split their news factors into three groups that they labeled "Impact", "Pragmatism" and "Audience Identification". The "Impact"-group contains the news factors Threshold, Frequency, Negativity, Unexpectedness and Unambiguity. The "Pragmatism" category encompasses the factors Consonance, Continuity and Composition. The "Audience Identifiction" factors are labelled as Personalization, Meaningfulness, the presence of "Elite Nations" or "Elite Persons" in the context of the news item in question or the news item itself. Galtung and Ruge thus group factors that mainly pertain to three aspects of news production and consumption:

- The workflow and practice of the journalists themselves – i.e. the notion that a good alignment between the news event and the production cycle of the news organization in question is present ("Frequency"), or that the issue in question has been reported on by the same outlet before ("Continuity").
- The perceived or presumed societal impact of a specific news item on the intended audience – how many people are affected ("Threshold"), how close to the intended news audience is the event ("Meaningfulness"), how famous are those involved ("Elite persons")?
- The preconceptions and predispositions of the journalists, concerning questions like "How well does this item fit into the current news mix in our publication or program?" ("Composition"), or the question how well a specific news item fits into the preconceptions and the worldview of the journalists making the editorial decisions ("Consonance").

Different newsrooms and news organizations obviously don't apply those criteria in a consistent, invariable manner. They might, for example, put different weights on the different news factors. A tabloid paper will probably rely more heavily on Unexpectedness, Elite Persons and Personalization, while a high-brow paper or news program might stress Meaningfulness and Threshold aspects more.

Other authors have put forward alternative lists of news factors and alternative groupings of those factors. Weischenberg [31] for examples distinguishes between two groups of factors concerning the "Meaning", including reach and direct consequences of an event and the "Audience Interest" a certain news item is deemed to command/presumed to attract, including physical and psychological proximity, the celebrity of those involved, novelty and human interest aspects of an event.

At any rate, there is broad agreement between scholars that journalists follow certain, often implicit, rules and guidelines when making relevancy decisions. The "Gatekeepers" [29, 32], of the pre-internet era thus exerted a substantial amount of influence over what news did reach the eye of the public and which items didn't.

The new gatekeepers of the 21st century are the large platforms making available media content via the internet, the information intermediaries like search engines, video platforms and social networking sites (SNS) [33].

There is an important interplay here between the work of traditional news outlets using SNS [34] and search engines [35] as tools to reach a larger audience as well as particularly SNS serving as platforms for the dissemination of original media items produced and uploaded by their users (e.g. [36]). The sheer amount of media content provided not only by media organizations but other companies, governments, non-governmental organizations, commercially motivated social media personalities ("Influencers", see e.g. [37, 38]) and average users makes, at least in some platform models, some kind of automated sorting of content almost inevitable. The volume of content would make it impossible to discover relevant content otherwise. YouTube is a good example: Every minute, over 500 h of content are uploaded to the platform [39].

Neither search engines nor social media platforms, however, apply the same or even similar sets of criteria for deciding which kind of content to surface for which users as journalists and newsrooms. Despite this, the algorithms that these platforms employ have been called "Relevancy Machines" [40].

2.2   User Engagement as a New Relevancy Signal

The selection and curation criteria employed by the large platforms are markedly different from those employed by journalists. This is due to the fact that they are aimed at optimizing certain metrics that are intended to allow them to maximize not only the benefit for individual users but also their own monetization opportunities.

For Facebook, for example, the central optimization goal is to maximize Engagement, a hybrid measure composed of the different ways users can interact with content on Facebook.

Engagement is computed by combining [41]:

- The so-called reactions a given user and all Facebook users as a whole produce towards a certain piece of content – reactions here meaning klicks on the like-button or other options like a laughing emoji and angry emoji and so on.
- The number of shares, i.e. the number of times individual users share a certain piece of content they encounter on Facebook with their online circle of contacts inside the SNS, using the built-in functionality to do just that.
- The number of comments a certain piece of content garners, i.e. the amount of individual language-based responses to said piece of content produced by users within the confines of the SNS's user interface.

Engagement is thus a compound measure of the amount of responses requiring at least some form of personal activity on part of the users other than purely passive consumption. The actual user and other signals fed into Facebooks ADM systems to curate the personalized newsfeed of every single user are way more numerous, however. We will return to these signals and those employed by two other platforms, Google and YouTube, in more detail in Sect. 3.

For Facebook as well as Twitter, another SNS, it's been shown that pieces of content with an emotional, particularly a negatively connotated emotional valence elicit higher rates of responses from other users [42, 43]. The question of the role of emotional valence in this regard is not quite as clear-cut as these two results seem to suggest, but an overwhelming number of studies with different methodologies, looking at different platforms and different kinds of content shows that emotionally charged content tends to elicit more Engagement within SNS and other shared online communication systems [44].

2.3   The Influence of the Users: Who Is Engaging?

One key factor in the complex interaction of users, signals and sorting algorithms responsible for creating the individual experiences of single users is of course the make-up and engagement level of the user base itself. As Hölig and Hasebrink [45] have shown for a German audience, a larger percentage of users classifying themselves as "far left" or "extreme left" as well as users who classify themselves as "far right" or "extreme right" on the political spectrum are particularly active both on social media as well as in the user comments sections of online news media. While, for example, 15% of respondents classifying themselves as politically "center" sometimes respond with a klick on a reaction button or emoji to news items found in SNS, the respective percentages are 19% for users classifying themselves as far or extreme right and 27% for users classifying themselves as far or extreme left. Similar distributions apply for other activities like commenting on articles found on SNS or sharing news articles within SNS: Users from the far ends of the political spectrum report activity in higher percentages than politically moderate users.

A second data point is equally interesting in this context: Among those who disagree with the statement "In general, the news can usually be trusted", the percentages of users "reacting" to, commenting on and sharing news articles is higher than among those who are undecided or agree with that statement. In other words: People who trust the news media and traditional journalism least currently are most active at producing Engagement signals within SNS.

2.4   User Interface Design and the Psychology of Cognitive Heuristics

There are a number of studies showing that, in the words of Andrews and colleagues [46], "estimates concerning the number of times an individual used their phone across a typical day" do "not correlate with actual smartphone use." This and the astonishing number of times average users unlock their smartphones every day and total usage time [47] as well as the "habit forming" [48], some even say "addictive" [49, 50] qualities of current smartphones have their roots in core design principles of these devices and some of the applications running on them.

The scientific and design principles of these devices and platforms were developed in the 1990s by behavioral scientists like B.J. Fogg of the University of Stanford. Fogg coined the term "Captology", as shorthand for Computer Aided Persuasive Technology as early as 1996 [51]. He defined this new discipline as focused on "the design, research and analysis on interactive computing products created for changing people's attitudes or behaviors" [52]. In his 2003 book "Persuasive Technology" quoted here Fogg asserted that "in the future we'll see more and more computing products designed for the primary purpose of persuasion". "The potential for using (or, unfortunately, abusing) such technology is enormous", he wrote prophetically.

He also pointed out five main advantages that computers have over traditional media when it comes to changing attitudes and behaviors: Interactivity, anonymity, storing, accessing and manipulating huge volumes of data, using many modalities, scalability and potential ubiquity: "Applications are becoming commonplace in locations where human persuaders would not be welcome, such as the bathroom or the bedroom." All of this was published four years before the first iPhone was brought to market in 2007, i.e. four years before the era of truly ubiquitous, mass market mobile computing devices with graphical user interfaces began.

The persuasive technology Fogg talks about here owes a lot to classical learning and behavioral psychology. The basic principles of operant conditioning in the tradition of Thorndike [53], Watson [54] and Skinner [55] are combined with newer approaches to learning like those put forward by Bandura [56], motivational psychology and the possibilities that interactive computing devices offer.

A number of researchers and entrepreneurs very influential in the product design field of Silicon Valley over the last decade learned their trade in Fogg's persuasive technology lab in Stanford, amongst them Mike Krieger, one of the founders of the immensely popular photo sharing service Instagram [57]. Instagram was acquired by Facebook in March 2012 for about one billion US Dollars. Another influential ex-student of Fogg is Nir Eyal, author of a product design book called "Hooked – How to build habit forming products" [58], extensively quoting not only Fogg but a whole host of behavioral and learning psychologists, including Thorndike, Skinner and Bandura.

"Hooked" is a good and very outspoken example of the way the original concepts of Captology were reconfigured and adapted by Silicon Valley product designers to best serve the needs of companies whose primary business model is advertising, i.e. acquiring, packaging and selling users' attention to advertising customers [59]. "To initiate action, doing must be easier than thinking", Eyal writes. "The more effort – either physical or mental – required to perform the desired action, the less likely it is to occur" [58].

He also describes in detail how reinforcement signals from the user's own social circle can be and in many cases already are employed to drive engagement and retention in SNS user interfaces. Eyal calls these reinforcement signals "variable social rewards", directly referencing the reward schemes that were developed with rats and pigeons in Skinner boxes and have been a staple of, for example, slot machines for many decades: "Logging in reveals an endless stream of content friends have shared, comments from others, and running tallies of how many people have 'liked' something. The uncertainty of what users will find each time they visit the site creates the intrigue needed to pull them back again."

These design principles create user interfaces that are in many ways conceptually similar to the classic Skinner boxes: Instead of lights, speakers, levers, food pellets and electric shocks, the user interface designers of today employ multimedia content, like, share and reaction buttons, likes, reactions and comments as stimuli, actions and rewards. Even Eyals language is reminiscent of the way behaviorists talked about the animals used in their experiments: "As users pass through the cycles of the Hook Model, they learn to meet their needs with the habit-forming product."

In "Persuasive Technologies", Fogg wrote: "In my view, the evolution of persuasive technology systems should not be left to accident or to market forces alone" [52]. In 2016 he told a journalist: "I look at some of my former students and I wonder if they're really trying to make the world better, or just make money. What I always wanted to do was un-enslave people from technology" [51].

The potential societal problem arising from this type of user interface and interaction optimization towards maximizing "engagement" becomes clear when one asks the question what kind of cognitive processing this kind of optimization encourages – "doing must be easier than thinking".

This kind of design goal encourages modelling for a cognitive style that psychologist and Nobel laureate Daniel Kahneman would identify as "System 1": Processing here is automatic, quick, effortless and occurs without voluntary control, as opposed to "System 2" cognition which Kahneman defines as effortful, conscious, logical, mediated by attitudes and controlled [60]. Kahnemans model is part of a larger family of psychological models distinguishing between cognitive processes that are fast, automatic, and unconscious and those that are slow, deliberative, and conscious, generally referred to as dual-process models (for a recent overview, see [61]).

User interface design expert Nir Eyal encourages interface designers to strive for interfaces that reduce the mental effort needed to interact with their products as much as possible: "As recent history of the web demonstrates, the ease or difficulty of doing a particular action affects the likelihood that a behavior will occur. To successfully simplify a product, we must remove obstacles that stand in the user's way." In other words: The goal here is to optimize, in Kahnemans terminology, for System 1 type processing. That in turn goes some way to explain the fact that people dramatically underreport their mobile phone usage and regularly spend more time with digital platforms than they intended to (see above): A lack of effort is intrinsically linked to relinquishing a certain amount of control and oversight.

This, however, becomes problematic when the platforms in question are also used to disseminate, consume and discuss information relevant to political and societal opinion formation and decision making. "Contrary to the rules of philosophers of science, who advise testing hypotheses by trying to refute them", Kahneman wrote in "Thinking, Fast and Slow" [60], "people (and scientists, quite often) seek data that are likely to be compatible with the beliefs they currently hold. The confirmatory bias of System 1 favors uncritical acceptance of suggestions and exaggeration of the likelihood of extreme and improbable events."

A prime example of the kind of cognitive distortions more likely under processing conditions of System 1 is the availability heuristic: "People tend to assess the relative importance of issues by the ease with which they are retrieved from memory – and this is largely determined by the extent of coverage in the media" [60].

Not just the confirmation bias and the availability heuristic but all kinds of cognitive heuristics and biases like the representativity heuristic, the bias of confidence over doubt, anchoring and priming effects, risk assessment heuristics and many others [60] become much more likely when the processing goes through System 1. To put it briefly and succinctly: The user interface design principles of modern smartphones and smartphone apps very often encourage a cognitive style that is detrimental to rational, fact-based information processing and decision making, particularly when it comes to complex issues. This, it should be noted, is not an intentional effect but a by-product of optimizing for certain behavioral metrics that are in turn intimately connected to the monetization models of the large digital media content platforms.

3 User Signals and Their Effects on Content Curation

Let's have a closer look at some examples of outcomes of this interplay of optimization goals, user interface design, user behavior and content on three exemplary platforms: Facebook, Google and YouTube. The concrete examples presented here represent a number of different problematic aspects that these ecosystems seem to foster: political extremism, especially politically motivated disinformation, and conspiracy theory content relating to a number of topics reaching from anti-vaccination sentiment to climate change and wild and false, but very damaging conspiracy theories about the victims of mass shootings. The examples were chosen for their breadth and their political and societal relevance: The mechanisms at work here seem to touch many areas, and many of those areas are of high importance to a functioning democratic society.

3.1 Example No. 1: Facebook

As mentioned earlier, Facebooks chief optimization metric currently is "engagement", i.e. the combination of all possible user interactions with a given piece of content: shares, reactions and comments.

The signals Facebook measures and employs to make inferences about the presumed engagement rate a certain piece of content will receive from a certain user include (for a more comprehensive overview see [41]):

- The relationship of sender and receiver of the piece of content in question, in turn measured by likes, clicks, shares and comments between the two, by the number of times the two have tagged each other in pictures, by direct page or profile visits, scrolling speed and clicks.
- Past interactions of the receiver with other pieces of content, like has he or she responded to certain media formats (e.g. videos, quizzes), as he or she hidden similar content in the past?
- Past interactions of other users with the content in question, including dwell/watch time, return rate, likes, shares, comments and so on.
- Attributes of the content itself, e.g. is it a video, a picture, how old is it, how have human testers responded to this content or this type of content?
- Human evaluation of the content at Facebook or its subcontractors, including polls, tests and the question whether there were requests for content moderation.

The German journalist Karsten Schmehl used data from a commercial social media data provider called BuzzSumo to sift through the news content popular on Facebook between 2012 and 2017, focusing on news items concerning the German chancellor Angela Merkel (CDU). He identified the top ten items in terms of engagement about Merkel and ranked them according to the total number of shares, reactions and comments each received. He then went on to fact-check each of these top ten items. It turned out that seven of the top ten news items by engagement were plainly false, including the top two. One claimed that Merkel was advocating simply accepting violence perpetrated by migrants, another that she had announced her resignation. Another two out of the ten were opinion pieces with a strong anti-Merkel message. Only one of the top ten was an actual news item [62].

The factors discussed above should now make clear how this kind of distribution can be explained:

- Users with extreme political views tend to be more active on social media, at least in Germany.
- Facebook's user interface is optimized for maximum engagement and thus for minimal cognitive effort, encouraging a processing style that in turn facilitates cognitive bias and emotional responses.

- Emotionally engaging content garners more engagement on social media platforms, probably not least because of these design decisions.
- Engagement is also a prime factor in algorithmic sorting of content on Facebook, i.e. the emotionally charged messaging of disinformation providers is often a perfect fit for the content ecosystem Facebook provides.
- Emotionally charged content, politically extreme users, an interface design that encourages thoughtless interaction and an algorithmic system that interprets user signals created under these conditions as relevancy signals creates a vicious circle that will inevitably make more users aware of the content in question and thus create more opportunities for engagement, creating new user signals and so on.

Facebook as a social media platform is a special case, but the disconnect between the quality or veracity of the information provided and the curation decisions ADM systems make extends further.

Further examples of questionable types of content that have in the past garnered a lot of engagement and thus reach on Facebook include anti-vaccination propaganda [63], misleading information about the spread of the Zika virus [64], and bizarre right-wing conspiracy theories that the Federal Bureau of Investigation now deems [65] a domestic terror threat [66].

3.2   Example No. 2: Google's Search Engine

Google, by far the dominant search engine in the German and many other markets, has a problem with recurring disinformation in top spots as well. Google itself does not publish detailed information about the criteria it uses to sort content on search result pages, citing the need to battle malicious or purely commercially motivated search engine optimization. A product manager called Rachel Garb in 2008 revealed a small number of data points used at the time by the search engine provider to make decisions about personalized search results: The user's location, inferred by GPS data on a mobile device or the IP address for users on stationary computers, recent search queries and the web or search history of the user in question [67].

Much longer lists of criteria Google employs are regularly published by companies or individuals specializing in search engine optimization. Dean [68] for example names, as part of a long list, a number of "User Signals" including the click-through rate, i.e. how many users have in the past clicked on a certain URL on a results page, the bounce rate, i.e. how many users immediately come back to the results page after clicking a certain link, the direct/repeat traffic a certain web page attracts – these data are generated by people using Googles own web browser, Google Chrome, as well as the number of users who have bookmarked a certain page in Chrome, and the dwell time, i.e. the amount of time a user spends on a given page after clicking on a link in the search results before returning to the results page. Longer dwell times are taken as an indicator that the user has found what he or she had been looking for.

These criteria and presumably hundreds of others, combined with the judgements of human quality raters [69] employed by Google, are used to automatically decide for billions of search queries every day how to rank the results. In many cases, this process works well enough for Google to have achieved a quasi-monopoly in many markets. In other cases, the results surfaced by applying these criteria are disinformation or even criminal violations.

When one typed, for example, "ist der holoc" into the search window on Google's German site in the January of 2017, using an anonymous, not logged-in browser, the autocomplete function of the site suggesting popular searches beginning with these letters suggested completing the phrase with, at number two or the drop-down list automatically generated by the site, "ist der Holocaust eine Lüge", translating as "is the holocaust a lie". Holocaust denial is a criminal offense that can carry a prison sentence in Germany, so this in and of itself was surprising.

Even more surprisingly, among the top six of the results on the first results page were four pages transporting the messages of holocaust deniers. When this was brought to Google's attention by the author of this chapter, the company tried to amend the issue. Four months later, however, in May of the same year, the autocomplete suggestion "is the holocaust lie" had travelled to the top of the autosuggest list and the first page of results still contained four holocaust denial sites, albeit some of them now a little further down on the list. Some of those results were new, indicating constant search engine optimization activity by the people creating and maintaining holocaust denial sites.

Today, Google blocks most autocomplete suggestions around the term holocaust, as well as a number of other search queries like "women are" or "Jews are" that had been shown to produce some highly questionable search suggestions. This seems to be a direct consequence of some high-profile reporting on these issues in publications like the British newspaper "The Guardian/Observer" [70].

Other contested issues, however, still produce highly contentious results pages and autocomplete suggestions. When one typed, again, with an anonymous, not logged-in browser, "Impfungen sind" ("vaccinations are") into a German Google search window in February of 2019, the first autocomplete suggestion turned out to be "Impfungen sind Gift" ("vaccinations are poison"). Four of the five top results to this query were sites by activists opposed to the scientifically and medically sound and most advisable practice of vaccination. Once again, a small number of highly motivated users seem to play a role here, in this case members of the so-called anti-vaxx-movement that is driven mainly by conspiracy theories and disinformation about allegedly harmful effects of vaccinations and sinister plans by medical practitioners.

The British newspaper "The Guardian" reported on this scene and its online presence in a series of articles in the first months of 2019. One article describes "networks of closed Facebook groups with tens of thousands of members" that are engaged in targeted harassment campaigns against people arguing for the individual and societal benefits of vaccinations.

Since Google relies mostly on the activities of users and other website owners by counting links, its results can in certain areas be easily gamed by highly motivated groups that generate a lot of traffic and produce a lot of online activity around a certain topic, be it holocaust denial or anti-vaccination activism. Also, holocaust denial sites and anti-vaccination websites have one feature in common: They most likely attract attention from users who are either curious or even unsure about the issue in question and want to find out more.

When they hit on a page that contains information that's contrary to what the "mainstream" is saying, they might spend a long time looking at that intriguing content. This, however, produces a dwell time signal that the search engines ADM curation systems automatically interpret as a relevancy signal. This effect seems to be so deeply ingrained that even actively trying to counter this kind of promotion of disinformation on the part of Google is of limited success, as the examples above show. Changing a running system is obviously hard, especially when it is as vast and complex as a large internet search engine with billions of users, billions of indexed web pages and billions of search queries a day.

3.3   Example No. 3: YouTube

YouTube is a video upload and hosting platform acquired by Google in 2006. It's main optimization goal for the recommendation system that is part of the core of the platform is view time, as a developer revealed in 2012 [71]: "Now when we suggest videos, we focus on those that increase the amount of time that the viewer will spend watching videos on YouTube, not only on the next view, but also successive views thereafter."

In 2016, a group of YouTube developers presented a paper at a large international conference about automatic recommendation systems that detailed the introduction of machine learning, i.e. deep neural network architectures for generating video recommendations that again stressed the importance of watch time for the platform [11]: "Ranking by click-through rate often promotes deceptive videos that the user does not complete ("clickbait") whereas watch time better captures engagement."

YouTube has been criticized for the effects that this focus on watch times involuntarily generates a number of times. A former YouTube developer came forward in 2018 [72] and demonstrated with a piece of software that he had developed for that purpose how YouTube recommendation systems leads users who simply keep watching recommended videos towards ever more extreme, often conspiracy theory content [72]. Information science scholar Zeynep Tufecki described in an opinion piece for the "New York Times" her experiences with YouTube's recommendation system during the US election campaign of 2016 when she watched videos about rallies by the then-candidate Donald Trump [73]: "YouTube started to recommend and, autoplay videos for me that featured white supremacist rants, Holocaust denials and other disturbing content." The author of this chapter had reported similar conclusions in an opinion piece for German news outlet "Spiegel Online" a few weeks earlier [74].

This brings us back to the example from Sect. 1.2, the aftermath of deadly knife attack in Chemnitz, Germany on YouTube. The Chemnitz demonstrations after this killing, just to remind readers, were joined by unabashed neo-nazis, some of them chanting extremist paroles, some of them displaying the illegal "Hitler salute". According to Ray Serrato's analysis, seven of the ten most viewed clips related to the killing and the subsequent demonstrations on YouTube were from far right or conspiracy theory accounts, the US alt-right or the state sponsored Russian television channel RT deutsch, many of them rife with disinformation and propaganda. An eighth was an interview with a leader of the far right German AfD party with the title "The people in the country are angry". Only two of the top ten videos are content that can be classified as independent journalism.

In the light of the recommendation principles outlined above, the data obtained by Serrato [28] in the aftermath of the right wing riots after the stabbing should come as less of a surprise. He subsequently used his access to the application programming interface of the platform to obtain not only the most viewed videos about the events in Chemnitz, but also the videos that YouTube suggested to viewers as "related" when they had watched these clips.

What he found shocked him so much that he immediately published the results via the SNS Twitter: The bulk of the videos that YouTube's recommendation system considered "related" to the top ten Chemnitz videos were, according to Serrato's own classification, mostly products either of people connected to the right wing, anti-muslim "Pegida" movement active in Germany at the time, content from white nationalists, refugee-related content from sources connected to the right wing AfD party, right wing extremist content or outright conspiracy theories. Only a small number of the suggested videos didn't fit into either of those categories. It has to be noted, however, that Serrato didn't publish in-depth information about the method he used for the classification for these videos.

This result is nevertheless disturbing not least because "the related video recommendation is the main source of views for the majority of the videos on YouTube", according to Zhou et al. [75].

Once again, the focus of the designers of the ADM system in question on maximizing a certain metric, in this case total watch time, had unintended consequences: It amplifies extremist, misleading and disinformation content.

Serrato is not the first researcher to obtain results pointing to a problem relating to YouTube's recommender system and extreme right (ER) video content. O'Callaghan et al. reported in 2015, based on a content categorization system applied to English and German language YouTube channels, that "a process is observable whereby users accessing an ER YouTube video are likely to be recommended further ER content, leading to immersion in an ideological bubble in just a few short clicks".

The effect also does not seem to be restricted to extreme right political content, and not just to the recommender system but also the search function of YouTube. Allgaier found, for example, that, when searching for videos related to the issue of man made climate change, "the majority of the videos in the sample (107 videos) supports worldviews that are opposing scientific consensus views". 16 of the 200 videos that were obtained through a number of different related searches within YouTubes large archive of videos denied the fact that CO_2 emissions cause climate change, while "91 videos in the sample propagate straightforward conspiracy theories about climate engineering and climate change" [76].

The recommendation mechanism seems to foster extremist and conspiracy theory content, concludes Albright [77], drawing on several hundred YouTube videos that a search for the term "crisis actors" turned up as a seed sample and subsequently cataloguing the recommendations YouTube's system attached to these videos. The term "crisis actor" is part of the conspiracy theory that school shootings and other mass shootings in the United States did not really take place at all and that the victims and their bereft relatives are in fact just actors playing roles, all to create a basis for tighter gun control laws. These theories have terrible real-world consequences for some of those affected: The parents of children killed in the Sandy Hook school massacre for example have been harassed by conspiracy believers for years, prompting them to take some of the purveyors of those conspiracy theories to court [78].

"Every time there's a mass shooting or terror event, due to the subsequent backlash, this YouTube conspiracy genre grows in size and economic value", Albright concludes, "the search and recommendation algorithms will naturally ensure these videos are connected and thus have more reach." The numbers are not trivial: According to Albright, his search turned up a total of 9.000 recommended videos that had been watched a combined four billion times. The most heavily watched clips had collected view counts in the tens of millions.

4   Summary and Conclusion: Disinformation Spreading as Collateral Damage

Some current online ecosystems reward emotional and emotion-eliciting content. Politically or otherwise extreme users produce outsized engagement, which in turn feeds back into the signals measured by the platforms as input for their recommendation and content curation systems. Not just the audience, but also the producers of disinformation content are often highly motivated and also organized. Both they and their audience often feel like the so-called mainstream media cannot be trusted. They may thus be more interested in explicitly anti-mainstream messaging, again generating engagement, dwell time and other signals.

The principles used in the design of the user interfaces of some of these platforms are particularly conducive environments for a certain style of cognitive processing that Daniel Kahneman has, as a shorthand, labeled "System 1": quick, automatic, effortless, without voluntary control. The desire of interface designers to create user experiences that are as frictionless as possible, that "don't require thinking to act", create conditions ideal for a whole host of well-known cognitive distortions to play a major role, e.g. the availability heuristic, the confirmation bias and many other biases and heuristics that are often detrimental to a rational, fact-based kind of information seeking, processing and decision making.

The recommendation systems themselves are based on machine learning and optimize for maximizing signals that are highly correlated to the kinds of user behavior that the platforms can monetize – dwell time, bounce rate, watch time and engagement, i.e. interaction with content, are prime examples. These metrics, however, often do not reflect relevance, quality or other desirable properties. In many cases, they can instead amplify the messaging and content of disinformation providers and thus distort public discourse and contribute to the spread of misinformation and propaganda.

The core of the issue seems to be the same for all three of the described platforms: The goals that the platforms optimize for are based on descriptive data from previous users. Obviously, many people who typed "Impfungen sind", i.e. "vaccinations are" into Google's search window went on to type the word "gift" or "poison". A purely descriptive algorithm will take this descriptive result as a primer for future recommendations: Since many people have typed this combination of terms in the past, it suggests the same combination to new users starting with a similar phrase. The interaction with the search results displayed in this case are the next step, and they are again evaluated on a more or less purely descriptive basis: Many users have clicked on this link, they did not return immediately to the results page (bounce rate), they even stayed away, probably on the site they had clicked on, for a comparatively long time. This is interpreted as a signal for relevance or even the quality of the result. The reasons for these results might be somewhat different though: For example, many of the users typing in such queries might be young parents unsure about what vaccinations to subject their children to. When they see a page that seems to contain credible warnings, backed up with long arguments and seemingly convincing data or anecdotes, they might spend a long time perusing this intriguing, if dangerously misleading, content. The dwell time thus signals something completely different. Laboratory studies observing actual user behavior might shed some additional light on these mechanisms.

Extremist and conspiracy groups have also learned to fill what Golebiewski and boyd [79] have called "Data Voids": "Search terms for which the available relevant data is limited, non-existent, or deeply problematic."

Similar mechanisms can be assumed for extremist or conspiracy theory content on YouTube and Facebook: Content that creates a lot of engagement or keeps people watching is not necessarily of a better quality, veracity or other desirable quality. It might just be more entertaining, elicit fear, curiosity, outrage or other strong emotions. Future research might look into the cognitive and emotional factors at play here in more depth, although the basic fact that highly emotional content is particularly useful for eliciting engagement is empirically well established by now [44].

The fact that emotion-eliciting content seems to be so successful in terms of engagement and watch time should not be surprising in and of itself – "if it bleeds, it leads" is a well-established saying among tabloid news editors. The new dimension of the problem in an age of ADM systems serving up content to billions of users daily is, on the one hand, a simple question of scale – and on the other hand a function of the dramatically increased amount and the new types of content that are now available for these distribution systems to choose from.

To sum up: There is a complex interaction between available content, the attitudes parts of the audience that are particularly motivated to produce what counts as engagement, user interface design, psychological heuristics and cognitive distortions, the optimization goals and ranking algorithms of the platforms themselves. This complex interaction or rather: bundle of interactions can lead to highly questionable content gaining large audiences. Other factors that are beyond the scope of this chapter, like the influence of automated accounts on SNS sites ("social bots") might also play a role by creating fake signals that in turn feed into the criteria of the ranking and recommender systems.

This is a large and complex problem, and there is no easy and quick way to fix it. A simple, fairly easy approach is, however, at least as a first step, to make the public, the users of these platforms aware of these mechanisms. Only an audience that is made aware of the functionality of the systems providing its media content can make informed choices and judgements about the kind of content it is served on these platforms and about the way those platforms are used. The most important aspect to bring across here is the difference between the descriptive data that most of the ranking decisions are based on and normative cues: The audience needs to understand that something that appears high up in the search results for a given query, for example, is not necessarily "better", more relevant, more truthful content, but might instead just reflect the behavior of previous users and other factors that have little to nothing to do with the actual quality of the content behind the link.

A more laborious approach that ties in with the concept of "data voids" cited above is trying to generate more high-quality content around sensitive issues and invest more time and effort into making them visible on search and SNS platforms. The news content of publicly funded German television stations, for example, is, partly due to legal constraints, often not accessible via YouTube. Some progress towards this goal of creating and disseminating quality content has been made already, however, for example when it comes to information about vaccination practices. The vaccination information provided by the German Robert-Koch-Institute for example explicitly names and debunks many of the criticisms leveled against vaccinations by anti-vaxxers [80]. It also ranks highly in the respective search results.

Facebook in particular has tried a different approach by co-operating with institutions that fact-check widely distributed pieces of content that create a lot of engagement and, if the content is found wanting, incorporating certain warnings into its presentation [81]. This system has, however, faced criticism, on the one hand about a perceived lack of transparence [82]. On the other hand, at least one organization involved in the program has pulled out, citing an overwhelming amount of content and the necessity to manually update fact-checks [83]. Indeed, manual solutions for a problem created by algorithmic sorting algorithms that are in place because of the overwhelming amount of content available will likely always end up falling short of what would be necessary to weed out all misleading and disinformation content.

A harder, slower, but nonetheless advisable approach is political and (self-)regulatory: The platforms themselves need to change their optimization targets, the metrics that their ADM systems optimize for, to avoid collateral damage like the examples described above in the future. This kind of intervention, however, is tricky and potentially risky. To quote O'Callaghan et al. from their 2015 study on extremist content on YouTube: "Many of these suggested interventions raise the specter of social media companies policing political thought, which is palatable to neither the companies nor many users, and is especially problematic in the absence of rigorous empirical research that analyzes the Internet's role in processes of radicalization."

On the other hand, the companies themselves seem to only slowly come to terms with the collateral damage that their monetization-oriented mechanisms cause in certain areas of public discourse and information. A broad, continued societal debate about these issues is necessary to inform the public on the one hand and to create a situation where the responsibility of the new gatekeepers towards their audience is acknowledged more than it is at present.

References

1. Schmid, C.E., Stock, L., Walter, S.: Der strategische Einsatz von Fake News zur Propaganda im Wahlkampf. In: Sachs-Hombach, K., Zywietz, B. (eds.) Fake News, Hashtags & Social Bots, pp. 69–95. Springer Fachmedien Wiesbaden, Wiesbaden (2018). https://doi.org/10.10 07/978-3-658-22118-8_4

2. Allcott, H., Gentzkow, M.: Social media and fake news in the 2016 election. J. Econ. Perspect. **31**, 211–236 (2017). https://doi.org/10.1257/jep.31.2.211
3. Frischlich, L.: "Propaganda3" – Einblicke in die Inszenierung und Wirkung von Online-Propaganda auf der Makro-Meso-Mikro-Ebene. In: Sachs-Hombach, K., Zywietz, B. (eds.) Fake News, Hashtags & Social Bots, pp. 133–170. Springer Fachmedien Wiesbaden, Wiesbaden (2018). https://doi.org/10.1007/978-3-658-22118-8_6
4. Tucker, J., et al.: Social media, political polarization, and political disinformation: a review of the scientific literature. SSRN Electron. J. (2018). https://doi.org/10.2139/ssrn.3144139
5. Neuberger, C., Nuernbergk, C., Rischke, M.: "Googleisierung" oder neue Quellen im Netz? In: Neuberger, C., Nuernbergk, C., Rischke, M. (eds.) Journalismus im Internet, pp. 295–334. VS Verlag für Sozialwissenschaften, Wiesbaden (2009). https://doi.org/10.1007/978-3-531-91562-3_9
6. Bruns, A.: Gatewatching: Collaborative Online News Production. P. Lang, New York (2005)
7. Bruns, A.: Vom Gatekeeping zum Gatewatching. In: Neuberger, C., Nuernbergk, C., Rischke, M. (eds.) Journalismus im Internet, pp. 107–128. VS Verlag für Sozialwissenschaften, Wiesbaden (2009). https://doi.org/10.1007/978-3-531-91562-3_3
8. Greenberg, K.J.: Counter-radicalization via the internet. Ann. Am. Acad. Polit. Soc. Sci. **668**, 165–179 (2016). https://doi.org/10.1177/0002716216672635
9. Thompson, R.: Radicalization and the use of social media. J. Strateg. Secur. **4**, 167–190 (2011). https://doi.org/10.5038/1944-0472.4.4.8
10. Ricci, F., Rokach, L., Shapira, B., Kantor, P.B. (eds.): Recommender Systems Handbook. Springer, Boston (2011). https://doi.org/10.1007/978-0-387-85820-3
11. Covington, P., Adams, J., Sargin, E.: Deep neural networks for YouTube recommendations. In: Proceedings of the 10th ACM Conference on Recommender Systems - RecSys 2016, pp. 191–198. ACM Press, Boston (2016). https://doi.org/10.1145/2959100.2959190
12. Digital 2019: Global Internet Use Accelerates. https://wearesocial.com/blog/2019/01/digital-2019-global-internet-use-accelerates. Accessed 26 Sept 2019
13. Google Search Statistics - Internet Live Stats. https://www.internetlivestats.com/google-search-statistics/. Accessed 26 Sept 2019
14. Search Engine Market Share Worldwide. https://gs.statcounter.com/search-engine-market-share. Accessed 26 Sept 2019
15. Desjardins, J.: How Google retains more than 90% of market share. https://www.businessinsider.de/how-google-retains-more-than-90-of-market-share-2018-4. Accessed 26 Sept 2019
16. Social Media Stats Worldwide. https://gs.statcounter.com/social-media-stats. Accessed 26 Sept 2019
17. Spangler, T., Spangler, T.: YouTube Now Has 2 Billion Monthly Users, Who Watch 250 Million Hours on TV Screens Daily. https://variety.com/2019/digital/news/youtube-2-billion-users-tv-screen-watch-time-hours-1203204267/. Accessed 26 Sept 2019
18. Datanyze: Online Video Platforms Market Share Report | Competitor Analysis | YouTube, Vimeo, Wistia, /market-share/online-video. Accessed 26 Sept 2019
19. Napoli, P.M.: Automated media: an institutional theory perspective on algorithmic media production and consumption: automated media. Commun. Theory **24**, 340–360 (2014). https://doi.org/10.1111/comt.12039
20. Napoli, P.M.: On automation in media industries: integrating algorithmic media production into media industries scholarship. Media Ind. **1** (2014)
21. Napoli, P.M.: Social media and the public interest: governance of news platforms in the realm of individual and algorithmic gatekeepers. Telecommun. Policy **39**, 751–760 (2015). https://doi.org/10.1016/j.telpol.2014.12.003
22. Schwarz, C., Gensing, P.: Fakes nach Tötungsdelikt: Das Trauerspiel von Chemnitz. http://faktenfinder.tagesschau.de/inland/chemnitz-fakes-trauerspiel-101.html. Accessed 22 May 2019

23. Bangel, C.: Chemnitz-Prozess: Im Zweifel für den Mob (2019). https://www.zeit.de/gesells chaft/zeitgeschehen/2019-08/chemnitz-prozess-urteil-alaa-s-toedliche-messerattacke-rechts extremismus

24. Friedrichsen, G.: Das Chemnitz-Urteil stellt dem Rechtsstaat kein gutes Zeugnis aus (2019). https://www.welt.de/debatte/kommentare/plus199063453/Das-Chemnitz-Urteil-stel lt-dem-Rechtsstaat-kein-gutes-Zeugnis-aus.html

25. Gürgen, M.: Urteil im Chemnitz-Prozess: Kein Mittel gegen den rechten Mob (2019). https:// taz.de/!5617542/

26. Lakotta, B.: Urteil nach Bluttat von Chemnitz: Im Namen des zornigen Volkes (2019). https://www.spiegel.de/panorama/justiz/chemnitz-im-namen-des-zornigen-volkes-k ommentar-zum-urteil-a-1283266.html

27. Biermann, K., Grunert, J., Polke-Majewski, K., Schönian, V., Thurm, F., Eckert, T.: Video von Chemnitz: Wurden in Chemnitz Menschen gejagt? (2018). https://www.zeit.de/politik/d eutschland/2018-09/chemnitz-video-sachsen-hans-georg-maassen-verfassungsschutz-angrif f-mob-fakten

28. Serrato, R.: #Chemnitz on YouTube. https://threadreaderapp.com/thread/103634916739479 5527.html. Accessed 13 Sept 2018

29. Lippmann, W., Noelle-Neumann, E.: Die öffentliche Meinung: Reprint des Publizistik-Klassikers. Brockmeyer, Bochum (1990)

30. Galtung, J., Ruge, M.H.: The structure of foreign news. J. Peace Res. **2**, 64–91 (1965)

31. Weischenberg, S.: Nachrichten-Journalismus: Anleitungen und Qualitäts-Standards für die Medienpraxis. (2001)

32. White, D.M.: The "Gate Keeper": a case study in the selection of news. J. Bull. **27**, 383–390 (1950). https://doi.org/10.1177/107769905002700403

33. Neuberger, C.: Welche Medien sind für unsere Meinungsbildung von Relevanz? Symposium Meinungsbildung und Meinungsvielfalt in Zeiten der Konvergenz"der KEK am., Berlin (2015)

34. Weeks, B.E., Holbert, R.L.: Predicting dissemination of news content in social media: a focus on reception, friending, and partisanship. J. Mass Commun. Q. **90**, 212–232 (2013). https:// doi.org/10.1177/1077699013482906

35. McGee, M.: Facebook Cuts into Google's Lead as Top Traffic Driver to Online News Sites [Report]. https://marketingland.com/facebook-cuts-googles-lead-top-traffic-driver-onl ine-news-sites-report-75578. Accessed 27 May 2019

36. Stöcker, C.: Terrornews aus Mumbai: Netzgeschwätz übertönt Augenzeugenberichte (2008). https://www.spiegel.de/netzwelt/web/terrornews-aus-mumbai-netzgeschwaetz-uebe rtoent-augenzeugenberichte-a-593173.html

37. Freberg, K., Graham, K., McGaughey, K., Freberg, L.A.: Who are the social media influencers? A study of public perceptions of personality. Public Relat. Rev. **37**, 90–92 (2011). https://doi.org/10.1016/j.pubrev.2010.11.001

38. Trammell, K.D., Keshelashvili, A.: Examining the new influencers: a self-presentation study of a-list blogs. J. Mass Commun. Q. **82**, 968–982 (2005). https://doi.org/10.1177/10776990 0508200413

39. Jhonsa, E.: How Much Could Google's YouTube Be Worth? Try More Than $100 Billion. https://www.thestreet.com/investing/youtube-might-be-worth-over-100-billion-145 86599. Accessed 30 May 2019

40. Katzenbach, C.: Die Ordnung der Algorithmen – Zur Automatisierung von Relevanz und Regulierung gesellschaftlicher Kommunikation. In: (Un)berechenbar? Algorithmen und Automatisierung in Staat und Gesellschaft, pp. 315–338 (2018)

41. Lischka, K., Stöcker, C.: The Digital Public. Discussion paper Ethics of Algorithms (2018). https://doi.org/10.11586/2017049

42. Stieglitz, S., Dang-Xuan, L.: Emotions and information diffusion in social media—sentiment of microblogs and sharing behavior. J. Manag. Inf. Syst. **29**, 217–248 (2013). https://doi.org/10.2753/MIS0742-1222290408
43. Stieglitz, S., Dang-Xuan, L.: Impact and diffusion of sentiment in public communication on Facebook. In: ECIS 2012 Proceedings (2012)
44. Stöcker, C.: Bedeutung von Emotionen in den Sozialen Medien, Emotionalisierung durch Soziale Medien: Emotion bringt Reichweite? In: Besand, A., Overwien, B., Zorn, P. (eds.) Politische Bildung mit Gefühl. Bundeszentrale für politische Bildung, Bonn (2019)
45. Hölig, S., Hasebrink, U.: Reuters Institute Digital News Report 2018: Ergebnisse für Deutschland. Hans-Bredow-Institut für Medienforschung, Hamburg (2018)
46. Andrews, S., Ellis, D.A., Shaw, H., Piwek, L.: Beyond self-report: tools to compare estimated and real-world smartphone use. PLoS ONE **10**, e0139004 (2015). https://doi.org/10.1371/journal.pone.0139004
47. Andone, I., Błaszkiewicz, K., Eibes, M., Trendafilov, B., Montag, C., Markowetz, A.: How age and gender affect smartphone usage. In: Proceedings of the 2016 ACM International Joint Conference on Pervasive and Ubiquitous Computing Adjunct - UbiComp 2016, pp. 9–12. ACM Press, Heidelberg (2016). https://doi.org/10.1145/2968219.2971451
48. Oulasvirta, A., Rattenbury, T., Ma, L., Raita, E.: Habits make smartphone use more pervasive. Pers. Ubiquit. Comput. **16**, 105–114 (2012). https://doi.org/10.1007/s00779-011-0412-2
49. Samaha, M., Hawi, N.S.: Relationships among smartphone addiction, stress, academic performance, and satisfaction with life. Comput. Hum. Behav. **57**, 321–325 (2016). https://doi.org/10.1016/j.chb.2015.12.045
50. Haug, S., Castro, R.P., Kwon, M., Filler, A., Kowatsch, T., Schaub, M.P.: Smartphone use and smartphone addiction among young people in Switzerland. J. Behav. Addict. **4**, 299–307 (2015). https://doi.org/10.1556/2006.4.2015.037
51. Leslie, I.: The scientists who make apps addictive. https://www.1843magazine.com/features/the-scientists-who-make-apps-addictive Accessed 30 May 2019
52. Fogg, B.J.: Persuasive Technology: Using Computers to Change What We think and Do. Morgan Kaufmann Publishers, Amsterdam, Boston (2003)
53. Thorndike, E.L.: Animal intelligence: an experimental study of the associate processes in animals. Am. Psychol. **53**, 1125–1127 (1998). https://doi.org/10.1037/0003-066X.53.10.1125
54. Watson, J.B.: Psychology as the behaviorist views it. Psychol. Rev. **20**, 158–177 (1913). https://doi.org/10.1037/h0074428
55. Skinner, B.F.: The Behavior of Organisms: an Experimental Analysis. Copley Publishing Group, Acton (1991)
56. Bandura, A.: Social Learning Theory. Prentice-Hall, Englewood Cliffs (1977)
57. Lagorio-Chafkin, C.: Inside Instagram's Humble Beginnings. https://www.inc.com/30under30/2011/profile-kevin-systrom-mike-krieger-founders-instagram.html. Accessed 30 May 2019
58. Eyal, N.: Hooked: How to Build Habit-Forming Products. Portfolio/Penguin, New York (2014)
59. Wu, T.: The Attention Merchants: The Epic Scramble to Get Inside Our Heads. Alfred A. Knopf, New York (2016)
60. Kahneman, D.: Thinking, Fast and Slow. Penguin Books, London (2012)
61. Evans, J.St.B.T.: Dual-processing accounts of reasoning, judgment, and social cognition. Annu. Rev. Psychol. **59**, 255–278 (2008). https://doi.org/10.1146/annurev.psych.59.103006.093629
62. Schmehl, K.: 7 der 10 erfolgreichsten Artikel über Angela Merkel auf Facebook sind Fake News. Buzzfeed.de

63. Wong, J.C.: Anti-vaxx propaganda has gone viral on Facebook. Pinterest has a cure (2019). https://www.theguardian.com/technology/2019/feb/20/pinterest-anti-vaxx-propaganda-search-facebook
64. Sharma, M., Yadav, K., Yadav, N., Ferdinand, K.C.: Zika virus pandemic—analysis of Facebook as a social media health information platform. Am. J. Infect. Control **45**, 301–302 (2017). https://doi.org/10.1016/j.ajic.2016.08.022
65. Wilson, J.: Conspiracy theories like QAnon could fuel "extremist" violence, FBI says (2019). https://www.theguardian.com/us-news/2019/aug/01/conspiracy-theories-fbi-qanon-extremism
66. Kozlowska, H.: Facebook is a perfect place for conspiracy theories like QAnon to evolve. https://qz.com/1348635/facebook-is-a-perfect-home-for-conspiracy-theories-like-qanon/. Accessed 26 Sept 2019
67. Garb, R.: More transparency in customized search results (2008). https://googleblog.blogspot.de/2008/07/more-transparency-in-customized-search.html
68. Dean, B.: Google's 200 Ranking Factors: The Complete List. http://backlinko.com/google-ranking-factors. Accessed 05 Mar 2017
69. Google: General Guidelines (2017). https://static.googleusercontent.com/media/www.google.com/de//insidesearch/howsearchworks/assets/searchqualityevaluatorguidelines.pdf
70. Cadwalladr, C.: Google, democracy and the truth about internet search (2016). https://www.theguardian.com/technology/2016/dec/04/google-democracy-truth-internet-search-facebook
71. Meyerson, E.: YouTube Now: Why We Focus on Watch Time. https://youtube-creators.googleblog.com/2012/08/youtube-now-why-we-focus-on-watch-time.html. Accessed 12 Sept 2018
72. Lewis, P., McCormick, E.: How an ex-YouTube insider investigated its secret algorithm (2018). http://www.theguardian.com/technology/2018/feb/02/youtube-algorithm-election-clinton-trump-guillaume-chaslot
73. Tufekci, Z.: Opinion | YouTube, the Great Radicalizer (2018). https://www.nytimes.com/2018/03/10/opinion/sunday/youtube-politics-radical.html
74. Stöcker, C.: YouTube, Facebook & Co.: Sehend ins Verderben (2018). http://www.spiegel.de/wissenschaft/mensch/youtube-facebook-co-sehend-ins-verderben-kolumne-a-1192615.html
75. Zhou, R., Khemmarat, S., Gao, L.: The impact of YouTube recommendation system on video views. In: Proceedings of the 10th Annual Conference on Internet Measurement - IMC 2010, p. 404. ACM Press, Melbourne (2010). https://doi.org/10.1145/1879141.1879193
76. Allgaier, J.: Science and environmental communication on YouTube: strategically distorted communications in online videos on climate change and climate engineering. Front. Commun. **4**, 36 (2019). https://doi.org/10.3389/fcomm.2019.00036
77. Albright, J.: Untrue-Tube: Monetizing Misery and Disinformation. https://medium.com/@d1gi/untrue-tube-monetizing-misery-and-disinformation-388c4786cc3d. Accessed 26 Sept 2019
78. Williamson, E.: Sandy Hook Families Gain in Defamation Suits Against Alex Jones (2019). https://www.nytimes.com/2019/02/07/us/politics/alex-jones-sandy-hook.html
79. Golebiewski, M., Boyd, D.: Data Voids: Where Missing Data Can Easily Be Exploited. https://datasociety.net/output/data-voids-where-missing-data-can-easily-be-exploited/. Accessed 30 Sept 2019
80. RKI - Bedeutung von Impfungen - Antworten des Robert Koch-Instituts und des Paul-Ehrlich-Instituts zu den 20 häufigsten Einwänden gegen das Impfen. https://www.rki.de/DE/Content/Infekt/Impfen/Bedeutung/Schutzimpfungen_20_Einwaende.html. Accessed 30 Sept 2019
81. Hilfebereich für Facebook Media und Publisher. https://de-de.facebook.com/help/publisher/182222309230722. Accessed 30 Sept 2019

82. Lu, D.: Facebook's fact-checking process is too opaque to know if it's working. https://www.newscientist.com/article/2211634-facebooks-fact-checking-process-is-too-opaque-to-know-if-its-working/. Accessed 30 Sept 2019
83. Snopes pulls out of fact-checking partnership with Facebook. https://phys.org/news/2019-02-snopes-fact-checking-partnership-facebook.html. Accessed 30 Sept 2019

Between Mainstream and Alternative – Co-orientation in Right-Wing Populist Alternative News Media

Lena Frischlich[1]([⊠]) [ID], Johanna Klapproth[1], and Felix Brinkschulte[2]

[1] Department of Communication, University of Münster, Münster, Germany
{Lena.frischlich,j_klap04}@uni-muenster.de
[2] Münster, Germany

Abstract. Alternative news media with a right-wing populist leaning are flourishing. They pitch themselves as opposition to a hegemonically interpreted mainstream news media system. Yet, at the same time, they rely on the so criticized others to justify their own existence. Using a co-orientation framework, the current study asked in how far right-wing populist alternative news media orient themselves towards the mainstream. Using a qualitative content analysis of all 658 websites referenced by a popular right-wing conspiracy-theoretical YouTuber in Germany, we demonstrate that distinct source types were quoted. References ranged from mainstream news media up to ultra-right wing truther blogs. A quantitative examination of the content-analytical categories confirmed significant differences between mainstream news media and right-wing populist blogs, with special interest and alternative news media ranging in between these poles. Alternative news media were overall found to orient themselves stylistically strongly towards the mainstream but less so regarding their content selection. Particularly, the top sources, accounting for over 76% of all references, were mostly rooted in the alternative ultra-right-wing ecosystem. In sum, our analyses showed how stylistic co-orientation is used to build a bridge towards the mainstream while content-related co-orientation towards other ultra-right-wing alternative sources allows for validating one's own right-wing populist worldview.

Keywords: Alternative news media · Co-orientation · Mainstream news media · Qualitative content analysis

1 Introduction

The global success of participatory online-media has fundamentally altered public communication. The boarders between traditional mass- and interpersonal communication are converging [1], and traditional information authorities are losing their control about

© Springer Nature Switzerland AG 2020
C. Grimme et al. (Eds.): MISDOOM 2019, LNCS 12021, pp. 150–167, 2020.
https://doi.org/10.1007/978-3-030-39627-5_12

information flows [2]. It has never been so easy to produce and upload own content including own news[1] for a global mass audience.

Although traditional news sources such as print and broadcast as well as online offerings associated with these two, remain the dominant venue for news in most countries [3], new intermediaries such as search-engines and social network sites[2] become more and more relevant, fueling the "hybridization" [4] of the news media system.

In this environment, *alternative news media,* which present themselves as correctives of the hegemonically interpreted "mainstream", are flourishing. Although alternative news media have been traditionally studied often in the context of progressive formats and associated with social movements, the last years have witnessed a global uprising of alternative news media with an ultra-partisan, right-wing political leaning [2, 3, 5]. Drawing from research and theorizing on journalistic *co-orientation,* the current study explores the emerging ecosystem of these alternative news media. Using a qualitative content analysis of all media sources cited by a popular German right-wing populist conspiracy-theorist, "der Honigmann" (English: the honey man), the study offers initial insights into co-orientation processes within the right-wing populist media ecosystem.

2   Alternative News Media

News media play a crucial role in democratic systems. From Habermas' [6] normative perspective, professional journalists – together with political actors– are "the coauthors and addressees of public opinions" [6] defining which political issues are discussed, and—in best-case scenarios—ensuring "the formation of a plurality of considered public opinions." (p. 416).

Although the boarders of what constitutes "journalism" are increasingly hard to define in the networked society, this normative function is traditionally associated with the legacy or "mainstream" media. We understand mainstream media as the journalistic eco-system formed by specific news media organizations which fulfills the societal function of enabling public discourse by providing topics of general interest which are oriented on facts, selected by professional actors, and published following professional rules [7, 8]. Although particularly smaller news media are increasingly under economic pressure and struggle for their place in the public arena, these mainstream news media still reaches the largest share of audiences [3].

---

[1] In line with Weischenberg, we understand news as an generic communication of general interest, being both "publicist material and journalistic form of expression [55, p. 17]". Ideally, news are formulated along professional standards of professional, non-partisan reporting about events without adding own evaluations [ibidem, p. 18] – however, the ideal of "objective truth" has gained substantial critique due to its lack of considerations of aspects such as framing, news selection etc. [ibidem p. 19]. That is not to say that news media do not report in an *objective manner,* by adhering to quality criteria such as the reliance on at least two sources and the attribution of statements to individuals to formally distinguish between reporter and subject of the report [ibidem p. 22].

[2] In line with boyd and Ellison [56] we understand social network sizes as a "set of web-based services that allows individuals to (1) construct a public or semi-public profile within a bounded system, (2) articulate a list of other users with whom they share a connection, (3) view and transverse their list of connections and those made by others within their system (p. 221)."

Alternative news media, as the opposite pole of the continuum under study, are the "proclaimed and/or (self-) perceived corrective[s], opposing the overall tendency of public discourse emanating from what [they] perceive as the dominant mainstream media in a given system" [9, p. 3]. Alternative news media stage their "alternativeness" on different levels, by providing space for alternative voices and/or publishing alternative content, by relying on alternative distribution channels (although these differences are less prominent in unifying social media streams were all news look equal at first glimpse) up to forming alternative news organizations (e.g., activist or partisan newspapers) and being part of an alternative news media ecosystem [ibid.]. Table 1 summarizes the key dimensions on which alternative news media stage their differences. Mainstream and alternative news media thereby are best understood as opposing poles rather than dichotomous opposites. Positions and relations can easily change [9] and different media organizations within each "ecosystem" are interwoven with each other in the networked digital public sphere [10].

Their counter-hegemonic agenda makes alternative news media an attractive source for information processes and opinion formation within so-called *counter-publics*. Counter-publics are those sub-publics directed *against* a hegemonically interpreted public sphere (for a nuanced discussion of the "counterpublics" term, see [11]). This similar "anti-systemness" [12] has motivated some authors to equate counter-publics and alternative media [e.g., 13].

Although alternative news media have been traditionally studied in the context of progressive movements and related to social-movements [14–16], they can be found across the political spectrum. Like in other Western democracies (see, for instance [2, 17]) the current German alternative news media landscape is heavily skewed towards the "alt-right" end of the political spectrum [18–20] and disproportionally attractive for right-wing populists [3, 21][3].

The association between right-wing populist attitudes and alternative news media is of little surprise. Alternative news media attract those who distrust the mainstream [26, 27] and accordant distrust is actively cultivated by right-wing populist actors, cumulating in accusations of the "liar press" [28] and "fake news" [29, 30] and by attempts to self-position as the only once legitimately stating critique upon the mainstream [17]. Paradoxically, prior research has repeatedly found that right-wing populists actors refer to both alternative and mainstream news media in their online communication [31–33] and recipients with right-wing populist attitudes consume both mainstream and alternative news sources [3], suggesting that the derogation of the mainstream is not absolute. The current paper builds upon this notion examining in how far alternative news media makers *themselves* relate to the mainstream media using a co-orientation framework.

---

[3] In line with Mudde [22], we understand populism as a 'thin-centred ideology' [...] that can be easily combined with very different (thin and full) other ideologies (p. 544), for instance ultra-right-wing beliefs, and that can be described along the three dimensions of anti-elitism, the preference for popular sovereignty, and a belief in the homogeneity and virtuousness of "the people" [23]. Following deVreese et al. [24], populist communication is content that transfers these key components via certain messages of frames, often by using a certain set of "presentational style elements" (p. 425), such as relying on emotion-inciting content [25].

Table 1. Key dimensions of alternativeness

	Mainstream news media	Alternative news media

Macro-level	• Major institutions and networks in a given system with their ethical and legal regulations
	• Societal function of enabling public discourse by providing topics of general interest, that are:
	  – Oriented on facts
	  – Selected by professional actors
	  – Published following professional rules
		• Institutions outside and largely unsupported by the major networks with unclear/contested ethical and legal regulations
		• Aim at complementing "the agenda" and provide topics of niche/ counter interest, that are:
		  – Oriented on specific values
		  – Not necessarily selected by professional actors,
		  – Published without adhering to professional rules

Meso-level	• Traditionally, commercially or state-funded (i.e. public broadcasters) • Comparably large reach	• Can be non-commercially funded (e.g. ideologically-motivated) • Tend to have a smaller reach and address a more specific audience (counter-public)

	• Gatekeeping, agenda setting, news values, etc
	• Established editorial routines
	• Relatively clear relationships between
	  – Journalists and editors
	  – With sources and/or the audience
		• Different forms of gatekeeping (e.g., the inclusion of lay voices), news values etc
		• Different, and less stable editorial routines
		• Can have less hierarchical and pre-defined relationships
		  – Within the organization
		  – To sources and/or audiences

Micro level	• Professional journalists • Regulated employment structures (including freelancers) • Journalistic role interpretation	• Alternative content producers (e.g., bloggers, citizen journalists etc.) • Various employment structures, including non-paid relationships • Alternative role interpretations

	• Typical "news style" (articles, (audio-) visual reports, comments and the like
	• Striving for objective reporting (i.e. two-source rule, attribution of quotes
	• Typical news values, epistemologies etc
	• Characteristic
	  – Meta information (e.g., headlines, leads)
	  – Environment (e.g. an (online) newspaper)
		• Alternative accounts, depictions and interpretations of political and social events
		• Content proclaims to be complementary, oriented at special interest and potentially different from traditional news regarding its
		  – Core information (e.g., news values, epistemology etc.)
		  – Meta information (e.g., headlines, images, author information)
		  – Context in which it is embedded (e.g. website design)

Notes. The descriptions of the two poles represent idealized extremes. We do not think that most or even any mainstream or alternative news medium (constantly) fulfills all of them, or that this is a necessary precondition to deem a medium as "alternative" – we do, however, think that the more a given medium stages its alternativeness on these different dimensions, the more likely it is perceives as alternative by its producers, competitors, and audience

3 Co-orientation

The concept of co-orientation has been originally introduced as a psychological state by Newcomb [34]. He describes co-orientation as the essential outcome of communicative acts: Allowing two or more individuals to orient themselves towards each other and the same object without a need for constant "translation" (p. 395) of the other ones' actions. Co-orientation not only reduces error sources in social interactions, but also consensually validates everyone's behavior in a given situation therewith satisfying existential human needs for the reduction of uncertainty [35].

Co-orientation has been studied extensively in the context of journalism. From a functionalist perspective, a central democratic function of (mainstream) news media is to allow for the co-orientation of the societal systems [36]. At the same time, journalist themselves heavily co-orient towards each other to validate their routines, their selection of newsworthy topics and the frames they apply [37]. Co-orientation allows them to reduce the inherent uncertainties they face in the rapid news-cycle. As Kepplinger [38] summarized it "the most important reference person for a journalist is another journalist (p. 97).

Krämer, Schroll, and Daschmann [37] differentiate three main forms of journalistic co-orientation: (1) *stylistic co-orientation* in terms of (a) the appearance and formal characteristics of typical "news" (e.g. the use of headlines, leads, etc.) as well as (b) the adherence to journalistic reporting norms (e.g. separating news and opinions, providing fact-oriented content, etc.). (2) *content-related co-orientation* regarding topics, frames, master-narratives and so on. (3) *Organizational co-orientation* (e.g., regarding editorial routines). Krämer et al. argue that each of these forms has a distinct function. Stylistic co-orientation allows the public to form expectations and recognize news media at the first glance. Content-related co-orientation allows for validating the own agenda and establishing a joint agenda [39]. Finally, organizational co-orientation allows for an easy transfer of journalists from one organization to another and a general exchangeability of "best-practices".

Co-orientation processes are not always observable. Often, co-orientation is only implicit (e.g. visible in the latent establishing of joint quality criteria), or needs to be inferred from the published product (e.g. intermedia agenda-setting, framing etc.) [40]. Explicit media-references to other outlets thereby are the most conscious, purposeful demonstration of co-orientation and allow for inferences about "opinion-leading" news media in a given system. The lead media are the "mass mediated partners of communication which a journalist prefers to consult" [41, p. 6].

Often, media opinion leaders tend to be the national quality media [10, 42] such as the New York Times, the Guardian, or the German Süddeutsche Zeitung or the Zeit. Yet, for certain issues, smaller and tabloid media can also drive the agenda [39] and topics can spill over from special interest and partisan outlets up to the ecosystem (for a German case, see [43], for a comprehensive overview for the US, see [44]). As Vargo and Guo [10] summarized it: "news media of different types set each other's network agenda to various degrees" (p. 1047).

Against this background, we asked the following research questions:

RQ1. Which sources do right-wing populist media makers refer to?
RQ2. Can we observe processes of co-orientation among alternative news media sources?

RQ 1(a) Is the co-orientation stylistic, providing an orienting function for the media users?

RQ 1(b) Is the co-orientation content-related, consensually validating a certain agenda?

4 Case Study "The Honey Man" – A Spy-Glass into the Right-Wing Populist Blogosphere

We answered our research questions via a database consisting of all media references shared by a German right-wing populist YouTuber, "Der Honigmann" [in English, "the honey man"]. Before his death in 2018, the "honey man" (full name Ernst Köwig), a right-wing conspiracy theorist and Holocaust denier[4], uploaded 1,565 YouTube videos on his channel in which he or his wife served as "news anchors" reading out reports from other sources. His (rather amateurish) mimicry of a news broadcasting, where he and his wife are filmed in their living room or garden, led to more than 10,500 subscribers and 5.6 million views till his death in 2018. Köwig extensively sourced each of his videos, providing insights into his co-orientation towards other media-sources and a unique spy-glass into the right-wing populist alternative news media ecosystem.

Between January 2012 and March 2018, Köwig shared a total of $N = 20,056$ URLs tracing back to $N = 778$ distinct websites. Most of these websites (86.58%) were still online at the time of data collection (October 10th till November 14th, 2018). These $N = 658$ websites formed the basis of our analysis. For each website, we saved a html version of the landing page, the lead article of the day and the imprint as material for the analysis.

The analysis entailed three steps: First, we did an extensive qualitative analysis of a random 10% of all websites in our sample ($n = 72$) in order to develop a comprehensive, qualitative typology of the source types referred to. Second, we used a quantitative analysis of the content-analytical coding of all websites to explore co-orientation in the entire database. Finally, we examined the 50 most frequently shared websites (top sites) to explore the dominance of different sources for the overall communication strategy.

5 Analytical Strategy

We used qualitative content analysis following Mayring [45] to answer our research questions. Qualitative content analysis assigns large proportions of text to predefined

---

[4] For a (German) media report, see https://www.ruhrbarone.de/honigmann-geht-wohl-in-den-knast/139765.

categories which are summarized in a category-system. The category system can combine super-ordinate categories (e.g. formal aspects versus content-related features) with sub-ordinated categories (e.g., right-wing versus left-wing political articles). Qualitative content analysis is one of the most frequently used methods of such kind of content analysis [46].

The final coding system developed for this study entailed four main categories of interest. (1) *Media type*, which we coded drawing from prior work [32], and where we distinguished between mainstream news media, non-traditional media, blogs, political actor sites, social networks sites, news ticker as well as "other" and non-definable websites. (2) *Structure of the website*, were we described the websites (a) appearance (neatness, aesthetic, clearness, harmony of colors, provision of resorts), and (b) whether animations, and/or social media links were provided. (3) the *formal characteristics* of the lead article (e.g. existence of a title image, a headline, or a lead, and timeliness of the information). Finally, (4) the *content*, was coded via sub-categories describing (a) the *focus* of the website (its emotionality, objectivity, and editorial leaning); (b) the *attitudes promoted* (Populist: anti-elitist sentiments and promoting homogeneity of the people and inferiority of the outgroup, see de Vreese et al. [24], extremist: anti-democratic, absolutist, compare Rieger, Frischlich and Bente [47]); and (c) the websites *prior aims* (e.g., information, entertainment, mobilization etc.). A translated version of the codebook the raw data and all analyses are available at the open science framework (https://osf.io/jpzhf/).

The qualitative content analysis following Mayring [45] combines deductively determined pre-set categories (e.g. media type as based on the literature) and inductively developed categories (such as website aims in the context of this research) emerging during an initial coding of a material subsample (here $n = 15$).

Once the category system is formulated, intersubjective reliability of category assignment is established by double coding a subsample of all materials by at least two independent coders. In our study, coding was done by a master coder and two independent coders extensively trained in advance. Intercoder-reliability was satisfying (Krippendorfs' $\alpha = .75$).

Once the intersubjective reliability of the coding scheme is established, the remaining material is coded without further modifying the categorization system. As such, the procedure ensures both openness towards the material and rule-based assignment. Depending on the formulation of the categories, the process results in a matrix of content-analytical codes that can be expressed by binary variables (category applies versus not) or ordinal data (category applies, respectively does not apply). This coding matrix can be used for further analyses such as type-building or quantitative examinations. As such, qualitative content analysis inherently combines qualitative methods "with the technical know-how of quantitative content analyses" [46, p. 543].

6   Results

6.1   Source Types Between National Newspapers and Professional Truthers

Our first research question (RQ 1) asked for the ecosystems of information, right-wing populist media makers refer to. To answer this question, we developed a typology based on an extensive qualitative review of a random 10% subsample ($n = 72$) websites.

The analysis revealed three distinct "ecosystems": The *mainstream media*, the *alternative media*, and *non-media sources* plus some *other* sources (Fig. 1). Most quoted websites were part of the alternative news media system, which entailed three distinct source types: *Blogs, alternative news media*, and *religious/esoteric media*.

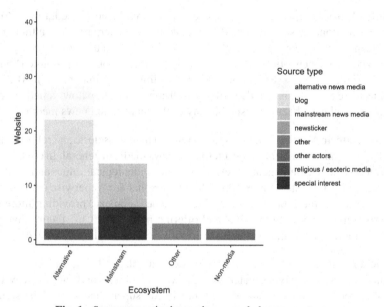

Fig. 1. Source types in the random sample by eco-system.

The second largest (though substantially smaller) eco-system were media organizations belonging to the traditional "mainstream", namely *mainstream news media* (e.g., public broadcast, or national newspapers), and *special interest outlets*. Finally, one *non-media sources*, the university of the German city Osnabrück was cited.

Three websites belonged to none of these ecosystems but directed the user to a professional association ("airliners.de"), a website for quotes and sayings ("sprueche-universum.de"), and a website for high-school materials ("levrai.de"). As we were interested in co-orientation towards other media sources, we focused on the five media source types in the following.

Mainstream News Media. This source type entailed typical German legacy media such as public broadcaster the "Tagesschau.de", national newspaper "Süddeutsche Zeitung", or the Suisse national newspaper "Tagesanzeiger". The websites ($n = 8$) were characterized by specific professional design rules (e.g. headlines, leads, or lead articles) and the providing of content informing its users about variety of topics spread across different resorts (e.g. politics or sports). The editorial leaning was mostly neutral, and the articles were written in rather balanced, objective way.

Special Interest Outlets. The special interest sources ($n = 6$) were characterized by similar professional design rules like the mainstream news media. In contrast to them, however, the content provided was narrower (e.g. about health or finance). Overall, the editorial leaning was rather neutral, and the articles were written in a balanced, objective and non-emotional way. In the literature, special interest outlets are sometimes considered "alternative media" too [48] but those mentioned in our sample were content-wise and stylistically part of "press" (for a comparable argument, see [7]).

Alternative News Media. At a first glance, the alternative news media ($n = 6$) used the same professional design rules as their mainstream counterparts. Yet, although their editorial leaning was often neutral, a closer inspection showed that some openly recommended a right-wing news-ticker ("news25.de") and others explicitly promoted "positive images" of foreign states ("Russia beyond the headlines", "china.org.cn"). Alternative viewpoints were carefully inserted into the overall communication flow, veiled by articles that could as well have been published in any of the mainstream news media sites.

Religious/Esoteric Media. Like the special interest media, esoteric and religious media ($n = 2$) focus on narrower topics than alternative news media in general. In contrast to the special interest media, their agenda is clearly driven by ideological values and – as typical for alternative media – they aim for providing topics that are "otherwise ostracized" [9, p. 3]. For instance, the protestant magazine "idea.de", aims at "providing more space for Christian messages in the media" and offering news from Christianity that would "otherwise not […] be available" (self-description accessed online 2010/07/05).

News Ticker. The only news ticker in the random sample, collected and amplified content from different source types matching right-wing ideologies and painting a dystopian vision of Europe by mocking about the proclaimed "super alienation". The style was amateurish, although certain "news cues" such as headlines, author names, and dates were provided.

Truther Blogs. The $n = 19$ truther blogs in the random sample strongly pitched themselves as opposition to the mainstream in both stylistic and content-related manner while proposing unique truth-ownership—a typical propaganda characteristic [49]. Sources of this type entailed amateurish websites, strongly motivated by partisan and often conspiracy theoretical worldviews (e.g., the blog "the awakening of the Valkyries" (title translated), which claimed that fossils of giants were found around the world). The content was presented in a very opinioned, subjective and emotional manner, and the blogs partially promoted far right ideologies and anti-democratic attitudes without any attempts to veil their purpose.

Overall, the different source types were locatable along a two-dimensional co-orientation space with *stylistic co-orientation* on the appearance of mainstream news media as the first dimension, and *content and tone related co-orientation* on the journalistic norms of reporting as the second dimension. To explore these dimensions in more detail, we analyzed and mapped all sources in the next step using the matrix of content-analytical categories as database.

6.2 Dominant Voices

To explore how influential the different source types were for the right-wing populist communication strategy, we analyzed how often, the "honey man" had linked to each website in our sample. The number of references varied substantially between websites: From only one mention (most of the websites) to 1,286 mentions to the Russian state-sponsored alternative news medium *Sputnik*. Following a classical "long-tail" logic, the top 50 websites accounted for nearly 4/5 (76.25%) of all references.

Inspecting these top sources revealed a much less diverse picture than the entire sample (see Figs. 2 and 3). Alternative media, particularly truther blogs, clearly dominated. Mainstream sources were restricted to special interest outlets like the tech-magazine *heise.de*, the finance magazine *finanzmarktwelt.de*, or the popular science magazine *scinexx.de*. Furthermore, right-wing sources were disproportionally present.

In sum, the analysis of the top 50 sources showed that the "honey man" himself oriented most strongly towards the right-wing partisan pole of the alternative-mainstream spectrum. Answering RQ 1, the honey man referred to a variety of sources, however, when only the most relevant sources (as indicated by times of mentioning) were considered, his communication strategy clearly validated a far right-wing populist, conspiracy-theorist worldview.

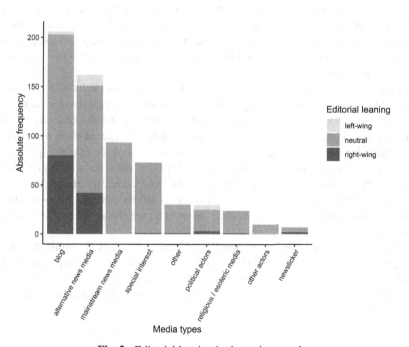

Fig. 2. Editorial leaning in the entire sample

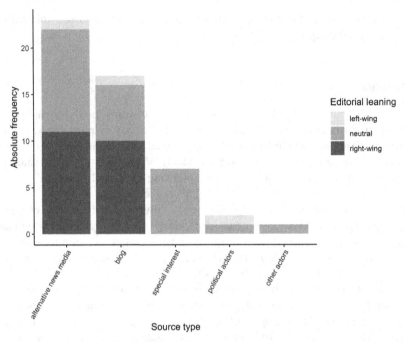

Fig. 3. Editorial leaning top 50 websites.

6.3 Stylistic Versus Content-Related Co-orientation - Mapping the Spectrum

RQ 2 asked whether processes of co-orientation among right-wing populist news media would be observable. To answer these questions, we inspected the association between the different source types and the stylistic and content-related categories using Pearson correlations. Figures 4, 5 and 6 visualizes these correlations as heatmaps, tackling the structure, formal characteristics, and content of the websites.

As regards to the *stylistic characteristics,* mainstream news media were statistically significantly associated with a more professional structure, e.g. the providing of different resorts, the use of a consistent, clear and harmonic design and the enabling of social media sharing. Their broadness, however, came at the charge of their neatness and aesthetical coherence. The truther blogs, in contrast, showed the opposite pattern and clearly emerged as the alternative pole of the continuum. All other source types laid in between. Although the correlation pattern for special interest and alternative news media was more similar to the pattern for mainstream news media, whereas religious/esoteric media were more similar to the truther blogs, none of these association reached statistical significance.

For *formal characteristics* of the articles, the pattern was less pronounced, although leaning in the same direction. Mainstream news media were significantly more likely to provide current content, report sources for their claims, assign their articles to a resort, and combine them with a lead and an image. Truther blogs, in contrast, were statistically significantly less likely to do so.

Structure

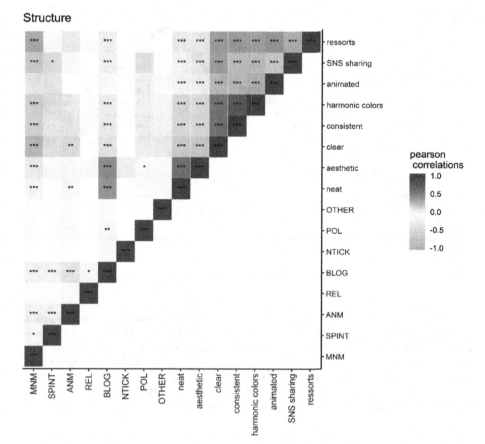

Fig. 4. Pearson correlations between source type and content-analytical categories related to the structure of the website. ($^{***}p < .001$, $^{**}p < .01$, $^{*}p < .05$ (two-tailed, Holmes corrected significance tested via the corr. test function embedded in the psych package [50]. MNM = mainstream news media, SPINT = special interest outlets, ANM = alternative news media, REL = religious/esoteric media, BLOG = personal or group blogs, NTICK = news ticker, POL = political actor, social movement, or political organization, OTHER = non-political actor. Non-definable "other" sources served as reference category.)

Finally, focusing on the *content*, both mainstream source types were significantly less likely to claim absolute truth-ownership or attack societal institutions (e.g. politicians or "the press"). The truther blogs, in contrast, were more likely to promote populist attitudes and anti-democratic content. Blogs were also less likely to provide content presented in an objective manner, whereas mainstream news media were more likely to do so. Again, all other source types ranged in between these poles without significantly strong associations with either the one or the other side.

To summarize, the quantitative analysis confirmed the existence of a spectrum of sources spanning from the alternative fringes up to the mainstream news media ecosystem. Both, special interest and alternative news media, showed a leaning towards the

Formal

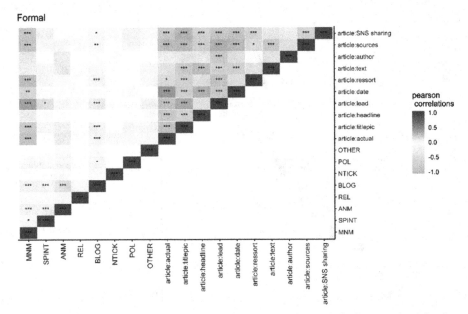

Fig. 5. Pearson correlations between source type and content-analytical categories related to the formal features of the lead article. ($^{***}p < .001$, $^{**}p < .01$, $^{*}p < .05$ (two-tailed, Holmes corrected significance tested via the corr. test function embedded in the psych package [50]. MNM = mainstream news media, SPINT = special interest outlets, ANM = alternative news media, REL = religious/esoteric media, BLOG = personal or group blogs, NTICK = news ticker, POL = political actor, social movement, or political organization, OTHER = non-political actor. Non-definable "other" sources served as reference category.)

"mainstream" pole when *stylistic co-orientation* was examined, but only special interest media did statistically significantly differ from the right-wing truther pole, when *content and tone related co-orientation* was considered.

7 General Discussion

In the current digital society, alternative news media are flourishing – particularly alternative news media promoting right-wing populist ideologies. Although alternative news media present themselves as opposition to a hegemonically-interpreted "mainstream", research has shown that right-wing populist actors refer to both mainstream and alternative news media sources in their online communication.

The current paper broadens the literature by showing how alternative news orient themselves towards the mainstream. Using a large database of over 600 websites, we explored the stylistic and content-related co-orientation of a right-wing populist media actor. Replicating prior work on right-wing populist movements ("PEGIDA", [31, 32]) and right-wing populist parties [33], we found no evidence for a closed "echo-chamber" of sources [51]. Even the right-wing populist media actor himself quoted mainstream and alternative news sources.

Content

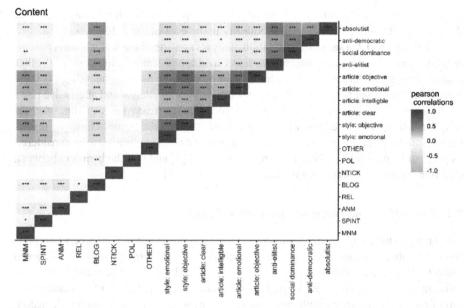

Fig. 6. Pearson correlations between source type and content-analytical categories related to the content of the website and the lead-article. ($^{***}p < .001, ^{**}p < .01, ^{*}p < .05$ (two-tailed, Holmes corrected significance tested via the corr. test function embedded in the psych package [50]. MNM = mainstream news media, SPINT = special interest outlets, ANM = alternative news media, REL = religious/esoteric media, BLOG = personal or group blogs, NTICK = news ticker, POL = political actor, social movement, or political organization, OTHER = non-political actor. Non-definable "other" sources served as reference category.)

The seven source types identified, span broadly media systems, entailing mainstream sources like traditional *legacy news media* such as public broadcasters or national TV ("mainstream news media") and *special interest outlets* (e.g. about finance or medicine) as well as *alternative news media* (e.g. Russian state-sponsored *Sputnik* or the German right-wing newspaper *Junge Freiheit*), *religious/esoteric "special interest" outlets,* right-wing *new stickers* and *truther blogs.*

These findings are meaningful in at least two ways: First, they contribute to the growing notion of a "paradoxical relationship" [31] between right-wing populist media and the mainstream they condemn. Although rejected and condemned, the mainstream news media are the blueprint against which conceptualizations of "news media" emerge – even in the so-called alt-right. Second, our results are consistent with prior studies questioning the echo-chamber hypotheses [52] – even when recipients would follow only the recommendations by the "honey man", they would be exposed to mainstream news media content.

Focusing only on the most referenced sources, the media "opinion leaders", showed that alternative sources dominated clearly. Among the top-sources Russian sponsored, right-wing, conspiracy-theorist, and populist content was over-represented. From a co-orientation perspective, these inter-reliance on other actors in the alternative news media network validates the right-wing populist attitudes promoted by the "honey man" and therewith is likely to increases their credibility in the eyes of the public too.

Answering RQ 2, a series of correlation analyses confirmed the stylistic and content-related opposition between mainstream news media and truther blogs, with all other sources ranging in-between. Although the other media were not significantly associated with either the one or the other end of the spectrum, special interest and alternative news media showed a correlation pattern more like the mainstream news media, whereas religious and esoteric media leaned more towards the other extreme. Thus, our results support the assumption that mainstream and alternative news media need to be considered as poles of a continuum rather than binary categories [9] and that the boarders between different media ecosystems are increasingly blurred [4, 7].

7.1 Limitations and Directions for Future Research

The present study had several limitations which should be considered when interpreting the results. First, we focused only on one German right-wing populist YouTuber to collect our database. Although the alternative news media in our sample are in line with those mentioned in prior work [e.g., 18], [33], and follow-up checks of audience overlap of the analyzed media with other media's audiences via the online-tool alexa.com showed no substantially share of non-analyzed websites, we cannot exclude that some alternative news media are not included here. In addition, although our database included some popular Russian, American, and Chinese websites, our results are not easily generalizable to other countries, where alternative news media might reach substantially larger audiences [53], or partisan media heavily'impact the news agenda [10]. Although we think that similar co-orientation processes of alternative news media towards their respective mainstream media will be found in different cultural context, exploring these processes in greater detail is a fruitful venue for further research.

Scond, the lifespan of truther blogs, particularly those with extremist, anti-constitutional content, can be short. As such our results present a cross-section snap-shot of this media ecosystem and long-term observations are necessary to understand how the network develops over time.

Further, our study focused on the stylistic and content-related co-orientation of alternative media on the mainstream. Future research examining orientations on the journalistic practices and routines in this media eco-system are necessary to get a more complete impression of the meso-level alternativeness and to understand what Atton (2002) terms *alternative production routines*, complementing the *alternative products approach,* we choose in this study.

Nevertheless, our findings provide new starting points for research in other disciplines. For instance, the features identified in our work might serve as features in the development of classifiers aiming at distinguishing between right-wing alternative and mainstream news media. Recently the Massachussets Institute for Technology (MIT) reported about a classifier that evaluates news-media sources using features such as biased reporting and emotional, subjective reporting styles [54]–characteristics that have also been found to characterize the alternative news media system in our sample.

Furthermore, social media analytics could be used to examine how the different media types identified in our sample use social network sites to reach their audience and how audience members interact with these sites or their content across platforms.

Finally, experimental social research could use our hand-coded material to select material for media effect studies.

7.2 Conclusion

Overall, our study provided an initial "spy-glass" into the right-wing populist alternative news media eco-system showing how these media stage their alternativeness while simultaneously orienting strongly on the mainstream in terms of stylistic means.

Acknowledgments. This research was supported by the Digital Society research program funded by the Ministry of Culture and Science of the German State of North Rhine-Westphalia.

References

1. Walther, J.B., Valkenburg, P.M.: Merging mass and interpersonal communication via interactive communication technology. Hum. Commun. Res. **43**(4), 415–423 (2017)
2. Bennett, W.L., Livingston, S.: The disinformation order: disruptive communication and the decline of democratic institutions. Eur. J. Commun. **33**(2), 122–139 (2018)
3. Newman, N., Fletcher, R., Kalogeropolous, A., Kleis Nielsen, R.: Reuters Institute Digital News Report 2019, Oxford, UK (2019)
4. Chadwick, A.: The Hybrid Media System - Politics and Power. Oxford University Press, Oxford (2013)
5. Marwick, A., Lewis, R.: Media manipulation and disinformation online. Data and Society Research Institute, pp. 1–104 (2017)
6. Habermas, J.: Political communication in media society: does democracy still enjoy an epistemic dimension? The impact of normative theory on empirical research. Commun. Theory **16**, 411–426 (2006)
7. Steindl, N., Lauerer, C., Hanitzsch, T.: Journalismus in Deutschland. Aktuelle Befunde zu Kontinuität und Wandel im deutschen Journalismus. Publizistik **62**(4), 401–423 (2017)
8. Weischenberg, S., Malik, M., Scholl, A.: Journalismus in Deutschland 2005. Zentrale Befunde der aktuellen Repräsentativbefragung deutscher Journalisten. Media Perspekt. (7), 346–361 (2006)
9. Holt, K., Ustad Figenschou, T., Frischlich, L.: Key dimensions of alternative news media. Digit. Journal. **7**(7), 860–869 (2019)
10. Vargo, C.J., Guo, L.: Networks, big data, and intermedia agenda setting: an analysis of traditional, partisan, and emerging online U.S. news. Journal. Mass Commun. Q. **94**(4), 1031–1055 (2017)
11. Squires, C.R.: Rethinking the black public sphere: an alternative vocabulary for multiple public spheres. Commun. Theory **12**(4), 446–468 (2002)
12. Holt, K.: Alternative media and the notion of anti-systemness towards an analytical framework. Media Commun. **6**(4), 49–57 (2018)
13. Engesser, S., Wimmer, J.: Gegenöffentlichkeit(en) und partizipativer Journalismus im Internet. Publizistik **54**(1), 43–63 (2009)

14. Downing, J.: Social movement theories and alternative media: an evaluation and critique. Commun. Cult. Critique **1**(1), 40–50 (2008)
15. Fuchs, C.: Alternative media as critical media. Eur. J. Soc. Theory **13**(2), 173–192 (2010)
16. Atton, C., Wickenden, E.: Sourcing routines and representation in alternative journalism: a case study approach. Journal. Stud. **6**(3), 347–359 (2005)
17. Ustad Figenschou, T., Ihlebæk, K.A.: Challenging journalistic authority. Journal. Stud. **20**(9), 1221–1237 (2018)
18. Schweiger, W.: Der (des)informierte Bürger im Netz Wie soziale Medien die Meinungsbildung verändern, 1st edn. Springer Fachmedien, Wiesbaden (2017). https://doi.org/10.1007/978-3-658-16058-6
19. Humprecht, E.: Where 'fake news' flourishes: a comparison across four western democracies. Inf. Commun. Soc. **21**(13), 1–16 (2018)
20. Neudert, L.-M., Kollanyi, B., Howard, P.N.: Junk news and bots during the German federal presidency election: What were German voters sharing over twitter? COMPROP DATA MEMO 2017.2/, no. March 2016, pp. 1–5 (2017)
21. Schultz, T., Jackob, N., Ziegele, M., Quiring, O., Schemer, C.: Erosion des Vertrauens zwischen Medien und Publikum? Media Perspekt. **5**, 246–259 (2017)
22. Mudde, C.: The populist zeitgeist. Gov. Oppos. **39**(4), 541–563 (2004)
23. Schulz, A., Müller, P., Schemer, C., Wirz, D.S., Wettstein, M., Wirth, W.: Measuring populist attitudes on three dimensions. Int. J. Public Opin. Res. **30**(2), 316–326 (2018)
24. de Vreese, C.H., Esser, F., Aalberg, T., Reinemann, C., Stanyer, J.: Populism as an expression of political communication content and style: a new perspective. Int. J. Press/Polit. **23**(4), 423–438 (2018)
25. Wirz, D.S.: Persuasion through emotion? An experimental test of the emotion-eliciting nature of populist communication. Int. J. Commun. **12**(25), 1114–1138 (2018)
26. Tsfati, Y.: Online news exposure and trust in the mainstream media: exploring possible associations. Am. Behav. Sci. **54**(1), 22–42 (2010)
27. Tsfati, Y., Peri, Y.: Mainstream media skepticism and exposure to sectional and extranational news media: the case of Israel. Mass Commun. Soc. **9**(2), 165–187 (2006)
28. Heim, T.: *Pegida* als leerer Signifikant, Spiegel und Projektionsfläche – eine Einleitung. Pegida als Spiegel und Projektionsfläche, pp. 1–31. Springer, Wiesbaden (2017). https://doi.org/10.1007/978-3-658-13572-0_1
29. Schulz, A., Wirth, W., Müller, P.: We are the people and you are fake news: a social identity approach to populist citizens' false consensus and hostile media perceptions. Commun. Res. 009365021879485 (advanced online publication, 2018)
30. Egelhofer, J.L., Lecheler, S.: Fake news as a two-dimensional phenomenon: a framework and research agenda. Ann. Int. Commun. Assoc. **43**(2), 97–116 (2019)
31. Haller, A., Holt, K.: Paradoxical populism: how PEGIDA relates to mainstream and alternative media. Inf. Commun. Soc. **22**(12), 1665–1680 (2018)
32. Puschmann, C., Ausserhofer, J., Maan, N., Hametner, M.: Information laundering and counter-publics: the news sources of islamophobic groups on Twitter. In: Workshops of the Tenth International AAAI Conference on Web and Social Media, Social Media in Newsroom, Technical Report WS-16-19, pp. 143–150 (2016)
33. Bachl, M.: (Alternative) media sources in AfD-centered Facebook discussions. Stud. Commun. Media **7**(2), 256–270 (2018)
34. Newcomb, T.M.: An approach to the study of communicative acts. Psychol. Rev. **60**(6), 393–404 (1953)
35. Jonas, E., et al.: Threat and Defense: From Anxiety to Approach. In: Olson, J.M., Zanna, M.P. (eds.) Advances in Experimental Social Psychology, vol. 49, 49th edn, pp. 219–286. Elsevier Inc., Burlington (2014)

36. Hanitzsch, T.: Integration oder Koorientierung? In: Löffelholz, M. (ed.) Theorien des Journalismus. Springer Fachmedien VS, Wiesbaden (2004). https://doi.org/10.1007/978-3-663-01620-5_9

37. Krämer, B., Schroll, T., Daschmann, G.: Die Funktion der Koorientierung für den Journalismus. In: Müller, D., Ligensa, A., Gendolla, P. (eds.) Leitmedien. Konzept - Relevanz - Geschichte, pp. 93–111. Transcript (2015)

38. Kepplinger, H.M.: Problemdimensionen des Journalismus. Theoretischer Ansproch und empirischer Ertrag. In: Löffelholz, M. (ed.) Theorien des Journalismus, pp. 81–100. Westdeutscher Verlag, Wiesbaden (2000). https://doi.org/10.1007/978-3-322-97091-6_4

39. Vonbun, R., Von Königslöw, K.K., Schoenbach, K.: Intermedia agenda-setting in a multimedia news environment. Journalism 17(8), 1054–1073 (2016)

40. Reinemann, C., Huismann, J.: Beziehen sich Medien immer mehr auf Medien? Dimensionen, Belege, Erklärungen. Publizistik 52(4), 465–484 (2007)

41. Krämer, B., Naab, T., Daschmann, G.: The effect of journalistic co-orientation on press coverage: a time series analysis. In: Annual Meeting of the International Communication Association, pp. 0–43 (2008)

42. Harder, R.A., Sevenans, J., Van Aelst, P.: Intermedia agenda setting in the social media age: how traditional players dominate the news agenda in election times. Int. J. Press/Polit. 22(3), 275–293 (2017)

43. Mathes, R., Pfetsch, B.: The role of the alternative press in the agenda-building process: spill-over effects and media opinion leadership. Eur. J. Commun. 6(1), 33–62 (1991)

44. Guo, L., Vargo, C.: 'Fake News' and emerging online media ecosystem: an integrated intermedia agenda-setting analysis of the 2016 U.S. presidential election. Commun. Res. 1–23 (advanced online publication,2018)

45. Mayring, P.: Qualitative Inhaltsanalyse. Grundlagen und Techniken. Beltz, Weinheim (2010)

46. Mayring, P., Fenzl, T.: Qualitative Inhaltsanalyse. In: Traue, B., Pfahl, L., Schürmann, L. (eds.) Handbuch Methoden der empirischen Sozialforschung, pp. 661–673. Springer VS, Wiesbaden (2014). https://doi.org/10.1007/978-3-531-18939-0_38

47. Rieger, D., Frischlich, L., Bente, G.: Propaganda 2.0: Psychological Effects of Right-Wing and Islamic Extremist Internet Videos, vol. 44. Wolters Kluwer Deutschland, Cologne (2013)

48. Atton, C.: Alternative Media. Sage Publications, London (2002)

49. Merten, K.: Strukturen und Funktionen von Propaganda. Publizistik 45(2), 143–162 (2000)

50. Revelle, W.: An overview of the psych package. Northwestern University, 7 January 2017. http://personality-project.org/r/overview.pdf. Accessed 11 Jan 2020

51. Sunstein, C.R.: Republic.com 2.0: Revenge of the Blogs. Princeton University Press, Princeton (2007)

52. Dubois, E., Blank, G.: The echo chamber is overstated: the moderating effect of political interest and diverse media. Inf. Commun. Soc. 21(5), 729–745 (2018)

53. Hájek, R., Carpentier, N.: Alternative mainstream media in the Czech Republic: beyond the dichotomy of alterative and mainstream media. Continuum 29(3), 365–382 (2015)

54. Conner-Simons, A.: Detecting fake news at its source Machine learning system aims to determine if an information outlet is accurate or biased, 04 October 2019. news.mit.edu

55. Weischenberg, S.: Nachrichten-Journalismus: Anleitungen und Qualitäts-Standards für die Medienpraxis. Springer-Verlag, Berlin (2001). https://doi.org/10.1007/978-3-322-80407-5

56. Boyd, D.M., Ellison, N.B.: Social network sites: definition, history, and scholarship. J. Comput. Commun. 13(1), 210–230 (2007)

Maintaining Journalistic Authority

The Role of Nigerian Newsrooms in "Post-truth Era"

Kelechi Okechukwu Amakoh[✉]

Department of Media and Journalism Studies, Aarhus University, Aarhus, Denmark
kelechi.amakoh@post.au.dk

Abstract. This study provides an insight into the practice of fact-checking in Nigerian newsrooms. Theoretically, this study draws upon the ability of the Nigerian media to maintain its journalistic authority in this supposed "post-truth era". Using the 2019 Nigerian presidential elections as a lens, this study applies qualitative thematic analysis in examining 28 fact-checked election stories by 15 Nigerian newsrooms under the aegis of *CrossCheck Nigeria*. This study is guided by the overarching question: How do the Nigerian newsrooms maintain its journalistic authority? Findings show that the Nigerian media maintain its journalistic authority through the following means: technological expertise, access to sources, spokespersons of real-life events and mastery of knowledge. This novel study shows how fact-checking activities by the media can maintain journalistic authority.

Keywords: Fact-checking · Nigerian media · Journalistic authority

1 Introduction

In 2016, Oxford Dictionaries declared 'post-truth' as the word of the year. This word asserts that appeal to emotion and personal belief influences and shapes public opinion more than objective facts (Oxford Dictionaries 2016). This has influenced the global discourse about the emergence of 'post-truth era'. Some argue that two global events in 2016 - the European Union referendum in the United Kingdom on June 23 and the United States of America elections on November 8 - influenced the popularity of the word (Ball 2017; D'Ancona, 2017). On the other hand, others argue that 'post-truth' is not new. It has 'flowered' - leading to the presence of fakery (fake news) and erosion of legitimacy in journalism practice (McNair 2018). This has raised concerns and research interests among scholars, especially in the fields of political communication, media and journalism studies.

Previous studies have examined the concept of fake news and the legitimacy crisis of journalism. These studies draw upon the unique role of journalists as the fourth estate of the realm (Akinfeleye 2003; Benkler 2011). On the concept of fake news, studies have looked at it from different perspectives. According to Egelhofer and Lecheler (2019), two broad dimensions of fake news emerge from the literature on fake news-fake news as a genre and as a label. While the former looks at the intentionality involved in misleading the public with fabricated news stories for a specific reason, the latter looks

C. Grimme et al. (Eds.): MISDOOM 2019, LNCS 12021, pp. 168–181, 2020.
https://doi.org/10.1007/978-3-030-39627-5_13

at how politicians make use of it to 'discredit' the media. Unlike Egelhofer and Lecheler (2019), a 2017 review by Tandoc, Lim and Ling identify six perspectives of fake news: satire, parody, fabrication, manipulation, propaganda, and advertising (Tandoc, Lim and Ling 2018). Despite the different perspectives of fake news, is the threat posed to the practice of journalism. This threat seeks to alter the journalistic authority conferred on the media to be listened to (Carlson 2017).

In maintaining its journalistic authority, studies show an increase in fact-checking practice (Graves and Cherubini 2016). This paper examines how the media maintains its journalistic authority through fact-checking activities in Nigerian newsrooms. Specifically, the fact-checking activities of fifteen newsrooms in Nigeria under the aegis of *CrossCheck Nigeria* are examined. Through the use of qualitative thematic analysis, 28 fact-checked stories related to the 2019 presidential election stories were analysed. This method of analysis is important in identifying, analysing and interpreting patterns (Clarke and Braun 2017) adopted by Nigerian newsrooms in maintaining its journalistic authority.

2   The Media, the Journalist and 'Post-truth Era'

In every clime, media organizations are charged with the sole responsibility of gathering and disseminating information to the general public. They are known as 'authoritative chroniclers' and 'spokespersons of real-life events' (Zelizer 1990). This confers on the media the authority as the fourth estate of the realm (Akinfeleye 2003). Journalists working in the media are expected to serve the public as watchdogs; be independent, objective in reporting, have a sense of immediacy; and legitimacy (Kovach and Rosential 2001) These functions empower the journalist to provide citizens with the necessary information needed to make informed decisions (Carlson 2017).

Today's journalism practice has changed with the emergence of new communication technologies and 'digital intermediaries' (Nielsen and Ganter 2018). Media organizations now compete with influential search engines like Google and platform companies like Facebook and Twitter in delivering news to the public. The public sphere which was once served by the media has now expanded to accommodate other news suppliers and aggregators. This development has given rise to the use of these platforms by media to reach wider audiences (Nielsen and Ganter 2018). Scholars posit that there is a need for partnerships such as this to maintain journalism's legitimacy to create discursive knowledge (Carlson 2017).

These platforms have led to the involvement of 'strangers' in the profession (Holton and Belair-Gagnon 2018). Their activities include the identification and gathering of news in different ways, effective dissemination of news and interactivity with the audience (Holton and Belair-Gagnon 2018, p. 72). Some scholars argue that the contribution made to journalism by these strangers are beyond boundaries (Carlson 2016). On the other hand, these strangers are believed to play a unique role as 'digital-periphery' and critics of the media thereby calling for a reconstruction of media boundaries (Eldridge 2018).

With the ongoing debate, the need to uphold truth in the profession is sacrosanct. In this supposed 'post-truth era', there is a digitized form of fake news peddling.

As surmised by Egelhofer and Lecheler (2019), fake news has been seen through two lenses: as a genre and as a label. These two lenses have aided the understanding of the erosion of the media's legitimacy and authority as 'spokespersons of real-life events' (Zelizer 1990).

2.1 Fake News

Fake news is not new. Its practice is as 'old as human civilization' (McNair 2018). With the emergence of new communication technologies, the method of dissemination has changed. On fake news as a genre, scholars examined the act of misleading the public through false content presented in a journalistic form with diverse intentions (McNair 2018). Allcott and Gentzkow (2017) posit that fake news are intentionally planted news stories in the media with the sole aim of confusing or/and misleading the public. The authors of fake news present lie using the conventional form of news presentation by journalists to deceive the unsuspecting audience. This could come in the form of misleading headlines, fabricated content of the news stories, tweaked facts and figures as well as cloning of online platforms of credible media organisations. As a label, politicians make use of fake news to 'discredit' the media (Egelhofer and Lecheler 2019). This strand of research sees 'fake news' as a buzzword (Ogwezzy-Ndisika and Amakoh 2019). The overarching aim is to criticise and erode the legitimacy of the media to influence the public (Quealy, 2017; Cheruiyot 2018).

Tandoc, Lim and Ling (2018) highlight six distinct perspectives of fake news: satire, parody, fabrication, manipulation, advertising, and propaganda. Satire refers to the use of exaggeration and humour by entertainers/comedians to "provide critiques of political, economic or social affairs" (p. 141). A distinction between satire and parody is the use of non-factual information to evoke humour.

Parody shows are seen as the "fifth estate of the realm" (Berkowitz and Schwartz 2016) while fabrication refers to the production of news items with no clear fact and it is intended to mislead. This perspective of fake news as noted by Tandoc, Lim and Ling (2018) aligns with fake news as a genre as highlighted by Egelhofer and Lecheler (2019). Both perspectives have the sole aim of misleading the public ultimately. The perspective of manipulation deals solely with photographs/videos (Tandoc, Lim and Ling 2018). This involves the manipulation of photographs or videos with the aid of new communication technologies (p. 144). On advertising, the journalistic form is applied to the selling of a product by advertising outfits. There is also the use of click baits headlines to attract the attention of people (p. 146). While propaganda involves the use of news stories and certain crafted narratives intended to influence the public by the political class.

In sub-Saharan Africa, fake news is not new. Wasserman and Madrid-Morales (2019) note that fake news in the region is primarily used in politics. Taking Nigeria as a case study, the practice of fake news can be traced back as 1989 when the first president of the country, Nnamdi Azikiwe was rumoured to have died. This rumour made the headlines on the Nigerian Television Authority (NTA) primetime news bulletin (Olatunji 2016).

In 2015, there were allegations of interference in Nigeria's 2015 presidential elections by Cambridge Analytica. A viral video portrayed one of the presidential candidates as a supporter of sharia law- showing people been mutilated and burned alive (Guardian UK 2018). This manipulated video was aimed at tarnishing the image of presidential candidate and reducing his votes at the poll. The presidential campaign also witnessed the use of acerbic comments and fake news by politicians and their supporters (Ogwezzy-Ndisika 2015; Ogwezzy-Ndisika 2018). These comments were "unguarded, offensive, uncouth, and uncultured" (Ogwezzy-Ndisika, Faustino and Amakoh 2019). The election was portrayed as a 'do-or-die' affair while the media provided the platform for election misinformation (Amakoh 2015).

During the 2019 presidential election campaigns, one of the fake news disseminated on social media platforms was the death of the incumbent president, Muhammadu Buhari and his impersonation by a man from Sudan known as Jibrin Al-Sudani. This fake news was orchestrated by separatist leader of the Indigenous People of Biafra (IPOB), Nnamdi Kanu. According to Kanu: "the man you are looking at on the television is not Buhari... His name is Jubril, he's from Sudan. After extensive surgery, they brought him back." The video showing Kanu speaking about Buhari and his double body from Sudan was shared by a Twitter user @sam_ezeh on September 3, 2017. This led to the reactions from Nigerians (Akinwotu 2018).

The traction gained by the rumour of Buhari's death can be linked to two factors: the increasing number of internet/social media users in Nigeria – 86 million Nigerians use the internet while about 34% of this population make use of social media (Internetlives-tats.com 2016; Statista 2019) - and the news space and airtime given to the story by both print, broadcast and online media organizations in Nigeria. This virality influenced the President's response during his visit to the Nigerian community in Poland on December 3, 2018. He noted:

"A lot of people hoped that I died during my ill health. Some even reached out to the vice president to consider them to be his deputy because they assumed I was dead. That embarrassed him a lot and, of course, he visited me when I was in London convalescing... Its real me; I assure you. I will soon celebrate my 76th birthday. I am still going strong." (Daka and Olatunji 2018).

In a bid to check this kind of stories bandied as truth, the media has continued to ensure they check and report only facts to the public. This has led to the practice of fact-checking journalism. The next section discusses the practice of fact-checking by mainstream media and periphery organizations in the media industry.

2.2 Fact-Checking Journalism

Journalism is no longer the same. Some years back, it was 'great' human interest story that was reigning. Then we shifted to 'great investigative stories. After that, 'great' data journalism was promoted. Now, it is the 'great' fact-checking journalism-Seun Akioye (Nigerian investigative journalist, February 19, 2019).

Ten years ago, the practice of fact-checking journalism was not as ubiquitous as it is now. Key activities included in fact-checking include: 're-reporting and researching purported facts' (Elizabeth 2014) as well as liaising with traditional and social media, educators and the public to change how information is communicated and interpreted (Cunliffe-Jones 2019). The first fact-checking organization is traced back to the 2000s in the United States of America (Graves and Cherubini 2016). Since then, the practice of fact-checking in the United States has turned into a professional movement (Graves 2018). This movement has also experienced growth in Europe. Since 2005, the growth has led to the establishment of over 34 dedicated fact-checking organizations (Graves and Cherubini 2016).

As of 2018, there were 156 active fact-checking projects in over 50 countries (Stencel 2018). This is an improvement from 2017 which had the total number of projects at 114. In 2014, Duke Reporters' Lab noted that there were only 44 fact-checking projects. The next year saw the addition of 20 projects while in 2016 there were 96 projects. (Stencel and Griffin 2018). In Africa, some of the dedicated fact-checking organizations include: Africa Check (South Africa, Nigeria, Kenya, and Senegal) Dubawa (Nigeria), Zimfact (Zimbabwe), Congo Check (Congo DR), Pesacheck (Kenya), Open Up (South Africa), Code for Africa (Cameroon, Ethiopia, Ghana, Kenya, Morocco, Nigeria, Sierra Leone, South Africa, Tanzania and Uganda).

Non-governmental organizations are lauded for being at the fore of the fact-checking movement in the continent while the mainstream media play catch-up (Cheruiyot and Ferrer-Conill 2018, p. 72). Contrary to the submission of Cheruiyot and Ferrer-Conill, Fifteen newsrooms in Nigeria (including major mainstream media from the print, electronic as well as online media houses teamed up to fact-check the 2019 presidential election stories. In a bid to combat election misinformation, the partnership was built to ensure newsrooms worked together to re-report and research facts reeled out by politicians. On the impact of fact-checking, scholars argue that the practice of fact-checking helps to mitigate the effects of fake news (Cheruiyot and Ferrer-Conill 2018, Nyhan, Putan, Reifler and Wood 2019). On the other hand, empirical studies show that fact-checked stories only play the role of informing the citizens. During the election, the fact-checked stories cannot influence who citizens will support (Nyhan, Putan, Reifler and Wood 2019).

Based on literature review conducted, there are three strands of research literature on fact-checking: impact of fact-checking (Nyhan, Porter, Reifler, and Wood 2019; Cheruiyot and Ferrer-Conill 2018; Pavleska, Skolkay, Zankova, Riberiro and Bechmann 2018; Amazeen 2017; Wintersieck 2017; Gottfried, Hardy, Winneg and Jamieson 2013); the role of new media in fact-checking (Coddington, Molyneux and Lawrence 2014; Al-Rawi 2018; Brandtzaeg, Følstad and Domínguez 2018) and a comparative study of fact-checking (Birks 2019).

There is a dearth of a global perspective to the study of fact-checking. From an African perspective, only two studies (Cheruiyot and Ferrer-Conill 2018; Wasserman 2017) discuss fact-checking practice and fake news on the continent. Through the lens of the Nigerian mainstream media and its first-of-its-kind fact-checking collaboration in 2019, this study contributes to the discourse of fact-checking practice globally. This study examines how the mainstream media through fact-checking election stories maintained its journalistic authority. The next section explains the media landscape of Nigeria and the partnership of the Nigerian newsrooms under the aegis of *CrossCheck Nigeria*.

3 Nigerian Media Landscape and *CrossCheck Nigeria* Model

Through the CrossCheck Nigeria model, it is evident that there is potency in newsrooms collaborating for a genuine cause. Today, the media landscape in Nigeria is regarded as the 'liveliest' in Africa (BBC 2017). There is a growing number of print, radio and emerging online platforms operating in the country. Before the emergence of online platforms, the media landscape was controlled by print, radio and television for a long time (Kolawole and Umejei 2018). This control can be traced back to the emergence of the first newspaper titled Iwe Irohin fun awon Egba ati Yoruba on December 3, 1859.

In a 2018 report by the International Telecommunication Union, Africa witnessed an increase in internet access from 2.1% in 2005 to 24. 4% in 2018 (ITU 2018). This has led to the emergence of hybrid and digital-only newsrooms in sub-Saharan Africa. Based on this, Nigeria has witnessed a growing number of online newsrooms. Nigeria ranks seventh on the 2016 internet users ranking with a total of 86 million people online (about 46% of the population) (Internetlivestats.com). According to Statista, there were about 29.3 million Nigerians who used social media platforms in 2018. This is projected to rise by 26% (36.8 million users) by 2023 (Statista 2019). According to Alexa.com top 20 most visited websites in Nigeria, there are three social media platforms- Nairaland.com (5th) – an indigenous microblogging website-, Facebook (7th) and Twitter (16th). Instagram ranks the 21st on the ranking (Alexa 2019). In terms of the messaging application, Whatsapp is the most popular messaging application across 40 countries in Africa (including Nigeria) (Hitchen, Fisher, Hassan and Cheeseman 2019).

With an increased digitized Nigeria media landscape, the CrossCheck Nigeria collaboration of 15 newsrooms included four digital-only newsrooms such as Premium Times, The Cable, The Niche, Sahara Reporters.

This collaboration aimed to combat fake news and election misinformation. This was established through the efforts of the International Centre for Investigative Reporting (ICIR), a non-profit investigative media organization in Nigeria and First Draft News, a UK-based investigative journalism outfit (Oluwole 2018).

Before coming in partnership with ICIR, First Draft worked on combating voters' suppression during the 2016 United States of America elections, combatting of fakes through a collaborative project, Cross Check in France, United Kingdom and Germany before and during their elections in 2017 and the use of Comprova before and during the Brazilian presidential election in October 2018 (First Draft 2018a; Cross-Check 2018; Comprova 2018). These successes led to the partnership between ICIR and First Draft in Nigeria. This partnership led to the collaboration of 15 newsrooms in Nigeria to launchCrossCheck Nigeria.

They include: Premium Times (Online), Daily Trust (Print), News Agency of Nigeria, AFP (Agence France-Presse), The Nation (Print), Tribune (Print), The Guardian (Print), Punch (Print), The Sun (Print), Channels Television (Broadcast), The Cable (Online), The Niche (Online), Sahara Reporters (Online), Freedom Radio (Broadcast). Other members of the collaboration include Africa Check (Fact-checking organization), Dubawa (Fact-checking organization), University of Lagos (Researchers from the Department of Mass Communication), and CODE (Social Accountability Movement). Every collaborator agreed to abide by the following principles: transparency, accuracy, independence, fairness and impartiality, and ethical responsibility (FirstDraft 2018b).

CrossCheck Nigeria fact-checked election stories and published their findings on https://crosschecknigeria.org/ and social media platforms. The public had the opportunity to send stories circulating online about the election for verification. Through a dedicated WhatsApp number, the members of the public could convey their message to CrossCheck Nigeria. The project sought to give every Nigerian voter the "best information" about the 2019 election and to clarify or dispel rumours that circulate online.

This collaboration can be seen as a good example of participatory journalism in practice with the deployment of new communication technologies and the inclusion of the public (Thurman and Hermida 2010; Domingo et al. 2008). Members of the public were able to end in their stories to be fact-checked by CrossCheck Nigeria.

This study's overarching question is: To what extent do Nigerian newsrooms maintain its journalistic authority?

4   Data Collection

A total of 32 stories was published by CrossCheck Nigeria on www. crosschecknigeria.org. Each story was researched, written and cross-checked by collaborators of *CrossCheck Nigeria*. These stories were published between November 28, 2018, and March 1, 2019. The time frame covered the period of the general election campaign (the campaign started on November 10), the presidential election (Feb 23, 2019) and post-presidential election. I read every story published on the *CrossCheck Nigeria* website. A total of 32 stories were read. Out of these, five stories were removed. The removed stories were not related to the 2019 presidential elections (Fig. 1). A total of 28 stories were thematically analysed.

Fig. 1. A screenshot showing the title of one of the five stories removed before data analysis.

4.1   Method

To answer the overarching question for this study, a qualitative thematic analysis approach was adopted. This approach seeks to identify, analyse and interpret the patterns adopted by the Nigerian media to fact-check election stories. Clarke and Braun (2017) notes that this method can be applied across several theoretical frameworks. This study focuses on the latent level of thematic analysis (Braun & Clarke 2006; David and Sutton 2011, p. 342). This level helps to interpret and identify themes beyond description.

4.2 Analysis

Using the thematic analysis approach, 28 stories were read to be familiar with it. From the reading of the stories, I noted my general impression of how the fact-checked stories were presented. Based on the notes, I conducted the first cycle of coding each story in the sample. Similarities and differences in the stories published were identified (David and Sutton 2011, p. 339). During the exercise, I coded each story in quick succession as suggested by Charmaz (2006, p. 49). Each code generated at this stage were descriptive (Miles, Huberman and Saldaña 2014). The next step was the second-cycle coding. At this stage, I paid more attention to stories being coded with the intent to identify similar code patterns generated in the first-cycle coding applied (Miles, Huberman and Saldana 2014). Codes identified with similar patterns were collected and assigned themes on the latent level (Braun and Clarke 2006). The final stage of the coding process involved the evaluation of the assigned themes to ensure clarity.

5 Findings

Findings of this study show that Nigerian newsrooms maintain its journalistic authority through four major themes. These include technological expertise, access to sources, spokespersons of events and mastery of knowledge. The collaborators of *CrossCheck Nigeria*, who were drawn from across the Nigerian media exhibited and maintained their journalistic authority.

5.1 The Technological Expertise of Nigerian Newsrooms

The first theme generated from the stories studied is the portrayal of technological expertise by Nigerian newsrooms in fact-checking election stories. In displaying this expertise, the journalists highlighted their use of reverse image search - a geo-satellite search of videos, and online verification software, InVID to either confirm or dismiss viral election stories.

For example, in a fact-checked story posted on February 23 by Motunrayo Joel of Africa Check and cross-checked by seven collaborators, the image reverse search technique was used. This technique was used in confirming if Muhammadu Buhari, the All Progressives Congress presidential candidate voted for the opposition party, Peoples Democratic Party candidate, Atiku Abubakar in the election. This check was necessitated by the viral photograph online showing Buhari holding a thumb printed ballot paper which showed he voted for Atiku. Through the IRS technique, it was confirmed that the photograph was from the 2015 presidential election which showed Buhari voted for APC.

In maintaining its journalistic authority, Joel noted:

1. *CrossCheck Nigeria, through an image reverse search on the photo, confirms picture was dug out from the 2015 presidential election.*

Through reverse image search, the report provided background details about the viral photograph in question:

2. *The original also shows that President had voted for his party, All Progressives Congress, at the election, and not PDP*
3. *At Daura, Katsina State where President Buhari visited to cast his vote for this year's election, he was dressed in a dark blue native attire*

5.2   Access to Sources

The second theme generated from the stories is the portrayal of access to sources involved. In fact-checking some of the election stories, journalists went a step further in contacting the sources mentioned in the stories for them to offer their side of the story. This highlighted the relationship maintained by Nigerian journalists with sources.

In fact-checking a story titled: "Man caught with PVCs is [an] ex-officio member of PDP in Mpkat Enin LGA of Akwa Ibom State",CrossCheck Nigeria confirmed speaking with the spokesperson of PDP in the state. The story used phrases like: *"When Cross-Check Nigeria initially called"*, *"when he was called again by another reporter known to him"*.

2. *When CrossCheck Nigeria initially called PDP's spokesperson, Ini Ememobong, in Akwa Ibom State, he denied that the men in the picture belonged to the party in the state.*
3. *However, days later, when he was called again by another reporter known to him, Ememobong confirmed that one of the men in the photograph is, indeed, Aniete Isoenang, an ex-officio member of the party in Mpkat Enin local government area of Akwa Ibom state.*

In another story authored on January 24 by Lolade Nwanze of The Guardian, several sources were spoken to: the media aide of Atiku, Paul Ibe, the spokesperson of the Oyo State Police and fellow reporters in the state in order to ascertain if the wife of Abubakar Atiku, Peoples Democratic Party presidential candidate was attacked in Ibadan as reported.

We investigated the claim by speaking with Atiku's media aide, Paul Ibe, a spokesperson for the Oyo State Police, as well as other reporters covering politics in the state.

5.3 Purveyors of Real-Life Events

The third theme generated is the portrayal of journalists as purveyors of real-life events. Specifically, the fact-checkers referred to previous news reports by the Nigerian media to justify or dispel the rumours about the election.

An example of this theme can be seen in the story titled: "Amaechi was not arrested over corruption allegation" This story was authored by Damilola Ojetunde of The ICIR on January 24. In dispelling the rumour that Rotimi Amaechi, a Minister of Transportation and the Director-General of the presidential campaign of Muhammadu Buhari was arrested, Ojetunde referred to a news report published by one of the collaborators, News Agency of Nigeria and a live event aired by Nigeria Television Authority on January 23. The news report and live event aired justified the fact that Amaechi attended the presidential campaign of Buhari which held in Sokoto and Kebbi states on January 23 and was not arrested for corruption as widely reported. Part of the story highlighting this theme:

CrossCheck Nigeria confirms that Amaechi was not arrested and that he was at the presidential rally of President Buhari in both Sokoto and Kebbi states yesterday, January 23.

To verify this, CrossCheck Nigeria tracked the minister's public appearance on said date. The presidential rally of the APC was in Sokoto and Kebbi on January 23. A NAN report confirmed the APC campaign DG was in attendance. Live coverage of the event by the NTA also showed Amaechi addressing the crowd at the rally.

In another story fact-checked on February 9 by Opeyemi Kehinde of Daily Trust, clips from one of the collaborators of CrossCheck Nigeria - Channels Television were used to confirm a misleading viral collaged photograph showing the campaign rallies of both Muhammadu Buhari of APC and Atiku Abubakar of PDP. Part of the story reads:

4. *Though the photo of Atiku's presidential rally in Katsina as shown in the collage is original, it only revealed the crowded sections of the Karkanda Stadium, Katsina and neglected the scanty sections during the rally. A video of the campaign venue as shown in a Channels TV news clip (From 3:00–3:45 min) shows that several seats were empty during the rally.*

5.4 Mastery of Knowledge

The fourth theme generated from the fact-checked stories portrayed the media possess the mastery of salient knowledge to inform the public. In a story titled: "The USA Centre for Security Studies DID NOT declare Nigeria an SOS state," and published on February 6, the author, Lolade Nwanze of The Guardian authoritatively noted that there is no centre known as "USA Centre for Security Studies". This highlights the media's wealth of knowledge to inform the public correctly. Part of the story showing this theme reads:

There is no USA Centre for Security Studies. The video is of Frank Gaffney, the Founder and President of Centre for Security Policy, a US non-profit.

6   Discussion

Based on the findings from this study, the Nigerian media is waking up to its role of verification of information in this supposed "post-truth era". Cheruiyot and Ferrer-Conill (2018) surmised that the non-governmental organizations helped in filling the verification role of the mainstream media. The emergence of CrossCheck Nigeria in 2018 highlights how the Nigerian newsrooms are showing more interest in curbing the spread of fakery related to the election.

The themes of purveyors of real-life events and mastery of knowledge generated in this study agree with the submission of Zelizer (1990) and Carslon (2017). Zelizer (1990) noted the role of journalists as spokespersons of real-life events. For Carlson (2017), for journalists to retain their legitimate discursive role, they must be able to possess control over knowledge.

The success of this collaboration was based on the partnership between the newsrooms and relevant stakeholders- Africa Check (Fact-checking organization), Dubawa (Fact-checking organization), University of Lagos (Researchers from the Department of Mass Communication), and CODE (Social Accountability Movement) to ensure its success. Newsrooms must continue to build this kind of relationship within and outside the newsroom (Carlson 2017) to maintain its journalistic authority in this supposed "post-truth era".

7   Limitations and Agenda for Future Study

The sample studied in this paper was restricted to the fact-checked stories by CrossCheck Nigeria. This limited to the scope of the study in explaining the fact-checking activity that took place during the 2019 presidential elections in Nigeria. Despite this limitation, the sample provided a leeway in understanding how the Nigerian media maintain its journalistic authority during election reporting.

Four research areas require further study: one, a study on the reach recorded by these fact-checked stories on social media platforms. This will provide an insight into the degree of impact on voters by this novel collaboration of Nigerian newsrooms. Two, a study of the fact-checking activities of non-governmental organizations in Nigeria. This will help in understanding their goals, impact and role in metajournalistic discourse. Three, a study on the use of social media in propagating fake news, especially during elections. Studies show that Whatsapp was used during the 2019 elections in Nigeria to spread fake news (Hitchen, Fisher, Hassan and Cheeseman 2019). Fourth, a comparative study on the fact-checking activities of the media in sub-Saharan Africa especially during elections.

8   Conclusion

Notwithstanding, this study is novel in understanding how the journalistic authority of Nigerian newsrooms is maintained. It provides a global perspective on the discourse of fact-checking. Through qualitative thematic analysis, 28 fact-checked stories by Cross-Check Nigeria - a collaboration of 15 newsrooms in Nigeria were studied. Four themes - technological expertise, access to sources, spokespersons of events and mastery of knowledge- were identified through this study. The Nigerian media in this supposed 'post-truth' era portray a professional sense of duty as authoritative chroniclers.

References

Akinfeleye, R.: Fourth estate of the realm or fourth estate of the wreck: imperative of social responsibility of the press. University of Lagos Press, Lagos (2003)

Akinwotu, E.: There's no evidence that Nigeria's President Muhammadu Buhari has died and been replaced by lookalike. https://factcheck.afp.com/theres-no-evidence-nigerias-president-muhammadu-buhari-has-died-and-been-replaced-lookalike. Accessed 04 June 2019

Alexa. Top Sites in Nigeria (2019). https://www.alexa.com/topsites/countries/NG

Allcott, H., Gentzkow, M.: Social media and fake news in the 2016 election. J. Econ. Perspect. **31**(2), 211–235 (2017). https://doi.org/10.1257/jep.31.2.211

Al-Rawi, A.: Gatekeeping Fake news discourses on mainstream media versus social media. Soc. Sci. Comput. Rev. 89443931879584 (2018). https://doi.org/10.1177/0894439318795849

Amakoh, K.: Newspaper coverage of the 2015 Nigeria's presidential elections: a study of selected newspapers. Mass Communication, University of Lagos (2015)

Amazeen, M.A.: Journalistic interventions: the structural factors affecting the global emergence of fact-checking. J.: Theory Pract. Crit. 146488491773021 (2017). https://doi.org/10.1177/1464884917730217

Ball, J.: Post-Truth: How Bullshit Conquered the World. Biteback Publishing, New York (2017)

BBC: 'Post-truth' declared word of the year by Oxford Dictionaries. https://www.bbc.com/news/uk-37995600. Accessed 04 June 2019

Benkler, Y.: A free irresponsible press: Wikileaks and the battle over the soul of the networked fourth estate. Harv. Civ. Rights Civ. Libert. Law Rev. **46**(2), 311–398 (2011)

Berkowitz, D., Schwartz, A.: Miley, CNN and the Onion. J. Pract. **10**(1), 1–17 (2016). https://doi.org/10.1080/17512786.2015.1006933

Birks, J.: 12 Fact-checking, false balance, and 'fake news'. The discourse and practice of verification in political communication In: Price, S. (ed.) Journalism, Power, and investigation: Global and Activist Perspectives. Routledge, Taylor & Francis Group, London, New York (2019)

Brandtzaeg, P.B., Følstad, A., Chaparro Domínguez, M.Á.: How journalists and social media users perceive online fact-checking and verification services. J. Pract. **12**(9), 1109–1129 (2018). https://doi.org/10.1080/17512886.2017.1363657

Braun, V., Clarke, V.: Using thematic analysis in psychology. Qual. Res. Psychol. **3**(2), 77–101 (2006)

Carlson, M.: Metajournalistic discourse and the meanings of journalism: definitional control, boundary work, and legitimation. CT **26**(4), 349–368 (2016)

Carlson, M.: Journalistic Authority: Legitimating News in the Digital Era. Columbia University Press, New York (2017)

Charmaz, K.: Constructing Grounded Theory: A Practical Guide through Qualitative Analysis, pp. 42–60 (2006)

Cheruiyot, D.: Popular criticism that matters. J. Pract. **12**(8), 1008–1018 (2018). https://doi.org/10.1080/17512786.2018

Cheruiyot, D., Ferrer-Conill, R.: "Fact-checking Africa": epistemologies, data and the expansion of journalistic discourse. Digit. J. **6**(8), 964–975 (2018). https://doi.org/10.1080/21670811.2018.1493940

Clarke, V., Braun, V.: Thematic analysis. J. Posit. Psychol. **12**(3), 297–298 (2017). https://doi.org/10.1080/17439760.2016.1262613

Coddington, M., Molyneux, L., Lawrence, R.G.: Fact checking the campaign: how political reporters use twitter to set the record straight (or not). Int. J. Press/Polit. **19**(4), 391–409 (2014). https://doi.org/10.1177/1940161214540942

Comprova Home page. https://projetocomprova.com.br/

CrossCheck (2018). https://crosscheck.firstdraftnews.org/france-fr/. Accessed 04 June 2019

Cunliffe-Jones, P.: Fighting falsehood, reducing harm? Lessons from Africa's complex countries (2019). https://africacheck.org/2019/05/31/comment-fighting-falsehood-reducing-harm-lessons-from-africas-complex-countries/. Accessed 04 June 2019

Daka, T., Olatunji, K.: Buhari in Poland, says 'I'm not Jubril (2018). https://guardian.ng/news/buhari-in-poland-says-im-not-jubril/. Accessed 04 June 2019

D'Ancona, M.: Post Truth: The New War on Truth and How to Fight Back. Ebury Press, London (2017)

David, M., Sutton, C.: Coding Qualitative Data: Qualitative Content Analysis in Social Research: An Introduction, pp. 338–348. Sage Publications, Thousand Oaks (2011)

Domingo, D., Quandt, T., Heinonen, A., Paulussen, S., Singer, J., Vujnovic, M.: Participatory journalism practices in the media and beyond. J. Pract. 2(3), 326–342 (2008). https://doi-org.ez.statsbiblioteket.dk:12048/10.1080/17512880802281065

Egelhofer, J.L., Lecheler, S.: Fake news as a two dimensional phenomenon: a framework and research agenda. Ann. Int. Commun. Assoc. 43(2), 97–116 (2019). https://doi.org/10.1080/23808985.2019.1602782

Eldridge II, S.A.: Online Journalism from the Periphery: Interloper Media and the Journalistic Field. Routledge, London (2018)

Elizabeth, J.: Who are you calling a fact checker? (2014). https://www.americanpressinstitute.org/fact-checking-project/fact-checker-definition. Accessed 04 June 2019

First Draft: Comprova Wraps in Brazil (2018a). https://medium.com/1st-draft/comprova-wraps-in-brazil-99de54a01d14. Accessed 04 June 2019

First Draft: *CrossCheck Nigeria* launches to fight information disorder (2018b). https://firstdraftnews.org/crosscheck-nigeria-launches-to-fight-information-disorder. Accessed 04 June 2019

Gottfried, J.A., Hardy, B.W., Winneg, K.M., Jamieson, K.H.: Did fact checking matter in the 2012 Presidential campaign? Am. Behav. Sci. 57(11), 1558–1567 (2013). https://doi.org/10.1177/0002864213489012

Graves, L.: Boundaries Not drawn: mapping the institutional roots of the global fact-checking movement. J. Stud. 19(5), 613–631 (2018). https://doi.org/10.1080/1461670x.2016.1196602

Graves, L., Cherubini, F.: The rise of fact-checking sites in Europe. University of Oxford: Reuters Institute for the Study of Journalism (2016)

Hitchen, J., Fisher, J., Hassan, I., Cheeseman, N.: Whatsapp and Nigeria's 2019 Elections: Mobilising the People, Protecting the Vote (2019). https://www.africaportal.org/publications/whatsapp-and-nigerias-2019-elections-mobilising-people-protecting-vote/

Holton, A., Belair-Gagnon, V.: Strangers to the game? Interlopers, intralopers, and shifting news production. Media Commun. 6(4), 70–78 (2018). https://doi.org/10.17645/mac.v6i4.1490

Internetlivestats.com: Internet Users by Country (2016). https://www.internetlivestats.com/internet-users-by-country/

Kolawole, S., Umejei, E.: Nigeria – Media Landscape (2018). https://medialandscapes.org/country/nigeria/. Accessed 06 June 2019

Kovach, B., Rosenstiel, T.: The Elements of Journalism: What News People Should Know and the Public Should Expect, 1st edn. Crown Publishers, New York (2001)

McNair, B.: Fake News: Falsehood, Fabrication and Fiction in Journalism. Routledge, London (2018)

Miles, M.B., Huberman, A.M., Saldaña, J.: Qualitative Data Analysis: A Methods Sourcebook, 3rd edn. SAGE Publications, Inc., Thousand Oaks (2014)

Nielsen, R., Ganter, S.A.: Dealing with digital intermediaries: a case study of the relations between publishers and platforms. New Media Soc. 20(4), 1600–1617 (2018). https://doi.org/10.1177/1461444817701318

Nyhan, B., Porter, E., Reifler, J., Wood, T.J.: Taking fact-checks literally but not seriously? The effects of journalistic fact-checking on factual beliefs and candidate favorability. Polit. Behav. 1–22 (2019). https://doi.org/10.1007/s11109-019-09528-x

Ogwezzy-Ndisika, A., Faustino, B., Amakoh, K.O.: Curbing hatred: the ethnic diehards' agitations and 2015 presidential election campaign in Nigeria. J. Hate Stud. (2019). https://doi.org/10.33972/jhs.169

Ogwezzy-Ndisika, A.: Hate speech, media ethics and 2015 electioneering campaign: insights from relevant codes and the electoral act (2015)

Ogwezzy-Ndisika, A.: Towards a peaceful 2019 Nigeria general election. A paper delivered at the official launch of the Nigerian Verification Project, CrossCheck Nigeria on Wednesday, 28 November 2018 in Lagos (2018)

Ogwezzy-Ndisika, A., Amakoh, K.O.: Curbing fakes: the role of nigeria online news media. Paper presented at the Multidisciplinary International Symposium on Disinformation in Open Online Media, University of Applied Sciences, Faculty Design, Media and Information, Hamburg, Germany (2019)

Olatunji, D.: The day Zik didn't die (2016). https://thenationonlineng.net/day-zik-didnt-die. Accessed 04 June 2019

Oluwole, J.: Platform to check fake news launched in Nigeria. https://www.premiumtimesng.com/news/top-news/298087-platform-to-check-fake-news-launched-in-nigeria.html. Accessed 04 June 2019

Oxford Dictionaries: Word of the Year 2016 is… https://en.oxforddictionaries.com/word-of-the-year/word-of-the-year-2016. Accessed 04 June 2019

Pavleska, T., Skolkay, A., Zankova, B., Riberiro, N., Bechmann, A.: Performance analysis of fact-checking organizations and initiatives in Europe: a critical overview of online platforms fighting fake news. In: EIDS6 (European Integration and Democracy Series), pp. 1–29 (2018). http://compact-media.eu/wp-content/uploads/2018/04/Performance-assessment-of-fact-checking-organizations_A-critical-overiview-Full-Research-1-1.pdf. Accessed 04 June 2019

Quealy, K.: Trump is on track to insult 650 people, places and things on Twitter by the end of his first term - the New York Times. https://www.nytimes.com/interactive/2017/07/26/upshot/president-trumps-newest-focus-discrediting-the-news-media-obamacare.html. Accessed 26 July 2017

Statista: Number of social network users in Nigeria from 2017 to 2023 (in millions) (2019). https://www.statista.com/statistics/972907/number-of-social-network-users-in-nigeria/

Stencel, M., Griffin, R.: Fact-checking triples over four years. https://reporterslab.org/fact-checking-triples-over-four-years/. Accessed 04–06 June 2019

Tandoc Jr., E.C., Lim, Z.W., Ling, R.: Defining "fake news". Digit. J. 6(2), 137–153 (2018). https://doi.org/10.1080/21670811.2017.1360143

Thurman, N., Hermida, A.: Gotcha: how newsroom norms are shaping participatory journalism online. In: Tunney, S., Monaghan, G. (eds.) Web Journalism: A New Form of Citizenship?, pp. 46–62. Sussex Academic Press, Eastbourne (2010). ISBN 1845192896

Wasserman, H., Madrid-Morales, D.: An exploratory study of "fake news" and media trust in Kenya, Nigeria and South Africa. Afr. J. Stud. (2019). https://doi.org/10.1080/23743670.2019.1627230

Wasserman, H.: Fake news from Africa: panics, politics and paradigms. J.: Theory Pract. Crit. 146488491774686 (2017) https://doi.org/10.1177/1464884917746861

Wintersieck, A.: Debating the truth: the impact of fact-checking during electoral debates. Am. Polit. Res. 45, 304–331 (2017)

Zelizer, B.: Achieving journalistic authority through narrative. Crit. Stud. Mass Commun. 7, 366–376 (1990)

State Propaganda on Twitter

How Iranian Propaganda Accounts Have Tried to Influence the International Discourse on Saudi Arabia

Bastian Kießling, Jan Homburg, Tanja Drozdzynski[✉], and Steffen Burkhardt

HAW Hamburg, Finkenau 35, 22081 Hamburg, Germany
{bastian.kiessling,jan.homburg,tanja.drozdzynski,
steffen.burkhardt}@haw-hamburg.de

Abstract. In recent years, a variety of studies has discussed the use of social media in the context of misinformation, fake news and manipulation of public opinion. Based on two data sets published by Twitter, including more than 1.7 million English-language tweets, this study focuses on the question whether Iranian propaganda accounts tried to influence the international online debate on the country's biggest rival, Saudi Arabia. The rivalry between both countries has been an ongoing fight deeply rooted in a regional, geopolitical, ideological and somewhat religious conflict. An analysis of the tweets published by the accounts which are believed to be connected to Iranian state-backed information operations has shown that they have tried to establish an anti-Saudi narrative on Twitter. Different strategies, including the spread of biased hashtags or retweeting internal and external propaganda sources, were used to promote their agenda. The propaganda activity on Saudi Arabia was especially distinctive during specific time intervals, correlating with political events, but has regularly failed to manipulate the international discourse. Although some content that negatively mentioned Saudi Arabia was actively retweeted, the vast majority did not influence the social media debate on the Gulf state.

Keywords: Propaganda · State-backed · Twitter · Iran · Saudi Arabia

1 Introduction

The role of social media was increasingly discussed in conjunction with the US presidential election in November 2016 in the context of fake news, disinformation, manipulation, propaganda and social bots. In the past, social media platforms such as Twitter and Facebook were noted as tools to foster democratic processes about social and political issues. Positive effects of social media usage and visibility pushed the general assumption that these kinds of social networks would promote democracy and civic engagement [14, 28, 43, 45]. Nevertheless, possibilities and instances of manipulating social media users were also documented in some studies [9, 18]. In combination with documented effects of influencing individuals' opinions and behaviors [3], the public perception of social media has partially changed over the past year. Several platforms started to be perceived as places for manipulative actors who are trying to alter the public opinion [7, 50]. So

© Springer Nature Switzerland AG 2020
C. Grimme et al. (Eds.): MISDOOM 2019, LNCS 12021, pp. 182–197, 2020.
https://doi.org/10.1007/978-3-030-39627-5_14

far, analysis of the social media sphere in the context of governmental interference has not been detailly conducted in the segment of English Twitter activity by Iranian actors. Researchers [15] are currently analyzing an Arabic proportion of tweets in a dataset published by Twitter that includes content in connection with Iranian propaganda efforts. They are alleging that the Arabic tweets are not aiming at interaction, but rather have informational purposes to push a pro-Iranian political narrative. This study is focusing on an English sample and its implications for the English-speaking world.

In order to present results that have a lasting effect on the scientific discussion, our focus is to analyze how these tweets by alleged Iranian propaganda accounts are influencing the perception of Saudi Arabia in the Twitter-sphere. A variety of datapoints serve as clusters to highlight how Iranian actions are shaping the discourse on Saudi Arabia. This paper summarizes findings based on the text analysis of two datasets published by Twitter in October 2018 including 770 accounts and January 2019 including 2320 accounts. The tweet information consists of 885 megabytes of text-based data. A media dataset that was included with the release of the tweets, amassing 267.7 gigabytes, is disregarded in this study.

2 Propaganda on Social Media

The rise of digital communication services, especially social media platforms, has changed the operational field of propaganda. Looking at the public discussion, there is no obligatory need for traditional media companies to be involved anymore. Smaller groups or even individuals are now able to spread their propaganda messages and reach an influential audience. The originators of these messages often remain unrecognized [10] due to a high level of anonymity online. Propaganda is defined as "information, especially of biased or misleading nature, used to promote a political cause or point of view" [37]. Spreading biased messages within a short period of time becomes easier and, as a result, more popular amid the growth of political communication on social media platforms. Social media accounts used for propaganda mostly share content on theological and religious topics, sectarian discussions, violence, or influential actors and political events [7]. Trolling is another increasingly important element of social media propaganda. A troll is defined as someone who purposely publishes disturbing messages online, in order to gain attention or cause trouble [11]. They are mostly sharing harassment and therefore generate lasting effects on the public discourse [20]. Troll armies are used to disturb debates by spreading propaganda messages on specific issues, causing other users to stop sharing their opinion online [5]. Regarding Twitter, propaganda accounts usually express the same content or opinion by sending a high volume of tweets over short periods of time. These accounts mainly retweet instead of publishing original content and collude with other, seemingly unrelated, accounts to circulate duplicate or similar messages simultaneously on the same topic [13]. These four characteristics have the potential to influence the public online debate and therefore the user's opinion on certain topics.

Many works in this field have analyzed social media propaganda in the context of terror groups [6, 7, 27, 35]. Terror organizations such as the so-called Islamic State (IS) use propaganda techniques as a central point of their communication strategy. The worldwide dissemination of social media services has fundamentally changed the dynamic.

They help terror groups to easily reach thousands of sympathizers on a global level [6]. Unsurprisingly, propaganda seems to be especially effective on users sharing the same opinion as the sender [38]. Messages and especially pictures, promoting extremist opinions, are purposefully used to recruit militants, spread extremist ideology, enhance the popularity of the discourse and educate a certain dogma [26]. Apart from terror groups, there are various political actors who use propaganda techniques on social media.

Some strategies include fake propaganda: by imitating the identities of political opponents and using these fake accounts to spread obvious propaganda messages, hateful and aggressive reactions are expected to be provoked [17]. During the presidential elections in Brazil in 2014 [4] and the US in 2016 [49], propaganda messages were automatically published by social bots. As per definition, propaganda accounts on social media differ from social bots as they are not programmed algorithms that behave automatically. However, social bots are often used to spread online propaganda, leading to the assumption that the propaganda accounts also indicate automated activity. The most powerful forms of computational propaganda involve both algorithms and human curation [50]. Political regimes and authoritarian governments have also adapted the mechanism of these new communication channels for propaganda purposes. They implement accounts that act like real citizens and push state compliant information on social media platforms, trying to silence opponents, swaying the vote or defaming critics [50]. Political actors in other countries are also addressed by state propaganda messages. Russian and Chinese propaganda campaigns have targeted political figures and activists in rivaling countries [51]. Russia's propaganda efforts on social media and the following counter activities by targeted countries are describes as "new cold war reincarnation" [40]. Communist states such as China and Cuba are also confronted with propaganda allegations, saying that they try to extend their state build authority by distributing propaganda on a national and international level [26].

Elswah, Howard and Narayanan [15] have already analyzed Arabic-language tweets by Iranian propaganda accounts. These were mainly used to link out to content published by pro-Iranian Arabic-language news websites instead of engaging with other users on Twitter. Many of the most shared websites have tried to establish a pro-Iranian narrative, criticizing Saudi Arabia while supporting the Syrian government and President Bashar al-Assad. They also retweeted each other to increase the reach of the published content. The most common hashtags used in the Arabic-language tweets were #SaudiArabia, #Yemen, referring to the Yemen conflict, and #TheMarchBreaking, a popular pro-Palestine hashtag. In conclusion, propaganda has always been an important instrument of political communication to influence the public debate and to share biased information.

With the growth of social media services as mainstream communication tools, the possibilities for online and automated propaganda have extremely increased.

3   Computational Propaganda and Social Bots

The automated publishing of propaganda messages is often referred to as computational propaganda. Woolley and Howard [51, p. 3] define this term as the "use of algorithms, automation, and human curation to purposefully distribute misleading information over social media networks". They directly connect the term to the distribution of misleading information which should not be equated with misinformation. While misleading information can also include truth, it is usually biased, as misinformation is false or inaccurate by definition. Nevertheless, computational propaganda often includes the spread of biased information, algorithmic manipulation and the distribution of misinformation to influence the public opinion [4]. In comparison to traditional propaganda techniques, computational propaganda additionally involves learning from and imitating humans to manipulate the public opinion on digital communication platforms [51].

Computational propaganda in social media is usually spread by social bots that can be understood as algorithms that imitate human behavior on social media platforms [24]. The bot phenomenon is not a new but has become more popular in recent years [18]. Bots are often one of the key tools to circulate the propaganda automatically across different social media platforms. A variety of types of social bots are prevalent on Twitter. They have adapted techniques and changed their behavior over time to avoid being detected by current scientific approaches. Bot networks are especially active in countries where Twitter is an important social media platform [51]. While some work in this field has highlighted positive applications of social bots [32], most of it has analyzed bots in the context of manipulation and malicious behavior related to harassment, spamming and defamation [18, 47]. Political bots are focused on political communication, often spreading online propaganda and hate campaigns in the context of elections, political events and crises [24]. They are used by political actors to attack human rights activists as well as journalists, making computational propaganda one of the "most powerful new tools against democracy." [51, p. 6]. Bots tend to massively retweet original content and post similar or identical messages. They can push specific topics and hashtags to be perceived as trending content on social media platforms such as Twitter. Political actors use bot networks as an agenda setting tool by trying to place events and topics on the public agenda [42]. They are applied to influence the public opinion and disrupt communication processes on social media platforms, especially during election times [19, 48].

Several studies in this field focused on the 2016 US presidential election. There is evidence that the social media sphere was targeted by political propaganda bots ahead of the election [10]. These actors have tried to affect the public debate by giving the illusion of an online sphere whose majority agrees on stances on specific issues and by passing on propaganda to amplify online conversations. During the election campaign, they were used as a widespread tool of computational propaganda, affecting political online processes on a significant level [49]. The use of the automated accounts was strategically assigned throughout the election. According to research, most of the automated content was published with hashtags supporting the Trump campaign to positively emphasize the following president [23].

Other work has analyzed the role of computational propaganda in the UK, Germany, Russia, Poland, Brazil and China. Regarding the UK, social bots played a small, but strategic role during the UK referendum on the EU membership. Political bots mostly published tweets with hashtags for leaving the EU. A high level of automation was noticed since less than one percent of the analyzed accounts generated almost a third of all content in the sample [24]. Despite of ongoing concerns, there is limited evidence that computational propaganda in the form of social bots is a serious problem in Germany with implications for the political landscape. There was only marginal bot activity during the 2017 German federal election. Nevertheless, the spread of misinformation and junk news is still a relevant problem in a political context [33], although the content seems to be published by non-automated accounts or, respectively, human users. The Russian social media sphere shows a contrary pattern, revealing a high presence of social bots [44]. In addition, the Russian government has also set up efficient tools to publish online propaganda and counterpropaganda, using the abilities of bots to disturb hostile and promote affirmative content on social media platforms [40]. A study on political online debates in Poland revealed that a small number of suspected bot accounts were responsible for a significant part of the overall traffic of political hashtags. Right-wing bot accounts were twice as active as their left-wing counterparts [20]. Overall, bots are mostly used to propagate ultranationalist positions [42]. During the 2018 presidential elections in Brazil, media outlets reported about the involvement of politicians and parties in activities to manipulate public debates on social media by using own campaigning teams as well as consultancy companies [31]. Computational propaganda techniques were also used to oppose the former president Dilma Rousseff's agenda which, to a certain extent, resulted in the removal from office in 2016 [4]. While most of the studies solely focus on Twitter, Bolsover and Howard [10] analyzed computational propaganda on Weibo, a Chinese microblogging service, and Twitter, showing that there is no significant automation on Weibo and little evidence of automation with state interest on Twitter. Debates on anti-state issues were influenced a lot more by automated behavior.

It should be noted that the current debate on social bots is controversial and simultaneously discussed with a lack of empirical findings. Bots are partially held responsible for election outcomes and the massive distribution of propaganda and misinformation on social media. There is an ongoing challenge for bot detection mechanisms. More sophisticated approaches are needed to identify propaganda activity carried out by bots on a reliable level [22]. Regarding computational propaganda, there is growing evidence that a series of political actors uses social media platforms to automatically circulate misinformation and biased information worldwide.

4   Regional Rivalry Between Iran and Saudi Arabia

The rivalry between Iran and Saudi Arabia has been an ongoing fight deeply rooted in a regional, geopolitical, ideological and somewhat religious conflict [30]. While Iran can be identified as a state with a strong majority of Shia Muslims, Saudi Arabia's strongest religious branch is Wahhabism, a puritanical interpretation of Sunni Islam. Former and ongoing proxy wars since the Iranian Revolution, ending in 1979, led to a further distancing of both countries from each other which, previously, aimed at cooperating in various fields. The Iraq-Iran war between 1980–1988 caused further political separation between the two nations. As of now, the conflicts in Syria, Yemen [39, 52] and previously in Bahrain [29] are examples of the ongoing rivalries between both nations in so-called proxy wars in the Middle East. Furthermore, alleged manipulation through external actors in coups d'état and rivalries in many areas caused an even stronger separation. Incidents during the Hajj pilgrimages in 1987 (between Shia pilgrims and Wahhabi police forces) and 2015 (mass panic and stampede with more than 750 casualties) further worsened the relationship, when Iran criticized the Saudi security forces [2]. Starting in 2011, the Arab Spring across the Gulf acted as a proxy conflict in which both parties stood against each other [32].

In recent years, the Arab Gulf states Saudi Arabia, the UAE and Bahrain entered an economic and security cooperation with Israel which is strongly opposed by Iran [1]. The Saudi-led Islamic Military Alliance to Fight Terrorism (IMCTC), established in 2015, does not include Iran as well as Iraq and Syria. Another peak in the conflict arose in January 2016 when Saudi Arabia conducted 47 death penalties, including a prominent Shia cleric Nimr al-Nimr who was closely connected to Iran, resulting in the termination of formal relations between the two countries. Ongoing tensions in international politics persisted since 2017, especially due to U.S. President Donald J. Trump's stance to endorsing Saudi Arabia and conducting his first foreign visit to the kingdom, hence, changing the U.S. position against Iran [41]. President Obama had previously restored formal relations with Iran and led efforts that helped to successfully pass the Joint Comprehensive Plan of Action (JCPOA or "Iran Nuclear Deal") with its signatories China, France, the European Union (EU), Germany, Iran, Russia and the UK. Affecting the Iran-Saudi relations even more, President Trump and his administration decided in August 2018 to reimpose U.S. sanctions against Iran, much to the astonishment of the EU which stressed that it would still back the agreement [41]. In hindsight of these political events, Hassan Rouhani, President of the Islamic Republic of Iran, used Twitter to criticize the U.S. decision. This was also the last chain of tweets published by Rouhani in English until the time of conducting the research presented. In May 2019 Iran suspended JCPOA commitments which it previously agreed to after the U.S. re-imposed sanctions and increased its Navy presence in the Persian Gulf. The Ministry of Foreign Affairs of the Kingdom of Saudi Arabia historically used Twitter many times to depict Iran in a negative manner by connecting it to terrorism.

In addition to Twitter's publication of data on Iran's alleged propaganda efforts, the social network Facebook released a public notice that it had removed 513 "pages, groups and accounts that engaged in coordinated inauthentic behavior" [16]. These approx. 1.5 million data points are stated as being in connection with Iran's historical anti-Saudi position. The move is based on a current working paper by Nimmo et al. [34], cooperating with Facebook since May 2018. It identifies Iran as a potential influencer. According to the study, page administrators and regular account owners used Facebook groups and fake accounts to impersonate political groups and media outlets. The state-owned Iranian Al Alam and Saudi-influenced Al Arabiya media networks were also used as platforms to influence public opinion by stressing their government's position and publishing negative headlines against Saudi Arabia and Iran on Twitter [8].

Regarding the available data set of Iranian propaganda accounts, this study follows the research question if these accounts tried to implement an anti-Saudi narrative in the international social media discourse. The analysis also aims at answering the question as to which strategies were used to spread targeted propaganda messages, ranging from retweeting original content to operating in specific Twitter networks.

5 Data Sample and Analysis

In this study, we are focusing our research on state propaganda on social media. Twitter itself has published two data sets, including tweets, images and videos circulated by, now deleted, propaganda accounts which are, according to Twitter, believed to be connected to Iranian state-backed information operations. The first data set was released in October 2018, including 1,122,936 tweets and retweets from 770 accounts. Twitter released the second data set in January 2019, containing 4,447,056 tweets and retweets from 2,320 accounts. All data is publicly available [46]. The research process is following the question if and how the Iranian propaganda accounts tried to influence the online debate on the country's biggest rival Saudi Arabia. In line with Twitter, Facebook also deleted Iranian propaganda accounts, pages and groups. According to the social network, this activity was directed from Iran and based on interconnected and localized operation networks to mislead other users [16]. Instead of focusing on the Arabic-language [15], we studied English-language content to analyze which strategies were used by the propaganda accounts to target international social media users.

5.1 Descriptive Analysis

In a first step, both data sets were merged and filtered for English-language tweets. Due to missing language labeling in the second data set provided by Twitter, Google's compact language detector (cld2) for R [36] was performed to categorize the tweets by their language. 1,744,696 of the overall tweets were published in English by 2,271 different Twitter accounts. All tweets directly mentioning Saudi Arabia (Saudi OR saudi) were subsequently filtered out to analyze if the Iranian propaganda accounts had a focus on the Gulf state. The filtering process shows that 2.56% (n = 44,651) of the English-language tweets were directly linked to Saudi Arabia, published by 1,345 different accounts. They had an average of 1,616 followers (SD = 6,090). All analyzed propaganda accounts in the filtered data sample were registered between June 17, 2008 and October 24, 2018. 62.55% (n = 27,930) of the content are original tweets, while 37.45% (n = 16,721) are retweets. The content was retweeted 1.12 (SD = 6.97) and liked 0.92 (SD = 9.65) times on average.

As seen in Fig. 1, the number of tweets mentioning Saudi Arabia strongly increased since the end of the third quarter of 2014. But instead of a linear monthly increase, the propaganda accounts were especially active during a short period of time, falling back to a more inactive level before getting highly active again. The first activity peak was observed in October 2014. At the same time, the popular Shia Sheikh Nimr al-Nimr was sentenced to death by a court in Saudi Arabia for terrorism offences. The sentence was strongly condemned by Iran and activist groups, accusing Saudi Arabia of carrying out a campaign against dissidents. Another activity peak correlated in time with a deadly accident at the Grand Mosque in Mecca in September 2015, where 111 people were killed and 394 injured. The third peak of attention was observed in January 2016, correlating with the execution of 47 alleged terrorists, including al-Nimr. The data shows the highest activity in a time interval between May and August 2017. During this time, U.S. President Trump conducted his first foreign visit to Saudi Arabia. Furthermore, several Gulf states including Saudi Arabia, the UAE and Bahrain cut diplomatic ties with Qatar, criticizing the country's relations with Iran and accusing it of supporting terrorism. Additionally, a deadly airstrike carried out by a Saudi-led military coalition killed 35 people in Yemen's capital Sana'a.

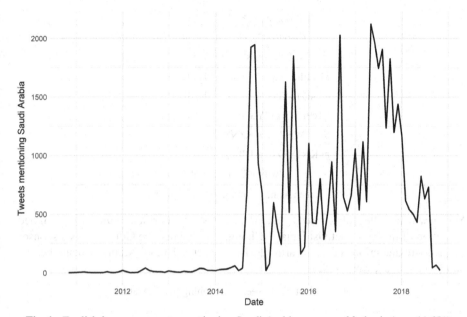

Fig. 1. English-language tweets mentioning Saudi Arabia on a monthly basis (n = 44,651)

The data sets do not include information on the number of tweets for every account. Nevertheless, it is possible to analyze the number of tweets and retweets published in the research period by allocating the content to a particular screen name. Table 1 shows the ten most active users and how often they mentioned Saudi Arabia. Accounts with less than 5,000 followers were anonymized by Twitter. All screen names were trimmed to 15 characters due to depiction requirements. The ten most active accounts in the filtered data set are responsible for 49.85% (n = 22,257) of the overall content published in connection with Saudi Arabia. Among these accounts are just two with more than 5,000 followers. Based on the profile description, the propaganda account @marialuis91 pretended to be an independent French journalist, while @MeettheNews described itself as an account that tweets about the latest incidents in the world and the Middle East. The overall average number of tweets published per day is 0.31 (SD = 8.25).

An analysis of the most viral tweets by the number of retweets mentioning Saudi Arabia shows that the Iranian propaganda accounts spread negative information about the Gulf state. Table 2 depicts the ten most retweeted tweets in connection with Saudi Arabia, showing that they were retweeted between 327 and 144 times by other social media users. Within the viral tweets, the propaganda accounts blamed the Saudi-led military coalition for the alleged killing of children in Yemen, accused the UN of not stopping Saudi Arabia from attacking Yemen, alleged that Saudi Arabia commits war crimes in the conflict by using white phosphorous bombs, mentioned a food crisis in

Table 1. Ten most active propaganda accounts mentioning Saudi Arabia (n = 22,257)

Screen name	n
marialuis91	8,416
cf35b18dbb39a8e*	2,655
a51115862ba4725*	2,339
cfb431d28838bc8*	1,917
MeettheNews	1,504
454d51cd3a15fe8*	1,201
Ij1c9FEJu447Y6 M*	1,119
SAvoWN7b5GpK3NY*	1,094
gyKN1SRZC6hT8BQ*	1,025
SWnvVY2wdjm4DLk*	987

* Screen name anonymized by Twitter

Yemen which is allegedly caused by Saudi Arabia, strongly criticized the falsely claimed execution of the rights activist Israa al-Ghomgham, blamed the Gulf state as a sponsor of terrorism and criticized Saudi arms deals and accused Saudi Arabia of being behind all terrorist attack worldwide.

Table 2. Most viral tweets mentioning Saudi Arabia

Tweet	Retweets (n)
Please share it widely. Heartbreaking video of a father crying after he saw his dead child's body on the car. Imagine if you were in his shoes and #Saudi led coalition killed your son in a school bus. This is #Yemen. #YemenGenocide #YemenChildren https://t.co/q3Jmynpa5F	327
The UN do nothing to stop Zio-Wahhabi Saudi war on #Yemen. #wahhabism https://t.co/tOUr43UaxU https://t.co/Cwr2qirQRD	323
Good Guy!!! Bad Guy!!! #Trump #SaudiaArabia #Iran https://t.co/yWO8DjTnAG	318
A #Yemeni child bombed with "White" Phosphorous by the #Saudi regime. #YemenUnderAttack http://t.co/Q2qhKWXlqR	240
Did you know only 2% of Yemen is arable? Did you know Yemen was completely dependent on imports of food even before the war? Did you know every 10 min 1 child dies in Yemen? Saudi Arabia's blockade on Yemen threatens more lives. #YemenCantWait #YemenWarCup https://t.co/xgw3nmCPP6	223
Saudi Arabia beheaded Human Right Activist & #Shia women "Esraa al-Ghamgam" from Qatif. She was sentenced to death for her criticism of Government over injustice to #Shia community. Her last words were b4 beheading: "I am being killed innocent, I will seek justice from God". https://t.co/ZlpQCaXYRH	218

(continued)

Table 2. (*continued*)

Tweet	Retweets (n)
'The Saudis committed two crimes: attacking a hospital and attacking a school bus with 40 or 50 innocent children on board. Do you have 8 or 9 year-olds at home? This is a dramatic tragedy. It truly breaks one's heart.' ~Ayatollah Khamenei https://t.co/haqVD8a0V8 https://t.co/uYkT8qD8s5	215
Sponsor Of Terrorism! #USA #SaudiaArabia #ISIS https://t.co/XQrZqcyrl3	182
US, UK & Saudis launch wars in ME so they can sell more weapons. Who benefits? #Israel #marr https://t.co/IKUHRzGKNU	146
#SaudiArabia is Behind all #TerroristAttack in the World by Funding #Wahhabism supported by the #US and #Israel https://t.co/dV4UhWf5r0 https://t.co/9bH95axXcr	144

The Iranian propaganda accounts used 5,453 different hashtags in tweets and retweets, mentioning Saudi Arabia. Table 3 shows the most common hashtags in descending order. While several of the most popular hashtags are neutral without the associated message included in the tweet (e.g. #Saudi, #Yemen, #US), some others directly attack Saudi Arabia. The hashtag #SaudiMustApologize was initiated in the aftermath of the 2015 Mina stampede in Mecca which led to the death of over 2,000 pilgrims during the annual Hajj pilgrimage. Many of the victims were Iranian citizen. In the following time range, social media users created this hashtag to blame Saudi Arabia for the incident. It now regularly reoccurs on the anniversary of the tragedy and is also particularly used to criticize Saudi Arabia in general. #StopTheWarOnYemen is directly connected to the Saudi-led military intervention in Yemen which was launched in March 2015. Social media users spread the hashtag to call on Saudi Arabia to stop the ongoing military campaign.

Table 3. Ten most popular hashtags included in tweets mentioning Saudi Arabia (n = 18,776)

Screen name	n
#Saudi	6,261
#Yemen	4,592
#SaudiArabia	3,300
#US	1,038
#Iran	672
#yemenpress	624
#Trump	601
#Israel	573
#SaudiMustApologize	570
#StopTheWarOnYemen	545

5.2 Retweet Network

In a next step, we analyzed the interactions of the propaganda accounts with other users on Twitter based on their retweet behavior. A social network analysis can reveal if the propaganda accounts mainly interacted with themselves, by mutually retweeting their own published content, or retweeted content posted by non-related Twitter accounts, with a similar point of view. Twitter can be used as a strategic tool to orchestrate networks of supporters and followers to spread propaganda via these networks [12]. The overall network is modeled by all retweets in the data sample, resulting in a directed graph of 3,273 nodes and 16,721 edges. Each node represents a single Twitter account, while the edges pose as the retweet interactions between all accounts in the network. 20.05% of the edges are directed paths within the propaganda accounts. 79.95% are links to public nodes, showing that the Iranian propaganda accounts mostly retweeted content published by external Twitter sources.

Figure 2 shows a central sequence of the retweet network. Gephi, an open-source network visualization software, was used to visualize the network. The layout is based on the ForceAtlas 2 algorithm [25], placing each node depending on the other nodes. The importance of a node is therefore determined by its induvial position within the network. It spatializes social networks and performs well for networks with less than 100,000 nodes. Larger nodes in the figure are accounts that were retweeted more often by the Iranian propaganda accounts. Measuring the indegree centrality, which counts the number of edges directed to each node, the analysis shows that the most retweeted accounts in the network are the Twitter accounts of (a) Press TV (@Press_TV, 327 neighbors), a news network run and financed by the Iranian government and therefore often accused of a biased news coverage; (b) RT (@RT_com, 228 neighbors), a Russian media network previously known as Russia Today funded by its government and also accused of spreading biased information and (c) an anonymized Iranian propaganda account (@df2dcvd4b4d8en7, 176 neighbors) which has depicted Saudi Arabia as a US "puppet". The data underlines that the propaganda efforts included different techniques to enable orchestrating their networks. Instead of just retweeting each other, the accounts actively retweeted content published by news organizations related to the governments of Iran and Russia.

Another central factor is the outdegree centrality, which describes the number of edges that each node directs to other nodes in the network. The accounts with the most outgoing links are (a) an anonymized propaganda account (@cf35b18dbb39a8e, 559 neighbors) which pretends to be a political analyst from the US, (b) another anonymized account (@3fXrw02Ese7Cy5A, 256 neighbors), an alleged founder of an Iranian news website and (c) @MeettheNews (208 neighbors), as previously mentioned one of the most active propaganda accounts. Especially accounts with fewer followers used the strategy to retweet content from a large variety of sources instead of focusing on a small network of accounts.

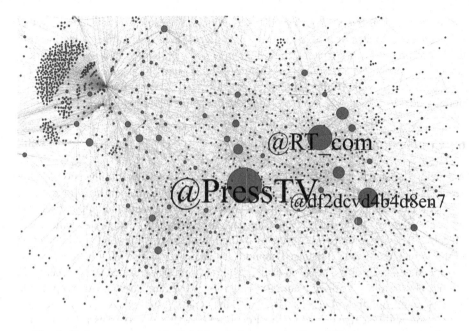

Fig. 2. Twitter accounts with the highest indegree centrality within the retweet network

5.3 Limitations

In review of this study, the classification of the accounts as propaganda accounts by Twitter itself is a limitation affecting the results. The micro-blogging service released the data sets with the goal of improving the understanding of foreign influence and information campaigns, saying it found malicious activity originating from Iran. Although Twitter has stated that the accounts are believed to be connected with Iranian state-backed information, there is no final proof of this statement. Some uncertainty about their origin remains, until Twitter is fully transparent regarding the classification process for the accounts. Twitter is also just a small part in the complex social media system in relation to propaganda, reducing the generalizability of our results. Other social media platforms, especially Facebook, need to be studied, to close the research gap in the context of state and automated propaganda. By analyzing the propaganda content, the effectiveness of the propaganda messages on one's mindset and the recipient's behavior cannot be measured and therefore provided. Experimental studies are necessary to get results on the individual impact level.

Due to the focus on English-language content mentioning Saudi Arabia, the analysis additionally did not reveal if the propaganda accounts have tried to influence the discourse in the Arabic social media sphere. The impact was solely examined for the international Twitter discourse and has furthermore highlighted content in connection with Saudi Arabia because of the historical rivalry between the Gulf kingdom and Islamic Republic of Iran. Further studies in this field should include all languages used by the accounts in the sample, to get a comprehensive pattern of their propaganda strategies. We used Google's compact language detector instead of Twitter's own language detection for separating English tweets from the rest of the content because the second data set of propaganda accounts released in January 2019 did not include a language identification field. The brevity of the content, multiple languages within single tweets and marked content, instead of natural language, such as hashtags and emojis, are challenging for language detection algorithms [21]. Therefore, deviations exist within the approach used in this study, in comparison with the language-detection field provided by Twitter.

6   Conclusion

A conclusion can be drawn when considering the research question if Iranian propaganda accounts tried to implement an anti-Saudi narrative: the data analysis has shown that a series of accounts indeed took an effort to influence the international online discourse on Iran's regional and political rival, using several propaganda strategies to achieve this objective. They opposed Saudi Arabia by frequently criticizing the country's interaction in the Yemen conflict or its alleged support of terrorism groups, such as the so-called Islamic State. According to Elswah et al. [15], Iranian propaganda accounts, tweeting in Arabic, also tried to establish an anti-Saudi narrative. The English-language propaganda activity about Saudi Arabia was especially distinctive during specific time intervals, correlating with events such as regional catastrophes, deadly airstrikes in Yemen, the execution of Shia people, state visits by high-ranking politicians and diplomatic disputes. The results are in line with previous work which has stated that propaganda accounts often share content on political events, violence and religious topics [7]. More than 60% of the published tweets were original content instead of retweets [13]. On average, the propaganda accounts were relatively inactive, apart from a few spam accounts. They published the majority of propaganda messages in the data set. Many of them were accounts with less than 5,000 followers. The most active account published 8,416 tweets on Saudi Arabia and 63,989 English-language tweets altogether, leading to the assumption that at least some propaganda accounts used automated scripts to circulate their messages.

The results support previous work, saying that social media platforms are used to influence the public debate [9, 18]. Nevertheless, an average of 1.12 (SD = 6.97) retweets and 0.92 (SD = 9.65) likes for each tweet related to Saudi Arabia implies that these attempts have regularly failed. Although some tweets that negatively mentioned Saudi Arabia for its intervention in Yemen and its alleged support of terrorism were actively retweeted, the vast majority did not influence the social media debate about the Gulf state. The propaganda accounts, nevertheless, used different strategies to promote their messages. Some accounts spread specific hashtags to target Saudi Arabia, others shared biased and misleading information published by further propaganda accounts or external sources. The network analysis examined a mix of internal and external propaganda, whereas external sources such as the governmental Iranian news network Press TV and the Russian state-funded media network RT were the most retweeted accounts. Iranian propaganda accounts did not stay in their own cluster by just retweeting each other: nearly 80% of the retweet activity consisted of messages from unrelated Twitter accounts which fit into their agenda.

Further research should analyze if Iran's rival Saudi Arabia is also operating an army of propaganda accounts, trying to negatively influence Iran's perception in the same way.

Due to fact that political regimes use propaganda techniques [50], there is a need for comparing state organized propaganda in social media worldwide. Furthermore, it is necessary to focus on the content of the published propaganda messages. Sentiment analyses can reveal the tonality of online debates and answer research questions about the extent of propaganda accounts circulating negative as well as biased content toward specific actors and issues. Topic modeling processes can support this approach by automatically clustering large data sets of social media data, giving more detailed insights about the agenda of propaganda accounts.

References

1. Ahmadian, H.: Iran and Saudi Arabia in the age of trump. Survival **60**(2), 133–150 (2018). https://doi.org/10.1080/00396338.2018.1448579
2. Amiri, R.E., Samsu, K.H.B.K., Fereidouni, H.G.: The Hajj and Iran's foreign policy towards Saudi Arabia. J. Asian Afr. Stud. **46**(6), 678–690 (2011). https://doi.org/10.1177/0021909611417546
3. Aral, S., Walker, D.: Identifying influential and susceptible members of social networks. Science **337**(6092), 337–341 (2012). https://doi.org/10.1126/science.1215842
4. Arnaudo, D.: Computational propaganda in Brazil: social bots during elections, p. 38 (2017)
5. Aro, J.: The cyberspace war: propaganda and trolling as warfare tools. Eur. View **15**(1), 121–132 (2016). https://doi.org/10.1007/s12290-016-0395-5
6. Awan, I.: Cyber-extremism: isis and the power of social media. Society **54**(2), 138–149 (2017). https://doi.org/10.1007/s12115-017-0114-0
7. Badawy, A., Ferrara, E.: The rise of Jihadist propaganda on social networks. J. Comput. Soc. Sci. **1**(2), 453–470 (2018). https://doi.org/10.1007/s42001-018-0015-z
8. Baghernia, N., Mahmoodinejad, E.H.: Al-Alam versus Al-Arabiya: Iran and Saudi Arabia's media propaganda tools. Asian Polit. Policy **10**(2), 388–391 (2018). https://doi.org/10.1111/aspp.12386
9. Bessi, A., Ferrara, E.: Social bots distort the 2016 US presidential election online discussion (SSRN Scholarly Paper No. ID 2982233). Social Science Research Network (2016). https://papers.ssrn.com/abstract=2982233. Accessed 9 May 2019
10. Bolsover, G., Howard, P.: Chinese computational propaganda: automation, algorithms and the manipulation of information about Chinese politics on Twitter and Weibo. Inf. Commun. Soc. 1–18 (2018). https://doi.org/10.1080/1369118X.2018.1476576
11. Cambridge University Press: Troll. Cambridge online dictionary (2019). https://dictionary.cambridge.org/dictionary/english/troll. Accessed 9 May 2019
12. Chatfield, A. T., Reddick, C.G., Brajawidagda, U.: Tweeting propaganda, radicalization and recruitment: Islamic state supporters multi-sided Twitter networks. In: Proceedings of the 16th Annual International Conference on Digital Government Research - Dg.o 2015, pp. 239–249 (2015).. https://doi.org/10.1145/2757401.2757408
13. Lumezanu, C., Feamster, N., Klein, H.: #bias: measuring the Tweeting behavior of propagandists. In: International AAAI Conference on Web and Social Media; Sixth International AAAI Conference on Weblogs and Social Media (2012). https://www.aaai.org/ocs/index.php/ICWSM/ICWSM12/rt/metadata/4588/4985. Accessed 9 May 2019
14. Effing, R., van Hillegersberg, J., Huibers, T.: Social media and political participation: are Facebook, Twitter and YouTube democratizing our political systems? In: Tambouris, E., Macintosh, A., de Bruijn, H. (eds.) ePart 2011. LNCS, vol. 6847, pp. 25–35. Springer, Heidelberg (2011). https://doi.org/10.1007/978-3-642-23333-3_3

15. Elswah, M., Howard, P.N., Narayanan, V.: Iranian digital Interference in the Arab World. In: Data Memo. Project on Computational Propaganda, Oxford, United Kingdom (2019)
16. Facebook: Removing Coordinated Inauthentic Behavior from Iran, Russia, Macedonia and Kosovo I Facebook Newsroom (2019). https://newsroom.fb.com/news/2019/03/cib-iran-russia-macedonia-kosovo/. Accessed 9 May 2019
17. Farkas, J., Schou, J., Neumayer, C.: Cloaked Facebook pages: exploring fake Islamist propaganda in social media. New Media Soc. **20**(5), 1850–1867 (2018). https://doi.org/10.1177/1461444817707759
18. Ferrara, E., Varol, O., Davis, C., Menczer, F., Flammini, A.: The rise of social bots. Commun. ACM **59**(7), 96–104 (2016). https://doi.org/10.1145/2818717
19. Forelle, M.C., Howard, P.N., Monroy-Hernandez, A., Savage, S.: Political bots and the manipulation of public opinion in Venezuela. SSRN Electron. J. (2015). https://doi.org/10.2139/ssrn.2635800
20. Gorwa, R.: Computational propaganda in Poland: false amplifiers and the digital public sphere (2017). http://trybun.org.pl/wp-content/uploads/2017/06/Comprop-Poland.pdf. Accessed 9 May 2019
21. Graham, M., Hale, S.A., Gaffney, D.: Where in the world are you? Geolocation and language identification in Twitter. Prof. Geogr. **66**(4), 568–578 (2014). https://doi.org/10.1080/00330124.2014.907699
22. Grimme, C., Preuss, M., Adam, L., Trautmann, H.: Social bots: human-like by means of human control? Big Data **5**(4), 279–293 (2017). https://doi.org/10.1089/big.2017.0044
23. Howard, P., Kollanyi, B., Woolley, S.C.: Bots and automation over Twitter during the second U.S. presidential debate (2016). https://ora.ox.ac.uk/objects/uuid:ad5ed49f-2ce3-4e74-a74b-74324f7dafba. . Accessed 9 May 2019
24. Howard, P.N., Kollanyi, B.: Bots, #Strongerin, and #Brexit: computational propaganda during the UK-EU referendum (SSRN Scholarly Paper No. ID 2798311) (2016). https://papers.ssrn.com/abstract=2798311. Accessed 9 May 2019
25. Jacomy, M., Venturini, T., Heymann, S., Bastian, M.: ForceAtlas2, a continuous graph layout algorithm for handy network visualization designed for the Gephi software. PLoS One **9**(6), e98679 (2014). https://doi.org/10.1371/journal.pone.0098679
26. Kalathil, S., Boas, T.C.: The Internet and state control in authoritarian regimes: China, Cuba and the counterrevolution. First Monday **6**(8) (2001)
27. Klausen, J.: Tweeting the Jihad: social media networks of western foreign fighters in Syria and Iraq. Stud. Conflict Terror. **38**(1), 1–22 (2015). https://doi.org/10.1080/1057610X.2014.974948
28. Loader, B.D., Mercea, D.: Networking democracy? Inf. Commun. Soc. **14**(6), 757–769 (2011). https://doi.org/10.1080/1369118X.2011.592648
29. Mabon, S.: The battle for Bahrain: Iranian-Saudi rivalry. Middle East Policy **19**(2), 84–97 (2012). https://doi.org/10.1111/j.1475-4967.2012.00537.x
30. Mabon, S.: Saudi Arabia and Iran: Soft Power Rivalry in the Middle East. Tauris, London (2013)
31. Machado, C., et al.: News and political information consumption in Brazil: mapping the 2018 Brazilian presidential election on Twitter (2018). The Computational Propaganda Project. https://comprop.oii.ox.ac.uk/research/brazil2018/. Accessed 9 May 2019
32. Matthiesen, T.: Sectarian Gulf: Bahrain, Saudi Arabia, and the Arab Spring that Wasn't. Stanford briefs, Stanford University Press, Stanford (2013)
33. Neudert, L.-M.N.: Computational propaganda in Germany: a cautionary tale, p. 31 (2017)
34. Nimmo, A.F., et al.: Guidelines for the safe practice of total intravenous anaesthesia (TIVA): joint guidelines from the association of Anaesthetists and the society for intravenous Anaesthesia. Anaesthesia **74**(2), 211–224 (2019). https://doi.org/10.1111/anae.14428

35. Ogun, M.N.: Terrorist use of internet: possible suggestions to prevent the usage for terrorist purposes. J. Appl. Secur. Res. **7**(2), 203–217 (2012). https://doi.org/10.1080/19361610.2012. 656252

36. Ooms, J.: cld2: Google's compact language detector 2 (Version 1.2) (2018). https://CRAN. R-project.org/package=cld2. Accessed 9 May 2019

37. Oxford University Press: Propaganda. Oxford online dictionary (2019). https://en. oxforddictionaries.com/definition/propaganda. Accessed 9 May 2019

38. Qin, B., Strömberg, D., Wu, Y.: Why does China allow freer social media? Protests versus surveillance and propaganda. J. Econ. Perspect. **31**(1), 117–140 (2017). https://doi.org/10. 1257/jep.31.1.117

39. Salisbury, P.: Yemen and the Saudi-Iranian 'Cold War'. Chatham House, London (2015)

40. Sanovich, S.: Computational propaganda in Russia: the origins of digital misinformation, p. 26 (2017)

41. Santini, R.H.: Between a rock and a hard place: trump's half-realist, half-mercantilist foreign policy in the Middle East. Interdisc. Polit. Stud. **4**(1), 7–16 (2018)

42. Schäfer, F., Evert, S., Heinrich, P.: Japan's 2014 general election: political bots, right-wing internet activism, and prime minister Shinzō Abe's hidden nationalist agenda. Big Data **5**(4), 294–309 (2017). https://doi.org/10.1089/big.2017.0049

43. Shirky, C.: The political power of social media: technology, the public sphere, and political change. Foreign Aff. **90**(1), 28–41 (2011)

44. Stukal, D., Sanovich, S., Bonneau, R., Tucker, J.A.: Detecting bots on Russian political Twitter. Big Data **5**(4), 310–324 (2017). https://doi.org/10.1089/big.2017.0038

45. Tufekci, Z., Wilson, C.: Social media and the decision to participate in political protest: observations from Tahrir square. J. Commun. **62**(2), 363–379 (2012). https://doi.org/10.1111/ j.1460-2466.2012.01629.x

46. Twitter: Data archive (2019). https://about.twitter.com/en_us/values/elections-integrity.html# data. Accessed 9 May 2019

47. Varol, O., Ferrara, E., Davis, C.A., Menczer, F., Flammini, A.: Online human-bot interactions: detection, estimation, and characterization. arXiv:1703.03107 [Cs] (2017). http://arxiv.org/ abs/1703.03107. Accessed 9 May 2019

48. Woolley, S.C.: Automating power: social bot interference in global politics. First Monday **21**(4) (2016). https://doi.org/10.5210/fm.v21i4.6161

49. Woolley, S.C., Guilbeault, D.R.: Computational propaganda in the United States of America: manufacturing consensus online. Computational Propaganda Research Project (2017)

50. Woolley, S.C., Howard, P.N.: Political communication, computational propaganda, and autonomous agents. Int. J. Commun. **10**(Special Issue), 4882–4890 (2016)

51. Woolley, S., Howard, P.: Computational propaganda worldwide: executive summary. Project on Computational Propaganda (2017)

52. Zweiri, M.: Iran and political dynamism in the Arab world: the Case of Yemen: Iran and political dynamism in the Arab world. Digest Middle East Stud. **25**(1), 4–18 (2016). https:// doi.org/10.1111/dome.12078

Author Index

Printed in the United States
By Bookmasters